SO FOUL AND FAIR A DAY

ALASTAIR DAWSON

SO FOUL AND FAIR A DAY
A HISTORY OF SCOTLAND'S WEATHER AND CLIMATE

BIRLINN

First published in 2009 by
Birlinn Limited
West Newington House
10 Newington Road
Edinburgh
EH9 1QS

www.birlinn.co.uk

ISBN: 978 1 84158 567 3

British Library Cataloguing-in-Publication Data
A catalogue record for this book is available
from the British Library

Designed and typeset by Mark Blackadder

Printed and bound by Bell & Bain Ltd, Glasgow

CONTENTS

For Sue, Greg, Laura and Euan

FOREWORD

In January 2005 a severe storm caused extensive damage to both the Inner and Outer Hebrides – beyond even what is often expected there during the winter months (and I know, because I used to live on one of those islands). On Canna, the bridge linking the two parts of the island was swept away, just after a mother and child had crossed (on their hands and knees, given the strength of the gale). At Balivanich, the primary school was shifted from its foundations, leading to a drastic shortening of its expected useful life, whilst at Poll-na-Crann seaweed and debris blocked the main coast road so severely that it took several weeks to clear.

Most tragically of all, when the weather was at its most ferocious, an extended family of five living at the top end of South Uist attempted to move to where they thought they might be safer. Instead they were swept to their deaths by the raging and swollen waters of what is known as the South Ford, the tidal strait which separates South Uist from Benbecula.

In the aftermath of the storm a vigorous debate raged about how to protect this area and its inhabitants from such tragedies. One problem was the possibility that a causeway built in 1982 had created changed patterns of tide and thereby increased the vulnerability of the existing community. Another was the effect of erosion and storm damage on Gualan Island, a drying sandbank lying at the western mouth of the ford.

Shortly after I was appointed Scottish Environment Minister in the spring of 2007 I tried to get some progress on these matters, not least finally to honour the commitments concerning safety that had been made to the islanders. In October 2007 I was able to make some Government money available to undertake a hydrographic survey, and a team of academics from Aberdeen University's Institute of Coastal Science and Management was appointed to carry out the work. Much to my surprise I discovered amongst them my old Marr College school friend Alastair Dawson (now a professor), whom I had not seen for more than thirty years.

Alastair's professional fascination for the effects of weather has led him to write this accessible and absorbing book, and his interest is one I share. Scotland's weather has imprinted itself not only on our landscape and shoreline but also on our people and our culture. The more we know about weather in the past, the more we are likely to know about why we are as we are, why we live in the way we live and why we may have to adapt our lifestyles in the future!

Our history is full of weather-related stories. King Alexander III fell to his death from the cliffs at Pettycur in a storm, an event which caused the Maid of Norway to become Queen of Scots – until she too perished as a result of bad weather. Another Queen of Scots – Mary Stewart – arrived back in her country from France on a day of mist and rain, prompting John Knox to draw the conclusion that 'sic a dark and dolorous day' was an ill omen for her future. The massacre of Glencoe took place in a snow storm, and the Tay Bridge fell when 'Boreas blew a terrific gale', according to William McGonagall.

Weather also permeates our literature. The action of Burns's epic *Tam O'Shanter* is set against a wild night – in more than one sense of the word – whilst plots of innumerable Scottish novels hinge upon fog, wind and rain. Even the rare spectacle of hot sunny weather gets recorded and embellished from time to time.

Weather makes us do things and stops us doing them. When I lived in the Western Isles there were times when travel simply was impossible because of gales or storms – a fact that most people who live in cities find difficult to believe. And Robert Burns recounts in a letter how he got trapped in Ecclefechan one night in February 1795 by ten-foot snow drifts. Forced to share the inn with a fiddler of no ability but great persistence, Burns had to choose 'either to get drunk, to forget the miseries; or to hang myself, to get rid of these miseries'. . . . 'Like a prudent man', as he puts it in a letter written that evening, 'I of two evils have chosen the least!'

Global warming may have worse in store, though as Alastair points out we have as a nation lived through more persistently wild weather and survived. Yet, whatever happens, it is certain that we will go on experiencing good days and bad, calm times and rough, wet weeks and dry, cold nights and warm. Now, thanks to Alastair, we can also start to understand how influential the weather has always been, and continues to be for us all.

Michael Russell

Minister for Culture, External Affairs and the Constitution. Argyll, July 2009

ACKNOWLEDGEMENTS

Many people have generously contributed to the preparation of this book. The compilation of weather records for Scotland started in the mid 1990s within a European Union research project concerned with storminess and coastal change. Thanks are expressed to David Smith for enabling this work to take place and to the huge efforts of Gillian West, who painstakingly transferred my various notes into an enormous database on Scotland's weather and climate history. To Gillian I owe the greatest debt of gratitude. Thanks are also expressed to the following for commenting on sections of text and also clarifying for me some aspects of science with which I was unfamiliar: Jane and Dick Broughton, John Gordon, Caroline Wickham-Jones, Doug Benn, Kevin Edwards, Paul Mayewski, Mike Cressey, Mike Wood and Mike Baillie. Others kindly gave of their time and effort to provide me with illustrative material: Stewart Angus, David Mackie, Colin Rendall, Tom Dawson, Sue Dawson, Sigurd Towrie, Andrew Black, John Rowan, Roland Gehrels, Jan Mangerud, Paul Fisher, Jim Allison, Donald Herd, Chris Caseldine, Brian Smith, Jason Jordan, Hans-Petter Sejrup and Richard Bates. Grateful appreciation is also expressed to Hazel Clement at the UK Met Office, Edinburgh for her patience and diligence in helping me wade through archive material, to Sarah Robertson at the St Andrews Preservation Trust, to staff at the National Museum for Scotland, Edinburgh, to Alison Sandison at the University of Aberdeen for the preparation of maps and diagrams, to Laura Dawson for help in preparing the Index, and finally to Andrew Simmons, Helen Bleck and Peter Burns at Birlinn for their enormous effort in helping me take the manuscript from its early stages to the final version. Finally, sincere gratitude goes to my wife, Sue, and family, without whom the making of this book would not have been possible.

Alastair Dawson
St Andrews, August 2009

PART 1
WEATHER AND CLIMATE CHANGE

CHAPTER 1
IT NEVER RAINS BUT IT POURS

In the bleak midwinter, frosty wind made moan,
Earth stood hard as iron, water like a stone;
Snow had fallen, snow on snow, snow on snow,
In the bleak midwinter, long ago.

Christina Rossetti, from 'In the Bleak Midwinter', 1872

INTRODUCTION

In Scotland, we have a fascination for weather – we are also intrigued by the ramifications of Scottish history. Yet we rarely learn how the two relate to one another. Open any history book and you will find very few references to past extremes of warmth or cold, storms or drought. Although you will find plenty of references to periods of famine, these are usually described from social and/or political perspectives and only very rarely will historic weather extremes be mentioned.

This book attempts to provide, for the first time, a detailed account of Scotland's past weather and climate. Since the last ice age, weather and climate have changed remarkably, and the story of how the landscape, and the people, adapted to such changes is a complex one. Beginning with the arrival of Scotland's first settlers around 9,000 years ago, floods, storms, blizzards, droughts and volcanic eruptions have influenced the development of Scottish society, culture and its history. The story leads ultimately to the present day, and how we view weather and climate in the light of current debates on 'climate change' and 'global warming'. It is a story that is vitally important to all of us.

To most people, Christina Rossetti's description of 'the bleak midwinter' evokes images of freezing cold Victorian winters. Equally, her words could be used to describe any of the winters in Scotland during the last ice age. They give a hint, too, that times have changed – we just don't have winters like that any more. Or, if we do, then they don't happen very often. So what were Scotland's weather and climate like in the past and are there things that we can learn that inform us better about how things might be in the future?

To explain the terms: a general definition of 'weather' is the state of the atmosphere at any moment in time. Defining 'climate' is much harder, but is usually considered as all the states of the atmosphere seen at a place over many years. The official view of the World Meteorological Organization (WMO) is that a thirty-year period ought to represent a climate timescale.

In any account of the history of Scotland's weather and climate, we have to recognise that there have been individual moments in history when a specific *weather* event has shaped aspects of Scotland's history. For example, the tragic Eyemouth fishing disaster, caused by a storm on 14 October 1881, lives long in the memory. Equally, however, there have been periods when the *climate* has influenced history – for example, the cold years and bad harvests of the 1690s, known as the 'dear years of King William'. When we discuss aspects of *climate change*, however, we move the discussion to longer intervals of time, when climate was subject to distinctive, and sometimes radical, changes. During recent decades the prevailing teaching in schools has been that climate in the past was essentially a constant thing, subject to random variations from season to season and year to year. Today, we have moved from that view to a type of thinking, expressed daily in the media, of how the rate of climate change is accelerating and that global warming will soon lead us to our doom.

The Brahan Seer, climate and weather

Kenneth MacKenzie, better known as Coinneach Odhar (the Brahan Seer) was born at the start of the seventeenth century at Baile na Cille in Uig Parish on the Isle of Lewis. He is reputed to have had 'second sight' and the 'Prophecies of the Brahan Seer' are well known – with numerous foretelling weather and climate disasters.

The legend tells that one night in Uig, Kenneth MacKenzie's mother witnessed all the graves in the churchyard opening up and allowing the dead to clamber from their resting places and run away in all directions (see account of the Uig Floods in Chapter 8). Later that night they all returned to their graves, which closed behind them as they climbed in – all, that is, except one. At that point a fair lady came rushing through the air. She said that she was the Maid of Norway (the daughter of the King of Norway), whose body had been found on a beach close to the graveyard and interred in the graveyard. She asked the woman to go to a nearby loch, where she would find a blue stone. She should collect the stone and give it to her son, Kenneth. The stone had a hole in the centre of it and when Kenneth looked through it, it made him blind in one eye but gave him the gift of second sight, and his fame spread far and wide.

He prophesied that civil disruption in the Highlands would follow a period of drought during which the River Beauly would dry up on three occasions. He also foretold that a period of drastic emigration would take place across the Highlands 'to islands now unknown, but which shall yet be discovered in the boundless oceans, after which the deer and other wild animals in the huge wilderness shall be extermi-nated and drowned by horrid black rains [siantan dubh]' – the latter analogous to the descriptions of ashfalls over Orkney and Shetland that accompanied past volcanic eruptions in Iceland. In a reference to coastal erosion, he described how an eight-ton boulder near Petty Bay between Culloden and Moray that was then 'high and dry upon the land as it appears to people this day . . . will be suddenly found as far advanced into the sea as it now lies away from it inland, and no one will see it removed or be able to account for its sudden and marvellous transportation' (see accounts of floods and storms at Findhorn in Chapter 5).

We all talk about the weather. From a morning shopping trip to the Co-op in Wick to the tearooms of Dumfries, the weather is always the main topic of conversation. One can hardly imagine the weather being such a key subject for discussion in other areas of the world, where the climate is more uniform between one season and another. In India, for example, most discussions about the weather start and end with the monsoon; there is relatively little discussion of the vagaries of the wet and dry seasons. Is the weather in Scotland in the forefront of our minds because it is so relatively unpredictable? Some summers, for example, appear to be characterised by incessant rain and cool weather, while others are dry and hot. Dry and wet spells seem to come and go with little predictability. We bask in the pleasure of a hot dry spell when it happens and moan when we trudge through the wet slush on a winter's afternoon. Then, if a dry spell lasts for a long time and develops into a drought, we complain that it is too hot and pray for rain to clear the air.

When we think of climate change over longer periods of time, we often remark on how few winters there have been recently when snow has been widespread. We listen at Christmas to the song which includes the line 'I'm dreaming of a white Christmas', yet for many Scottish children, snow is a rare thing indeed. Is our climate really changing – is it really becoming warmer? The media tell us that global warming is indeed taking place and that we face climatic disaster. Are we to believe them? If it is becoming warmer now, then when was the weather much colder? And how far back in time do we have to go to find patterns of weather quite unlike those that we experience today?

If it is indeed the case that climate has changed, how have such changes affected Scottish society? If we read any of the classic books on Scottish history, there is almost no mention of weather and climate. Could the political and social history of Scotland have been played out across a landscape where climate was indeed constant? Were past periods in Scotland's history when the spectre of famine loomed large entirely divorced from climate? When we read Andrew Fletcher's speech to the Scottish parliament in 1698, when he criticised wealthy Scottish landowners who still enjoyed their 'delicate morsels, when so many are already dead and so many are struggling with dearth' are we to conclude that the hunger he described was only socially – and politically – induced?

The climatic extremes of the 1690s serve to illustrate that Scotland's location in the mid latitudes of the northern hemisphere places it firmly within a zone of highly changeable weather and climate. On the one hand, the North Atlantic Ocean and its Gulf Stream result in the region being warmer than it otherwise would be given its latitude. On the other hand, Scotland is situated within an area of the northern hemisphere characterised by the collision of warm and cold air masses, the principal cause of storms and rainfall. During some periods when warm air masses are displaced further north than normal, we experience fine weather. By contrast, when cold polar air is displaced to the south, we may experience extremely cold winters. We therefore live on the edge of warm and cold, of rainfall and drought, of storminess and calm conditions.

So let us begin our journey into the past by first considering how weather and climate work. We need to do this in four ways:

1. We need to consider the *structure of the Earth's atmosphere* – what it looks like and what it consists of.
2. We need to understand the changing motion of *the Earth in space*, the main characteristics of its orbit around the Sun and how these processes affect weather and climate.
3. We need to consider the *dynamics of the Earth's atmosphere* and to learn how the movement of air masses affects us all.
4. We need to learn how Scotland's weather and climate are affected by the circulation of *the North Atlantic Ocean*.

THE STRUCTURE OF EARTH'S ATMOSPHERE

The gases

We are indeed fortunate on planet Earth. If we measure the temperature of the Earth across its continents and oceans, we find that the average temperature of the planet is +15°C. However, there is a difficulty with such a simplified figure, since readings of the Earth's temperature as measured from satellites and space stations tell us that our planet is emitting heat out to space as if it had an average temperature of -16°C. The difference in the figures is due to the fact that the gases in the lower atmosphere trap a lot of the outgoing radiation from the Earth's surface and prevent this radiation from reaching space. These gases are capable of effectively raising air temperatures by 31°C and are known as greenhouse gases. If we measured the temperature of the tops of clouds we would find an average temperature there of -16°C, exactly that needed to counter the incoming radiation from the Sun.

Although most of the gas in the atmosphere is made up of nitrogen (78%) and oxygen (21%), neither of these are greenhouse gases, which consist of water vapour (less than 1% of the Earth's atmosphere), carbon dioxide (less than 4 hundredths of a per cent of the atmosphere) and methane gas (less than a hundredth of that of carbon dioxide). Incredibly, our survival as a species depends on the effectiveness of these greenhouse gases keeping the temperature of the Earth's lower atmosphere much higher than it otherwise would be.

Beware the ions

Viewed from space, the Earth's weather systems appear extremely complex, yet display striking geometric patterns. From space, much of the Earth appears covered by swirling cloud systems, between which are some of the world's great deserts. Yet virtually all of the cloud that is visible from space occurs within a relatively thin layer of gas that extends no more than approximately 15km above sea level. Over the mid latitudes of the northern hemisphere this distance is much less – between 8 and 12km, roughly the distance between Edinburgh Castle and the Forth Road Bridge. The Earth's atmosphere, by contrast, extends above the cloud tops by an additional 4,000km, at which point it merges with space.

The lowest layer of the Earth's atmosphere within which our weather systems occur is known as the *troposphere*. It contains most of the gases in the atmosphere and allows us life. For the most part, the gases that occur in the troposphere (mainly oxygen, nitrogen and carbon dioxide) are the heaviest. They protect us to a large extent from harmful radiation from the Sun.

At the outer regions of the Earth's atmosphere, only the lightest elements occur and all of these are electrically charged. This is where most of the hydrogen and helium ions occur and it is these ions in our winter skies that create the majestic Northern Lights or *Aurora Borealis*. Thus, in our atmosphere there is a lowest layer where gas concentrations are very high but where there are no charged particles, and an upper layer where gas concentrations are negligible but where electrically charged ions are ubiquitous. In the inter-

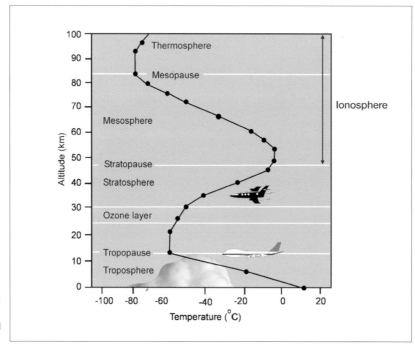

Profile of air temperature through the Earth's atmosphere. Note the inversion of the profile at the top of the tropopause that causes the majority of the gases necessary for life on Earth to be confined to the troposphere.

vening region of the atmosphere, we encounter intermediate gas concentrations and plenty of ions. This intermediate part of the Earth's atmosphere is known, not surprisingly, as the *ionosphere*.

Ozone holes, skin cancer and hope for the future

Ozone is a relatively heavy molecule composed of three atoms of oxygen. Ultraviolet radiation from the Sun creates oxygen ions in the upper stratosphere, which then sink into the lower part of the stratosphere, where they recombine to create triple molecules of ozone (O_3). Within the stratosphere, ozone has a tendency to re-form back to the double molecule (O_2). This process is accelerated by available chlorine, fluorine and bromine ions in the stratosphere. We need to be very aware of this since ozone protects us from harmful ultraviolet radiation. Our problem is that for over 100 years the concentrations of chlorine in the atmosphere have been steadily increasing. These gases are generally described as *chlorofluorocarbons* (CFCs). We are all responsible for producing CFCs – they are used in fridges, coolants, de-icers, solvents, fire extinguishers as well as being a product of jet aircraft exhaust. During the 1980s, scientists noticed stratospheric ozone concentrations over the Antarctic continent were depleted – to the extent that the depletion was described as a huge ozone hole. More recently, a similar ozone hole was noted over the Arctic. Fortunately for us all, the scientific community collaborated with governments of the world to ensure that CFC production was halted and that new, environmentally friendly compounds were used in their place. Today, CFC production has fallen and although stratospheric ozone concentrations have stopped their decline, they are still well above pre-industrial values.

When we sunbathe during summer we are always advised to use sun cream with an appropriate factor number. These creams are specifically designed to shield us against the harmful effects of ultraviolet radiation.

Between approximately 50 and 80km above the Earth's surface, solar radiation is very effective in creating ions of oxygen. These positively charged particles, largely because of their weight, descend slowly through the ionosphere to altitudes between approximately 15 and 30km. Here they recombine in groups of three to produce ozone. It is indeed fortunate for all of us that ozone is produced as it creates a shield above the troposphere in an area known as the lower *stratosphere* where the ozone intercepts harmful shortwave radiation from the Sun.

Good morning, sunshine

The continual bombardment of our atmosphere by solar radiation is never constant. Variations in the temperature of the Sun, normally fluctuating around approximately 7,000°C, lead to big changes in the amount of radiation that we receive. In general terms, the higher the temperature of the Sun's surface, the greater the amount of shortwave radiation that reaches our atmosphere. When the average temperature of the Sun is lowered, there is a corresponding decrease in the amount of shortwave radiation that is emitted from its surface. We know that sometimes parts of the Sun's surface are subject to flaring and sudden increases in temperature – in fact, during a period of strong flaring in the late 1980s, the increase in shortwave radiation was so severe that it disrupted military shortwave communications and displaced many satellites from their orbits. Relatively 'cold' areas known as *sunspots* also develop across parts of the Sun's surface. These frequently coincide with warmer than average temperatures across areas around the margins of the sunspots, and increased radiation from the Sun. So even though sunspots are relatively 'cold', in fact an abundance of sunspots means a hotter Sun, while an absence of sunspots means a colder Sun.

Scientists and astronomers have long known that the Sun's history has

Two images of the Sun showing (left) a quiescent and relatively cold Sun and (right) widespread solar flaring and a relatively warm Sun. (Courtesy of NASA.)

 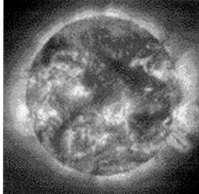

Early 1997 Late 1999

been characterised by different *sunspot cycles* – for example there is general agreement that the Sun experiences a distinctive eleven-year cycle in sunspot activity. Of considerable importance to our understanding of past weather and climate in Scotland is that almost no sunspots were observed during the periods 1400–1510 (known as the *Sporer Minimum)* and 1645–1710 (the *Maunder Minimum)*. It may not be a coincidence that these two periods of solar cooling broadly correspond with part of the era generally described as the *Little Ice Age.*

Climbing above the clouds

Imagine being on a morning flight from Aberdeen to Lerwick. Provided that you are not the unlucky one who has the aircraft seat with no window, the view on take-off is usually through thick cloud. After a while the captain informs you that the aeroplane is flying at a height of 28,000 feet (8.5km). Looking out of the window you see the tops of the clouds that form a blanket of white. They look solid enough to walk on, but the ice crystals making up the clouds wouldn't bear any weight. Above the clouds is clear blue sky. Outside, the air temperature is around -50°C, while the air pressure is about one fifth of what it is at sea level. In fact, the air pressure outside the aircraft is approximately what it is in the central part of a tornado; were the windows to open, most items would be sucked out of the plane.

The reason we nearly always witness the broad white carpet of cloud tops when we go on a flight in a jet aircraft is because most jets tend to cruise either at the very top of the troposphere or, more usually, at the base of the stratosphere. The reason they do this is to avoid the turbulence of the clouds themselves. It makes for the best fuel efficiency. But in terms of weather, the tops of the clouds represent a huge temperature inversion in the atmosphere (known as the *tropopause*; see p. 8). Apart from a very shallow layer of air near the ground surface, air temperatures progressively decrease upwards from near the ground surface to the top of the troposphere. At this altitude, the gases in the troposphere can no longer rise since the air above, at the base of the stratosphere, is warmer than the air beneath. From an early age we learn that hot air rises; to be more specific, air will always continue to rise as long as the parcels of rising air are warmer than the surrounding air.

Trapped air and wind

The view from our passenger seat on the aeroplane is of the base of the stratosphere and the very top of the troposphere. As stated earlier, this altitude tends to be between 8 and 12km in the middle latitudes of the northern hemisphere, but may be as high as approximately 15km over low latitudes. This restriction of the altitude to which air can rise effectively places a cap across the top of the troposphere (the aforementioned tropopause), and although there are a few gaps through which gases can be exchanged with the stratosphere, to all intents and purposes the existence of the temperature inversion at the tropopause means that the majority of gases in our atmosphere are trapped. It is within this relatively confined area that most of our weather is generated.

After landing in Lerwick there may be a relatively thin layer of fog, known in Scotland as haar, that has developed across the sea and land. As at the top of the troposphere, such low-level fogs are also temperature inversions, where the air temperatures over the sea and land are lower than those in the overlying air. Normally, haar will disappear when the land and sea surfaces are heated sufficiently to cause evaporation. Similar phenomena often occur within valleys overnight, when cold air descends from neighbouring hillsides into low-lying areas. The difference between these localised temperature inversions and the large inversion at the top of the troposphere is simply that, whereas the former will disappear as soon as sufficient heating has taken place, the latter is a permanent feature of the Earth's atmosphere.

Snowfall and blizzards

As mentioned earlier, all clouds are composed of ice crystals. The fundamental reason why it rains (rather than snows) most of the time is that as the ice crystals move down through the troposphere they are warmed rather than cooled. In this way, each ice crystal changes state from solid to liquid. We are all familiar with the moods of rain – from continuous drizzle to heavy rain. Drizzle is a characteristic of a warm front – namely an area where cold air at the ground's surface is gradually overridden by warm air. If the cold air is above freezing point, drizzle and light rain are produced. If the cold air is below freezing point, the ice crystals do not melt and fall as snow. Usually such an occurrence requires relatively still air conditions – it can be a characteristic of a warm front or of an occluded front.

Thus, we have the first stage of a snowfall event. Once the snow has fallen and a cold front approaches, the winds are capable of blowing snow around to create blizzard conditions – for the most part such winds act to transport snow that has already fallen, moving it into drifts rather than depositing new snow.

After this second stage, the cold front may pass and the country starts to experience high-pressure anticyclonic conditions. In winter, if such an anticyclone is long-lasting, the snow, having already fallen, may remain frozen for weeks. During such periods, the skies are clear and no snow falls, but freezing temperatures transform the fallen snow (and slush from traffic) into ice. The low Sun angles, together with the albedo (reflectivity) of the white snow surface, then make it difficult for the snow and ice to melt. For the snow to melt and finally disappear, an incursion of warm air is needed.

Colour, radiation and weather

Tramping over the slopes beneath the Paps of Jura on a clear summer's day, the sky is a translucent blue and the Atlantic Ocean to the west shimmers turquoise to the horizon. Yet why is the sky blue, why a turquoise sea and why do sunsets across the Paps cause the heather-covered hillsides to shimmer a golden colour?

A well-known law of physics states that the greater the temperature of an object emitting radiation, the shorter the wavelength of the radiation. The Sun, with its very high surface temperature, emits large quantities of shortwave radiation, together with quantities of radiation in the visible

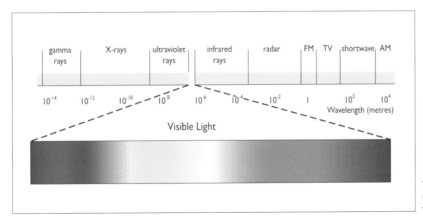

The electromagnetic spectrum, part of which is visible light.

spectrum as well as some radiation at longer wavelengths. The wavelengths of the radiation emitted from the Sun are extremely short and are measured in units known as *Ångströms,* each Ångström being equal to a millionth of a centimetre. The majority of solar radiation that makes up visible light lies within the wavelength range between 0.3 and 0.7 Ångströms. Shorter wavelength radiation is typically less than 0.3 Ångströms and is made up of X-rays, gamma rays and alpha particles, while longer wavelength radiation extends from approximately 1 Ångström to over 100 Ångströms and ranges from infrared radiation to radio waves.

The majority of solar radiation that is emitted occurs within the visible spectrum and represents light, with the kaleidoscopic sequence red, orange, yellow, green, blue, indigo and violet (ROYGBIV). Red represents the longest wavelength of colour in the spectrum and violet shortest.

When solar radiation passes through the Earth's atmosphere, the various wavelengths of radiation correspond approximately with the diameters of the gas molecules that are present. The radiation is scattered by the gas molecules and this effect results in the production of colour. This is why the sky is blue. It is also why the ocean is turquoise on some days and a dark, forbidding grey on others, and why reds and pinks predominate during sunsets. In cases where there is a lot of dust in the atmosphere, as often happens after a volcanic eruption, incoming radiation from the Sun is scattered by ash particles resulting in even more intensely pink and red evening skies.

Volcanic eruptions and climate

When a large volcanic eruption takes place, much of the ash is emitted into the troposphere. The ash then circles the Earth and is very quickly washed out within rainfall. If, however, the eruption is sufficiently violent and large-scale, causing the ash to pass vertically through the troposphere into the overlying stratosphere, the effects on climate are quite different. Ash within the stratosphere tends to remain there much longer. This is not surprising, since atmospheric gases do not exchange easily between the stratosphere and troposphere. Ash within the stratosphere tends to circle the Earth and remains there for months, or even years. When this happens, the presence of the ash is sufficient to block a certain amount of incoming solar radiation, causing cooling of the Earth's surface. Eruptions like this that have caused cooling of the

Earth's surface in recent history include those of Mt Tambora (Indonesia) in 1815, Krakatoa (Indonesia) in 1883 and Mt Pinatubo (Philippines) 1991. By contrast, when Mt St Helens erupted in Washington State in 1980, most of its ash was ejected into the troposphere and later washed out within rainfall.

Another issue that is vital in determining the impact of a large volcanic eruption on the Earth's climate is whether or not an eruption takes place in the low latitudes near the Equator, or if it happens in the middle or high latitudes of one hemisphere. Large volcanic eruptions that take place at high latitudes tend to affect the climate of that particular hemisphere but not the other. By contrast, large eruptions that take place in the low latitudes tend to result in the dispersal of ash into both hemispheres. Clearly, a very large eruption at low latitudes that is capable of ejecting ash into the stratosphere is liable to be associated with the spread of ash across the stratosphere in both hemispheres and thus is likely to have the greatest impact on the Earth's climate. This is why, for example, the eruption of Krakatoa produced remarkable orange and red sunsets in places as far apart as London and Buenos Aires. By contrast, some of Iceland's largest eruptions have a more geographically restricted impact. Unfortunately, Scotland's proximity to Iceland means that its climate is susceptible to volcanic eruptions in its own backyard.

Living in a greenhouse

Shortwave radiation is able to pass through the array of gases and reach the Earth's ground surface. It can penetrate even 1m or so into seawater, this being a reason why swimming in the sea on a hot summer's day with all but your head underwater will not protect you from the effects of shortwave radiation. Much of the shortwave radiation that reaches the Earth's surface is reflected back into the atmosphere. The catch is that, due to the relatively low temperatures of land and ocean surfaces, the outgoing reflected radiation takes place at much longer wavelengths, while the carbon dioxide molecules in the air are just the size to cause the outgoing radiation to be scattered and reflected. Much of the outgoing radiation is not able to get past the troposphere and as a result is heated to a greater degree that it otherwise would be. This effect is known as the *greenhouse effect*.

The enhanced greenhouse effect –
the flashing warning light

High up on a mountain top on the island of Mauna Loa in Hawaii, a scientific observatory is perched close to the summit of one of Hawaii's many ancient volcanoes. Here, in 1958, Charles Keeling started a series of measurements of the carbon dioxide content of the atmosphere. Part of his reasoning for having a scientific observatory near the top of an old volcano in the middle of the Pacific Ocean was that the location was ideal for measuring changes in the gas composition of the atmosphere, since firstly it was far away from any large cities, and secondly it was located high above sea level.

In the first years that measurements were made, Keeling's scientific team made very careful measurements of the carbon dioxide gas concentrations. In 1958, the average value of carbon dioxide concentration was measured at around 310 parts per million by volume (ppmv). As the graph

of measurements unfolded, it became clear that the values were increasing slightly each year while also displaying a seasonal zigzag variation. The reason soon became clear – the measurements were recording the annual cycle of photosynthesis by vegetation on a global scale, when carbon dioxide is seasonally abstracted from the atmosphere.

Since the time of the first measurements of carbon dioxide concentrations at Mauna Loa, the values have been increasing year by year such that at the start of the twenty-first century the average value had increased to close to 370 ppmv. But what sort of values existed for carbon dioxide concentrations prior to 1959? Remarkably, the answer to this question came from cores of ice sampled from Greenland and Antarctica.

Bubbles of air trapped between the ice crystals in the ice cores showed that at the end of the last ice age the carbon dioxide

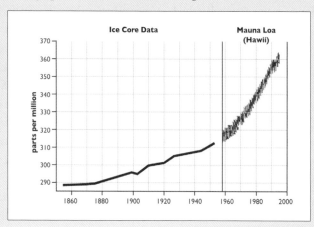

Atmospheric CO_2 record from ice cores and instrumental record from Mauna Loa in Hawaii show a recent accelaration.

concentration was around 280 ppmv and remained around this value until the Industrial Revolution. During the middle of the eighteenth century the values started to rise increasingly steadily through both the nineteenth and twentieth centuries. The most important lesson to be learned is that the greenhouse effect has always existed – civilisation faces the dilemma of an *enhanced greenhouse effect* caused by an anthropogenic increase in carbon dioxide concentrations. The additional carbon produced by human activities has come from two main sources. First, during the eighteenth and nineteenth centuries the main source of carbon was due to the clearance of forests and the creation of farmland for agriculture, together with the burning of wood and charcoal for fuel during the Industrial Revolution. After 1900, most of the extra carbon came from the burning of our fossil reservoirs of carbon, namely coal, oil and natural gas.

Nowadays the industrial emissions of carbon give great cause for concern while a second major area of worry is the amount of carbon released into the atmosphere through the cutting down of areas of tropical rainforest. At present approximately 55% of the excess carbon produced each year finds its way into the troposphere while another 25–30% ends up in the world's oceans. There seems to be no end in sight to annual increases in atmospheric carbon dioxide concentrations. A wide range of scenarios exist for the future, all with the principal aim of predicting what future concentrations are likely to be and what will be the likely effects on global climate. One thing is for sure – since these gases reflect back in the troposphere outgoing longwave radiation from the Earth's surface, the effect will be an inexorable rise in air temperatures.

As long as the Earth has had an atmosphere there has been a greenhouse effect. The problem that society has today is that carbon dioxide concentrations in the troposphere have been steadily increasing since the Industrial Revolution and have been rising even faster during recent decades. This can mostly be put down to the activities of humans, especially the effects of industrialisation and the destruction of rainforests. Whatever the pros and cons of the greenhouse effect and its consequences, it must never be forgotten that the greenhouse effect is a fundamental element of the Earth's atmosphere and weather. During the last ice age, the greenhouse effect was working effectively although the carbon dioxide concentrations (typically 250–270 parts per thousand compared with 350 parts per thousand at present) were much lower than today. The greenhouse effect itself is therefore not the problem. The real problem is the *enhanced* greenhouse effect.

THE EARTH IN SPACE

Spinning a yarn

At present the Earth rotates around the Sun approximately every 365 days and 6 hours. This is the modern Christian calendar, often referred to as the Gregorian calendar after its enactment in a papal bull by Pope Gregory XII in 1582. In order to allow the calendar to adjust to the extra 6 hours over the 365 days, a leap year is added every four years on 29 February. The preceding Julian calendar was only finally abandoned in 1752 and, as part of the adjustment, 2 September of that year was followed the next day by 14 September of the new Gregorian calendar.

The Earth rotates around the Sun in the form of an ellipse. The longest day coincides with the summer solstice on 21 June, while the shortest day in the northern hemisphere occurs on the winter solstice, on 21 December. The nature of the Earth's elliptical rotation means that the winter solstice in the northern hemisphere (between 20 and 22 December, when it is usually pretty cold in Scotland) corresponds almost exactly with the time in the elliptical orbit when the Earth is *closest* to the Sun: 3 January (known as *perihelion*). The same holds true for midsummer (21 June), which takes place when the Earth in its elliptical orbit is *furthest* from Sun; the precise day when the Earth is

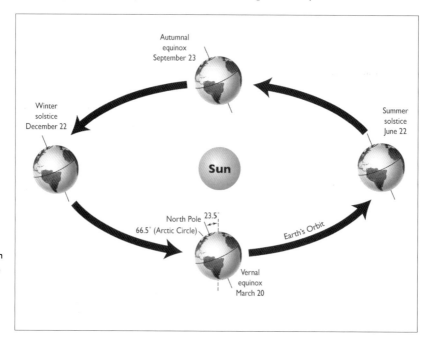

Pattern of Earth orbit changes around the Sun. Note that at present the Earth is closest to the Sun during January. However, the tilt of the Earth on its axis is sufficient to cause the northern hemisphere to experience cooling at this time of year.

furthest from the Sun is 13 days later, on 4 July (known as *aphelion*). In fact, aphelion coincides with the northern hemisphere summer, when the Earth receives approximately 3.5% less solar radiation than the annual mean (as measured at the outer edge of the Earth's atmosphere). Halfway through the Earth's rotation from winter to summer solstice, day and night are of equal duration (known as the *equinoxes*), with the spring equinox occurring on 20 March and the autumn equinox on 22 September.

So how on Earth can it be that at the time when we have our cold winters the Earth is at its closest to the Sun? The answer lies in the tilt of the Earth on its axis. At present the Earth is tilted approximately 23.44° to the vertical. This value changes slightly every year – over the last 3 million years the amount of tilting has varied between 21.39° and 24.36°. In fact this pattern of tilt changes from one extreme to the other and back again on a regular basis every 41,000 years. The significance to us of the 23.44° tilt angle is that during our winters the northern hemisphere of the Earth is tilted *away* from the Sun. As we all know, winter is the time of year when daylight hours are short.

Tilts, latitudes and a heat problem

As a result of these processes, all areas north of a latitude of 90° North less 23.44° North witness the Sun at, or only just above, the horizon for 24 hours each day during the winter. Conversely, these areas experience almost continuous daylight during the summer months. On maps, this latitude is routinely taken as 66.5° North and is known as the Arctic Circle, the area to the north also called the *Land of the Midnight Sun*. The latitude of Scotland is slightly less than this. The north of Unst in the Shetland Isles is at 60° 50" North while in the far south Dumfries lies at 55° 4" North. So Scotland is located a few degrees to the south of the Arctic Circle – in winter we live almost on the edge of permanent winter darkness.

These aspects of time, seasonal changes and the nature of the Earth's orbit around the Sun have very important effects on our weather in a number of ways. The most important relates to tilt. When we experience our winter, and the northern hemisphere is tilted away from the Sun, the land surface loses heat that cannot be compensated by heat from a Sun that barely rises above the horizon. The land-masses, as opposed to ocean areas, are most affected by this process. Of all the land areas that exist in the middle and high latitudes of the northern hemisphere, the Russian subcontinent is the most influential. In this area, there is considerably more heat lost in winter than gained during summer – causing ice to freeze in the ground. Over thousands of years this process has resulted in the growth in this area of great thicknesses of permanently frozen ground known as *permafrost*. Permafrost is also a feature in central and northern Alaska, the Canadian Arctic archipelago and most other islands bordering the Arctic Ocean – all due to the fact that more heat is lost from the ground surface during winter than is gained during summer.

El Niño, La Niña and world weather

El Niño refers to the irregular warming in the sea surface temperatures from the coasts of Peru and Ecuador to the equatorial central Pacific. When it occurs it can cause disruption to weather worldwide. This phenomenon is not totally predictable, but on average occurs once every four years. It usually lasts for about 18 months after it begins. The phenomenon of La Niña, by contrast, is almost completely the opposite to El Niño. When this happens, the tropical ocean cools down, reducing convection in the troposphere and changing weather patterns in quite different ways.

Several aspects of the atmosphere's behaviour are remarkable and entirely unique to the phenomenon of El Niño. Many areas of the world suffer abnormal drought, while others experience heavy rainfall and severe flooding. When the central and eastern Pacific Ocean heats up during an El Niño there is a corresponding increase in convection within the troposphere, leading to increased rainfall across the eastern Pacific. During El Niño events, there is a resulting reorganisation of the pattern of circulation through the troposphere. The biggest changes take place in the tropics, while further to the north the mid-latitude jet streams are also affected. It is this change to the mid-latitude jet streams that can affect Scotland's weather and climate. For example, the El Niño of 1982–83 caused droughts and fires across Australia and southern Africa as well as heavy rains extending from California in the north to Peru and Chile in the south. But due to changes in the jet stream, the winter of 1982–83 across Scotland was one of the stormiest in the entire twentieth century. In general terms, strong El Niño circulation during winter coincides with stormy winters across Scotland. Similarly the early phase of a major El Niño during 1997–98 was also associated with stormy weather across Scotland.

Together with an ice sheet over Greenland and an Arctic Ocean covered by sea ice in winter, the cold land surfaces that stretch around the high latitudes of the northern hemisphere result in a cooling of the overlying air. In the same way as air expands when it is heated, it shrinks when it is cooled. So in winter the lower part of the troposphere across the high latitudes of the northern hemisphere is chilled on a sustained basis, and as it is chilled it shrinks.

DYNAMICS OF THE EARTH'S ATMOSPHERE

Transfer of heat

The vigour with which atmospheric circulation transfers heat and energy from low to high latitudes (and compensates for the heat that is lost across high-latitude areas during winter) is at its greatest during winter, and with this come faster wind speeds. This situation is in striking contrast to midsummer in the northern hemisphere, when the Sun is overhead at the Tropic of Cancer. At midsummer, the region north of the Arctic Circle is tilted towards the Sun and experiences continuous daylight. Solar heating of polar regions is at its greatest at this time of year, and it is no coincidence that the rate of circulation in the troposphere is at its lowest then.

Inspection of the amount of heat we receive across Scotland each season shows very clearly that for our latitude our survival depends on the solar radiation that we receive during the summer months. In winter the amount of heat we receive at the ground surface is limited indeed. Fortunately for us, life is bearable, since we also receive heat from the North Atlantic Ocean.

Coping with pressure

For over 200 years people in Scotland have measured the pressure of the air. Many houses have barometers, which in the old days showed a dial with the words, 'Rain', 'Changeable' and 'Fair'. The older barometers contained a column of mercury and changes in air pressure caused the mercury column to rise and fall. Air pressure was initially therefore measured in 'inches of mercury'. The passage of a severe storm, for example, might be associated with a lowest air pressure of 28.6 inches of mercury, while clear skies and hot weather on a summer's day might cause air pressure to exceed 30 inches of mercury, this high value of air pressure reflecting the fact that warm air expands and increases the pressure on the air at the ground surface.

In the early years of the twentieth century, a change in measurement was made whereby inches of mercury were converted to a metric scale. The standard reference for mean air pressure at sea level was equated to 1 bar of pressure equivalent to 1,000 millibars (mb), or thousandths of a bar of pressure. This scheme of measurement is very convenient for meteorologists, who routinely measure air pressure at different altitudes above sea level. Air pressure falls with increasing altitude simply because the pressure of overlying air upon underlying air decreases with increasing altitude. Thus, halfway between sea level and the top of the troposphere, typical air pressure is in the order of 500 mb, while air pressure at the top of the troposphere is in the order of 200 mb. The most extreme storms and hurricanes that we experience on Earth are associated with air pressures that rarely fall below 950 mb. By contrast, the strongest areas of high air pressure (normally in the subtropics) rarely exceed 1,050 mb. Tornadoes do not conform to this pattern – these are much more extreme phenomena, the lowest pressure in a tornado frequently falling to between 200 and 300 mb (this is why the windows of buildings and cars tend to be sucked outwards during the passage of a tornado, since the air pressure outside the car or building is much lower than the air pressure inside).

Although we don't have to worry too much about the occurrence of tornadoes in Scotland, we do need to be aware of the way in which changes in air pressure influence our weather and climate. This takes us back to the notion of how air in the high latitudes cools and shrinks – especially during winter.

Shrinking and expanding air, and windy days

Suppose we were to embark on a programme of measuring air pressure across the northern hemisphere and at different heights between the ground surface and the top of the troposphere. A good place to measure would be the middle of the troposphere, somewhere around the 500 mb level and well above most mountain regions, where air flow is more streamlined. Around the high latitudes of the northern hemisphere this contour typically sits around 5,300m. By contrast, over North Africa, central Asia, China and the USA, the 500 mb contour is typically in the order of 5,800m. The higher value in the lower latitudes of the northern hemisphere is because of the fact that warm air expands and the overlying atmosphere is pushed upwards from beneath. This means that in the middle of the troposphere there is a *pressure gradient* between the middle and high latitudes of the northern hemisphere (with higher air pressure over the warmer parts of the Earth) and lower pressure over the colder regions. The same is true also for the southern hemisphere, although here the presence of an ice-covered Antarctic continent chilling the air from underneath causes an even stronger pressure gradient than exists in the northern hemisphere.

Were the Earth not spinning on its axis, this pressure gradient would result in a flow of air directly from low latitudes to the polar regions. However, owing to the Earth's anticlockwise rotation beneath the moving air, the flow of air instead takes place more or less *along* the lines of equal air pressure. As a result, near the top of the troposphere there is a tremendously powerful and sustained circumpolar flow of air travelling from west to east around the mid latitudes of both the northern and southern hemispheres known as the *jet stream*. The jet stream is never a purely circular flow around the mid latitudes of both hemispheres; instead its flow is characterised by a sinuous meander as it finds its way around the major mountain ranges of the northern hemisphere (e.g. the Rockies and the Ural Mountains).

Troughs, ridges and weather

In some areas of the mid latitudes where the pressure gradient happens to be greater than normal there is an acceleration in the flow of air from one area into another. Elsewhere, there may be areas where a decrease in the pressure gradient results in a deceleration or slowing down in the rates of air flow. In this way, a mass of air may accumulate over one particular area and remove air from another area. As a consequence, parts of the troposphere may experience higher than average air pressure (anticyclones) and lower than average air pressure (cyclones). These are the features with which we are familiar on our weather maps and which are responsible for our weather. Thus, for example, the eastern flanks of indentations (troughs) in the jet stream tend to be areas where cyclones form in the lower troposphere while the bulges (ridges) tend to be associated with the growth of anticyclones.

Sometimes the jet stream exhibits a very streamlined flow around the mid latitudes. When this happens, weather systems never tend to be long-lasting. Cyclones, for example, tend to form and decay quickly but are also rapidly replaced by new cyclones. When the flow of the jet stream is more sluggish, the ridges and troughs become more prominent. They result in cold air masses being displaced further southwards and warm air masses shifted further north than usual. Sometimes, the jet stream flow can be so sluggish that giant meanders frequently result in cells of displaced warm and cold air being isolated. Under such circumstances, when the brakes on the jet stream are fully down hard, the isolated air masses often lead to weather extremes characterised

Understanding weather maps

In the modern technological age, the detail on weather maps has been air-brushed out so that for most maps on the back pages of the daily newspaper all we see are symbols for clouds, rain, snow, wind direction and the occasional value for air temperature. Some newspapers still provide the contours of air pressure and the position of weather fronts. But what do they mean? Are there weather fingerprints on the map that tell tales of the circumpolar vortex? They are indeed there, but we need to know what to look for.

As an undulation or eddy develops at the boundary of the colliding cold and warm air masses, warm air starts to rise over cold. Along the eastern sector of the eddy and over distances of hundreds of kilometres, the warm air is progressively displaced to higher and higher altitudes. On weather maps the imaginary line across the ground surface where warm air comes into contact with cold is shown as a *warm front* and is drawn as a solid line with black semicircles regularly spaced along its length. Although the warm front refers to the boundary between the air masses at the ground surface, the same boundary extends above the ground and is represented by a gently rising slope.

In the western sector of the eddy, the dense cold air pushes beneath

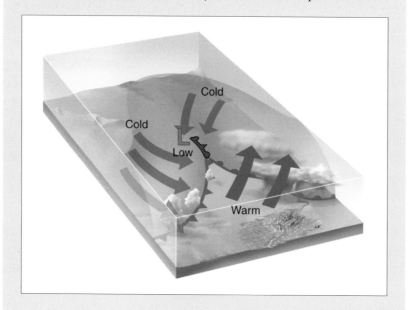

Three-dimensional model showing the development of warm and cold weather fronts as warm air comes into contact with cold air in the mid latitudes of the northern hemisphere.

the warm from behind and causes the warm air to rise. Here the boundary at the ground surface is known as a *cold front*. In general because of the pushing of the cold air against the warm air, the boundary between the cold and warm air is much steeper. This steepness results in air turbulence and the ascent and descent of moisture-laden air currents usually results in gusts of wind and heavy rain.

As the cyclone progresses the cold front tends to catch up with the warm front. When the two fronts come into contact at the ground surface, a wedge of cold air is driven beneath the warm, with the effect that the warm air between the cold and warm fronts is lifted off the ground. Meteorologists normally draw a line from the lowest part of the 'lifted' sector of warm air onto the ground surface. This line is known as an *occluded front* and the position of the line when drawn on a weather map shows the alignment of the part of the cyclone that is in its final stages of decay.

So on weather maps that show Scotland perched precariously on the edge of the North Atlantic Ocean, we see, especially during winter, sets of warm, cold and occluded fronts grouped together in distorted triangular shapes each showing the respective positions of the boundaries between the warm and cold air. Elsewhere on the map we can see isolated, usually sinuous occluded fronts, showing the approximate positions where former cyclones were but are no more.

by a persistence of one type of weather. Thus, in summer, the displacement northward and the isolation of a cell of warm air can lead to a prolonged drought. Conversely, the southward displacement and isolation of a cold air mass during winter can lead to a lengthy period of clear skies and freezing temperatures. Our weather is highly variable because the mid-latitude jet stream of the northern hemisphere is right over our heads.

What goes up must come down

Because of the orbital motion of the Earth around the Sun, during midsummer in the northern hemisphere the Sun is overhead at the Tropic of Cancer (23.5° North). The northern hemisphere is then tilted towards the Sun and this is when we experience days when the Sun does not set until late in the evening and wakes the cockerel so early that sleep is broken in the early hours. This is also the time of the year when we receive maximum amounts of heat from the Sun. Since the polar regions of the northern hemisphere experience continuous daylight during the summer months, the imbalance in heat between the Arctic and the mid latitudes is at a minimum. The summer months therefore represent the time of year when atmospheric circulation is generally much slacker than during winter – as a consequence, it is a time when stormy, inclement weather is rare. Summer is the time of the year when we *expect* fine weather. But this is not always the case, as we know, and often balmy summer days are replaced by weeks of rain and drizzle.

South of us in the subtropics, the effect of the Sun heating the air is to cause air to rise. The warm air keeps rising until it reaches the top of the troposphere, where it is cooled. As it starts to cool it sinks, creating a type of circulation known as a *Hadley* cell. As the air sinks it increases the pressure on the underlying air. The effect of this process is to produce gigantic areas of sinking air devoid of moisture, with higher than average surface air pressure. These areas of the northern hemisphere (and by the same token also across the southern hemisphere) coincide with a small number of cells of high pressure that traverse the circumference of the Earth and which coincide with some of the world's largest desert areas. These are the anticyclones that form along the warm flank of the jet stream, with winds that blow outwards around their margins and in a clockwise direction across the northern hemisphere. Some of these weather systems can be immense. It is not unusual for some of the biggest anticyclones to stretch up to 4,000km in length. Along the

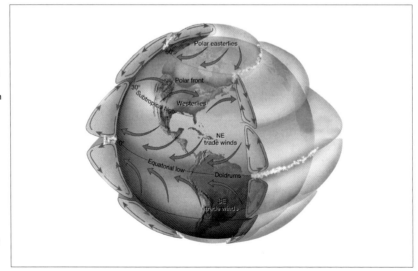

Schematic model of global atmospheric circulation. Note location of Scotland in the area where cold polar air collides with the westerly winds that are generated along the northern edge of the subtropical areas of high pressure. This collision of air masses results in significant air turbulence as warm air is forced above denser cold air and this, in turn, is responsible for the North Atlantic storm track.

southern flanks of the anticyclones the winds become part of the northeast Trade Winds, while along the northern flanks they form a belt of westerly winds. This flow of warm air out of the subtropics enables heat to be transported to higher latitudes experiencing heat loss. If there are significant ridges in the jet stream, this warm, dry air can move up into northern Europe during summer and allow some of us to spend days down on the beach or on mountain tops, while the rest of us are stranded in offices and factories, relying on electric fans to stay cool.

When cold air meets warm

During late December, when the Sun is overhead at the Tropic of Capricorn, heated air slowly rises to the top of the troposphere and starts to move towards the polar regions. To the north, heat loss from the ground surface during the dark winter results in a cooling of the overlying air from underneath. In part this is due to loss of heat from cold land surface, but is accentuated in areas covered by snow and ice, where the rate of heat loss from the ground surface is high. In addition, the presence of a cover of a relatively thin layer of sea ice across much of the Arctic Ocean adds to the chilling of the overlying air. Together, the cold air moves from high latitudes to low latitudes. Here it comes into contact with the much warmer air transported to high latitudes by the mid-latitude westerly winds. Like oil and water, cold and warm air do not mix easily.

When we consider these processes as a whole, we can be guided by the notion that hot air rises while cold air sinks. The analogy of a winter day in a draughty room is a good one. The hot air generated from the heater in the corner rises to the ceiling, where it is cooled. Frequently, the cooling is sufficient to induce condensation, while condensation may also take place in areas of the room where moisture-laden air comes into contact with colder surfaces (e.g. windows). At the same time, cold air finds its way into the room underneath a gap at the base of the door. The incoming draught causes cold air to spread across the surface of the carpet, causing one to huddle even closer to the electric heater. We can think of the same type of process happening across the northern hemisphere. To the south over the subtropics we have our great cells of high pressure, where sinking warm dry air sustains and protects our deserts. To the north the cold polar air formed across polar regions during winter spreads southwards and is incapable of rising.

The boundary between the two air masses of contrasting temperature and density is known as a *front*, while the collision of these two air mass types produces *frontal weather*. The nature of the collisions is often violent, and it is responsible for most of the extreme weather that we experience. The precise way in which collisions take place is reasonably well understood and is portrayed as the strange symbols and contours shown on weather maps. Before we look at the nature of these colliding air masses in more detail we need to remind ourselves that the battlefields where the cold and warm air masses stage their conflicts are determined largely by the behaviour of the mid-latitude jet stream high up in the troposphere.

Fronts – the battlefields of cold and warm air

Across the middle latitudes cold and warm air are continually coming into contact with one another. Since air is continually moving from west to east and is meandering to greater or lesser degrees through the troposphere, individual areas of weather instability are repeatedly generated in areas where troughs occur in the jet stream. Each region of instability develops into an area of low pressure, or cyclone, and having formed, it decays and disappears only to have a new disturbance generated in its place. Because of the greater vigour of atmospheric circulation during winter, cyclonic storms tend to be most frequent and violent during this time of the year.

Why it rains mostly in the west

One of the most striking aspects of Scotland's weather is the comparatively huge amounts of rainfall in the west of the country when compared with the east. A year in Skye, for example, would settle any debate regarding the truth of this statement. By contrast, rainfall in Fife is relatively low by Scottish standards. Even so, the people of Tiree or the Uists, for example, might disagree with this statement and point to the fact that, though they are located far to the west, the weather on these islands, although windy, is relatively dry.

The explanation lies in what happens to moisture-laden air when it is forced to rise. As mentioned, the first port of call for cyclones tracking eastwards across the North Atlantic is the west of Scotland. As the air reaches the mountains of the western and northern Highlands it is forced to rise, and as it rises it is cooled. In fact the rate at which air is cooled with increasing altitude is well known – for every 100m increase in altitude, the air temperature falls by 0.65°C. As air is cooled in this way, it shrinks and becomes less able to contain moisture. So as the air rises (known as *adiabatic ascent*) over the mountains of western Scotland, much of the moisture previously contained within the air is condensed out as rainfall. This type of rainfall is known to meteorologists as *orographic rainfall*.

Once the air has passed eastwards across the highest mountain ranges it is relatively dry. It is also progressively warmed as it descends to lower altitudes (known as *adiabatic descent*) in the course of its overall movement from west to east. Curiously the warming of the air during its descent takes place at a slightly greater rate than when it was rising. In this way, the air that is moved from west to east across the Scottish land mass during the passage of an Atlantic cyclone is much drier in the east of the country than in the west.

But although we have a simple explanation for Portree being much wetter than St Andrews, do we also have an explanation for why Tiree and the Uists, for example, are so dry? The answer is straightforward – many low-lying areas on the west coast are also relatively dry because the air in the eastward-tracking Atlantic cyclones is not forced to rise as it passes over these areas.

The weather disturbances begin their life as eddies or undulations in areas where cold and warm air come into contact. The cold air, being denser, tends to push under the warm air while the warm air tends to ride up over the cold air. As the cold air pushes beneath the warm, the respective *cold and warm fronts* become more accentuated. Eventually the area of warm air, as a result of it being 'squeezed' by the cold and warm fronts on each side, is removed from contact with the ground surface. As the base of the warm air is forced to higher and higher altitudes and replaced by cold air underneath, we witness the decay and disappearance of the cyclone, this stage on weather maps being indicated by an *occluded front* (see p. 24).

We experience the growth, maturity and decay of frontal cyclones in our daily lives. Rush hours during cold fronts can be horrendous, with high winds, driving rain, spray from lorries and windscreen wipers going at full tilt. Many times weak fronts pass over us without us realising that anything untoward has happened. But when a mature cyclone passes over us we know about it. The first sign is not so clear. This is the period of time in advance of the warm front when warm air rises above cold, often over distances of hundreds of kilometres, and as it does so it produces overcast skies and drizzle. As the warm front crosses over us, the air temperatures become slightly milder, quite often the humidity of the air increases drizzle and light rainfall continues while the wind direction may change slightly – often from a southerly to a south-westerly airstream. Then the cold front starts to pass over us. This is when there is a slight chill in the air and many of us sense that it will soon rain quite heavily. At the cold front, with wet-weather gear to the fore, currents of air are driven upwards from near the ground surface to high altitudes. The tremendous turbulence results in a short period of heavy rainfall. Then, as the cold front passes, the air becomes colder, the wind direction shifts to the northwest and the skies eventually clear of dark clouds. Depending on the depth of low pressure at the centre of the cyclone as well as the size of the low pressure system, some cyclones may develop into severe storms. When jet stream flow is streamlined with only poorly defined ridges and troughs, such cyclones tend to form and decay quickly with a conveyor belt of cyclones tracking from east to west after each other across the North Atlantic Ocean.

When the jet stream possesses strong meanders and the troughs are accentuated, large, severe and long-lasting storms may develop – the big storms of the movies. On 11 January 2005 such a storm struck the Outer Hebrides with incredible severity. It lasted over 15 hours and tragically led to the deaths of 5 people, while the ferocity of the hurricane-force winds inflicted damage to many buildings and even the causeways connecting the major islands were severely damaged by the storm waves.

We therefore live in a part of our planet where cold polar air comes into contact with warm air from the subtropics. We also live in the belt of the mid-latitude westerly winds, a spawning ground for winter storms. If the mid-latitude jet stream changes its behaviour, we move from winter storms to mild conditions or to extreme cold. The jet stream is our roulette wheel, where nature decides what happens when warm and cold air masses collide.

Continental land masses are cool – sometimes!

A characteristic feature of most solids is that they do not conduct heat well. The pavement slabs down by the seafront during summer can be very hot on our feet mid afternoon yet cold by evening. The same is true of continental land masses on Earth. During summer they heat up and, as they do so, they cause heating of the overlying air causing it to expand and rise. Across the mid latitudes of the northern hemisphere are two continental land masses affected in this way. One is the North American continent, the other is the vast land mass stretching from northwest Europe to northeastern Siberia. After emerging from the gloom and cold of winter both land masses are subject to heating. Across northern Canada and Arctic Russia, the heating is usually sufficient to melt the ground surface of the permafrost which had remained frozen all winter. The rising air results in a lowering of air pressure at the ground surface that starts during spring and culminates during the summer and autumn months. The development of low pressure has the effect of drawing air from surrounding areas into these regions. Across Asia, this process has the effect of setting in motion one of the world's great weather processes – the *monsoon* (from an Arabic word meaning 'season') – when warm air laden with moisture moves northward from the Indian Ocean and is drawn towards the Asian subcontinent. In northern Europe also, the lowering of air pressure across Scandinavia during spring and summer makes it easier for Atlantic cyclones to move from west to east across northern Europe.

Things change during winter, however. These vast land masses, deprived of sufficient heat, start to cool. As they lose heat, they chill the overlying air from beneath causing it to sink and, as it sinks, it creates high pressure as the air at higher altitudes presses down on the cold air underneath. This means that every autumn, high air pressure starts to develop across Russia and Scandinavia as well as across Canada. High pressure remains throughout the winter months and only starts to break down during spring. In meteorological language, these high-pressure cells that only exist for part of the year are known as *semi-permanent anticyclones*.

The principal effect of the creation of high air pressure during winter across such huge areas of terrain is to provide obstacles to the general west to east movement of surface winds. Cyclones that form over the North Atlantic, for example, are forced to divert around the area of Scandinavian high pressure. In some circumstances the North Atlantic cyclones are diverted northwards instead of towards the Arctic Ocean. At other times they are diverted along the southern flank of the Scandinavian high-pressure cell and travel eastwards across the Mediterranean, bringing stormy, wet winter weather. Quite often, the cyclones move into the North Sea where they start to decay – some even refer to the North Sea as a 'graveyard' of North Atlantic cyclones.

Cold comfort from Greenland ice

Apart from the big Hadley cells over the tropics that last all year round, there is only one other type of high-pressure cell that we need to know about in order to understand our weather. These are the anticyclone cells of high pressure that form over big ice sheets. Of these the biggest is the anticyclone that forms over the Antarctic continent. The one that has a direct effect on Scotland's weather is the anticyclone that forms over the Greenland ice sheet. The presence of surface ice chills the overlying air, making it stable and causing it to sink. Sometimes when such cold air descends into valleys along the margins of the Greenland ice sheet, the winds accelerate creating fearsome high-velocity *katabatic winds*. High air pressure occurs over Greenland all year round and, like elsewhere, it causes low-pressure cells to be steered around the subcontinent. Viewed another way, it acts as a constriction to the general west to east movement of mid-latitude cyclones, forcing them to move along a route towards northern Europe that is positioned to the south of the ice sheet yet north of the main area of subtropical high pressure located over the Azores.

THE NORTH ATLANTIC OCEAN – THE TRANSPORTER OF HEAT AND SALT

Basking in Gulf Stream warmth

So far the discussion of Scotland's weather has been confined to the context of atmospheric processes. However, it would be extremely foolish to imagine that we could account for most of our weather in terms of the atmosphere alone. Apart from anything else, we receive about one third of all our heat from the North Atlantic Ocean. So it is very important to understand the ways in which the ocean affects our climate.

The surface waters of the North Atlantic represent part of a bigger global system that transports heat from the low latitudes (in this case the central Atlantic Ocean) to the Arctic, thereby making up for the net loss of heat from the ground surface. Most of the heat is stored in the warm waters of the Gulf Stream. As water is moved progressively further north it cools and, as it does so, transfers heat from the ocean to the atmosphere. The Atlantic Ocean is also unusual amongst the world's ocean areas because it is the saltiest ocean. This is due to the occurrence of significant evaporation across the surface of the central Atlantic Ocean and also because the low-latitude easterly winds that blow across this area result in the transport of moisture out of the ocean area, across Central America and into the Pacific Ocean. Thus the northward moving flow of water into the North Atlantic Ocean not only brings heat, it also brings salty water.

The Gulf Stream forms an important component of the gyre-like flow of water. We often think of the Gulf Stream as a surface ocean current but we must remember that surface winds blowing over the ocean are able to impart drag on ocean waters to depths in excess of 100m below the sea surface. The prevailing winds that blow across the North Atlantic in the area of the Hadley cell that lies between the mid-latitude westerlies to the north and the north-easterly Trade Winds to the south normally develop as a clockwise spiral-type movement over the ocean surface. The spiral flow is favoured also by the effect of the Earth's rotation (known as the *Coriolis effect*) that causes the ocean currents to be deflected to the right of the direction of the prevailing winds. All these factors together cause the Gulf Stream to exhibit a right-spiralling type of water flow. Some authors have observed that the volume of water involved in this clockwise movement is equal to something like 100 times the volume of water transported by all the world's rivers. The main spiral of the Gulf Stream is of sufficient size that the northward transport of warm water as part of the overall circulation system results in a transfer of heat from the ocean to the atmosphere that is of a similar amount to that delivered to the area by heating from the Sun!

Too much salt is good for us

The northward flow of this water forms part of a larger global system of ocean currents known as the *global thermohaline conveyor* – namely ocean currents that transport heat and salt. Part of this conveyor involves surface currents that enter the South Atlantic Ocean from the Indian Ocean and then move north-wards into the central Atlantic and eventually via the North Atlantic into the

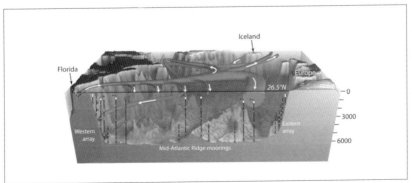

Principal ocean currents in the North Atlantic. The upper currents, which in part form the Gulf Stream, are warm and transfer heat and salt from low to high latitudes. As the cold and salty water sinks in the high latitudes, a set of cold, deep ocean currents are created causing a pattern of return flow from north to south. (Courtesy of the Natural Environment Research Council, UK.)

Norwegian and Greenland Seas. In these high-latitude seas, the cooled surface water is overturned and sinks to the floor of the ocean, where it then moves southwards as salty *Deep Water* ocean currents. This process of Deep Water formation is unique to the North Atlantic region and the oceans surrounding the Antarctic continent – nowhere else in the world does this happen. Deep Water formation is vital, since it represents the mechanism that exports salt from these oceans and prevents the surface currents creating a progressively saltier ocean.

The North Atlantic – one of the saltiest oceans in the world

The saltiness (salinity) of different ocean areas largely depends on a delicate balance between evaporation of moisture from the sea surface, the nature of the prevailing winds over ocean areas – and hence rainfall – together with the amount of fresh water entering the oceans from rivers. As far as the North Atlantic is concerned, the combined effect of these processes is to make the ocean one of the saltiest in the world. The response of the ocean to counteract increasing saltiness is to export the excess salt. The ocean does this by means of gigantic ocean currents – thus salt and heat are transported northwards by surface currents (of which the Gulf Stream is a part) and southwards by deep ocean currents. The area where the surface waters descend to the floor of the ocean is across a vast area east of Greenland. The surface and deep ocean currents in the North Atlantic form part of the global thermohaline conveyor, which represents all the ocean currents that transport heat and salt from one region of the world's oceans to another. There are relatively few places in the world where the surface waters sink to the floor of the ocean to create deep ocean currents. One important area is around parts of the Antarctic circumpolar ocean – the other is in the Greenland Sea. Water formed here by these processes is known as North Atlantic Deep Water, while the Deep Water formed off Antarctica is known as Antarctic Deep Water.

Oceanic and atmospheric fronts – the terrible twins

The mobile boundary between the warmer and less dense waters of the North Atlantic and the colder and denser waters of the northern seas is generally described as the *polar oceanic front*. Together the polar atmospheric front and the polar oceanic front interact in complex and dynamic ways to produce our weather and climate. They are the terrible twins. On the one hand, the development of storms along the polar atmospheric front is fuelled to a large extent by moisture evaporated from the ocean's surface. On the other hand, the polar oceanic front is much less visible, although very potent, its waters and currents responding to complex changes in water heat, saltiness and density. As we shall see later, there are grounds to believe that the position of the polar oceanic front across the North Atlantic has altered dramatically in recent years, and even more so during prehistory.

Deep Water formation – the joker in the pack

Considered at face value, if currents in the North Atlantic were incapable of causing overturning and Deep Water formation, the circulation of the Atlantic Ocean would effectively grind to a halt. If this were to happen, the Gulf Stream would be disrupted and a shutdown in the supply of heat from the ocean to the atmosphere would throw us into a new ice age. This is precisely how many envisage that past ice ages in northern Europe started. Therefore we need to understand the precise mechanisms of how Deep Water is produced, how it can slow down and speed up.

Deep Water formation in the North Atlantic takes place in two main areas, firstly in the Greenland Sea north of Iceland, and secondly in the Labrador Sea between eastern Canada and southern Greenland. One key process that enables water to overturn and sink to the floor of the ocean is an increase in water density. This can happen if ocean water is cooled as it flows further northwards and is chilled by cold air blowing over the ocean surface. The density of surface ocean water is also increased as a result of the formation of sea ice. If air temperatures are low enough, the surface of the ocean freezes – usually to no more than a maximum thickness of 1m. During the freezing process salt is expelled from the freezing water. The excess salt eventually enters the ocean, increasing the water density and causing plumes of cold, denser water to descend from the surface of the ocean to the ocean floor and thereafter move southwards along the floor of the Atlantic Ocean. In some high-latitude ocean areas, the production of sea ice is followed by its removal elsewhere by the prevailing winds. When this happens, the formation of new sea ice is accompanied by the production of new plumes of denser water. Such areas of open ocean are known as *polynyas* and are often referred to as sea ice 'factories'. They are hotspots of Deep Water production.

The enigma of sea ice formation

The formation of North Atlantic Deep Water is intimately linked to the development of sea ice in the Greenland Sea. When cold air originating over Greenland blows offshore across the Greenland Sea, the low air temperatures cause the surface of the ocean to freeze – producing sea ice. Sea ice is rarely more than a few metres thick. Once sea ice has formed, it is moved by winds and currents. When one floe collides with another, the ice frequently buckles to produce a chaotic and highly irregular topography. However, sea ice formation is vital to ocean circulation for a very special reason. When sea ice is produced, the freezing process results in the expulsion of salt. The excess salt enters the surrounding ocean waters and causes them to increase in density. Since the salty water produced in this way is denser than the surrounding ocean water, plumes of salty water descend to the floor of the ocean to produce North Atlantic Deep Water.

The formation of sea ice across the Greenland Sea can be viewed as the vital link that allows the deep ocean currents to export salt and hence enable the ocean thermohaline conveyor to operate. One should always remember that the surface ocean currents of the North Atlantic, of which the Gulf Stream is a part, represent the means by which heat is delivered to our shores. In fact, the Gulf Stream provides northwest Europe with approximately 30% of its atmospheric heat. Some have argued that in the relatively recent past, at the start of the last ice age, North Atlantic Deep Water formation may have ceased altogether and this may have been a contributory catalyst to ice ages.

So how can Deep Water formation be impeded?

Suppose that we wished to slow down the rate of Deep Water production and lead northern Europe towards cooling, what should we do? One obvious thing we could do is to reduce the amount of sea ice production. If we were able to do this, we could slow down the rate of Deep Water formation in the Greenland and Labrador Seas. Another thing we could do would be to allow huge volumes of fresh water to spread across the surface of ocean areas. This would have the effect of increasing the stratification of near-surface ocean waters with less dense fresh water on top of more dense saline waters.

Increased air temperatures linked to global warming can accelerate both of these processes. First, increased air temperatures over high latitudes make it more difficult for sea ice to form over the ocean surface. Second, increased air temperatures lead to increased melting of glaciers and ice sheets. As a result, there is an increased rate of discharge of glacial meltwater from the land into ocean areas. The above processes are counter-intuitive since at first sight one might expect global warming to lead to a heating-up of the oceans. But in the high latitudes of the North Atlantic Ocean and surrounding sea areas the opposite is the case.

A few years ago British and Norwegian government officials met to discuss climate change. Both countries noted that current views on the nature of climate change pointed in two completely opposite directions. On the one hand, scientists have made it quite clear that global warming was going to result in warmer temperatures accompanied by stormier and wetter weather. Others have put forward the contrary view that future changes in our climate will result in a shutdown or a slowdown in the oceanic thermohaline conveyor, linked to a reduction in the formation of Deep Water. Some scientists have pointed to the recent reduction in the extent and thickness of sea ice across the Arctic Ocean as an indicator of this change while others have observed a reduction in the rate at which warm North Atlantic waters are entering the Arctic Ocean as indicative of a slowdown in Deep Water formation.

POSTSCRIPT

It would be nice to be able to state here whether our future climate will become warmer or cooler but unfortunately science has not progressed far enough to provide us with a reliable answer of how our weather and climate are likely to be decades into the future. But there are pointers that can provide us with clues if we know where to look. First, we must develop a clearer understanding of how our weather and climate have changed in prehistory and at what rates. Second, we can learn an enormous amount from the study of historical accounts of past weather and climate in Scotland. With this information we will be much better placed to make more informed judgements on Scotland's future weather and climate.

PART 2
PREHISTORY

CHAPTER 2
OVER THE ICE TO SKYE

The Earth's climate system is a fearsome untamed angry beast that mankind had better be careful about messing with.

W.S. Broecker, *The Glacial World According to Wally*,
Eldigio Press, New York (1995).

INTRODUCTION

After a winter snowfall, the best snowballs are those where the snow packs easily under pressure from the hand. The process of making snowballs involves squeezing out the air that fills the voids between individual ice crystals. As the air is expelled, the density of the compressed snow increases until ice is formed. The more the ice is compressed, the more its density increases. As we all know, the fact that ice cubes float demonstrates that the density of ice is slightly less than that of water. Thus we have a simple explanation for the transition from snow to glacier ice and an explanation for why icebergs broken off from a glacier will float in the ocean with nine tenths of the ice beneath the sea surface.

The winter snows started to fall over Scotland approximately 2–3 million years ago, at the start of the last ice age. The failure of the snow to melt the following summer led to the development of ice on top of it, and its covering by the snows of the following winter. Thus the first glaciers in Scotland were eventually born. We have no idea where these first glaciers formed – we do know, however, that the glaciers eventually merged together to produce a large ice sheet. Most of what we imagine this first ice sheet looked like is almost entirely based on guesswork. At some stage the ice sheet melted, leaving behind a virgin landscape. The remarkable thing, however, is that this ice sheet was the first of approximately 20 separate ice sheets to build up and decay one after another during the course of the last 2–3 million years. The last of these ice sheets reached its maximum extent around 20,000 years ago.

The last glaciers disappeared from Scotland approximately 11,000 years ago. Compared with East Africa, where human remains over 3 million years old have been discovered by archaeologists, civilisation in Scotland is a relatively recent thing, with Scotland's original settlers making their first footprints on the landscape we know so well some time around 10–11,000 years ago.

With the growth and decay of so many ancient ice sheets, the concept of 'the last ice age . . .' takes on a new meaning. Instead of imagining our Highland corries and glens eroded by a single great ice sheet, we can start to think of the Scottish landscape sculptured by the erosive activity of a succession of separate ice sheets. Part of the reason we know so little about each of the 20 or so great ice ages is that the build-up of each successive ice sheet eroded the sediments deposited by the previous one. Thus the landscape that was uncovered 10–11,000 years ago from beneath the melting ice is mostly draped by sediments laid down by the last ice sheet and by the rivers that drained from the melting masses of ice.

How, therefore, do we know that Scotland has experienced so many separate ice ages? The answer lies within the sediment resting on the floors of the ocean. Cores of sediment taken from many locations on the ocean floor contain an archive of past climate changes, with each former ice age represented by layers of mud, silt and sand containing marine fossils deposited in glacial-age seas. Often these are accompanied by sediments that have fallen through the water to the ocean floor from the bottom of ancient icebergs as they progressively melted in the ice-age oceans. This record of largely undisturbed sediment on the ocean floor reveals the story of successive ice ages and of the intervals of intervening warmer climate that separated each period of cold. Scientists have even used the information gained from ocean floor sediments to estimate how much ice was locked up in ice sheets and glaciers throughout the world at different points in time. But this research is unable to tell us how much ice covered Scotland in any of these ice ages. There may even have been ice ages on Earth when there were large ice sheets on some continents but negligible ice cover over Scotland. Given such uncertainties, we can begin to understand why we *think* that Scotland may have experienced over 20 separate ice ages during that 2–3 million years, but have no idea what Scotland looked like during any of them except perhaps the last one.

Orbital rhythms and the beat of ice ages

During Victorian times, the Great Ice Age was generally considered to represent the last of the geological ages. Following the Tertiary Era, the

Quaternary Era was imagined as a single great ice age. During the 1860s, James Croll, a Scottish scientist, wrote a series of papers in which he outlined a theory by which the worldwide build-up of ice was related to changes in the nature of the Earth's orbit around the Sun. Not much changed during the early decades of the twentieth century until the early 1940s when a Serbian scientist, Milutin Milankovitch, wrote his treatise on an astronomical theory of ice ages. His first papers were written in Serbo-Croat and not widely read. However, by the 1960s his theory of ice ages was well known and, although now refined and improved, remains largely unchallenged.

James Croll

James Croll is not widely known to the public but he deserves to be in the Hall of Fame of illustrious Scots. James was born in 1821 near Wolfhill and as a young man worked as a mechanic in Banchory. He left school at 13 but loved reading and devoured as many books on philosophy, theology and physics as he could manage. By the time he was 16 he was keen to go to university but the cost of doing so was way beyond what his family could afford.

When he was 21 he gave up his job (as millwright by this time), and became a carpenter. This didn't last either, and he gave it up to run a tea shop and general store. He married Isabella MacDonald in 1848 and set up home in Elgin. Marriage and the store gave him the opportunity to read, and further his self-education, but he gave up the tea shop and tried his hand as a hotel keeper in Blairgowrie. That was not a success either. Then he tried his hand as an insurance salesman; that flopped also. In 1857 Isabella became ill, he gave up his job and they moved to Glasgow, where she could be taken care of by her sisters.

Unemployed, James spent his time writing. He had soon completed a booklet entitled *The Philosophy of Theism* and reached the elevated position of janitor at the Andersonian College and Museum in Glasgow. When he was not working he was studying in the Library. In 1864 he started to take an interest in the causes of the Great Ice Age. It occurred to James that changes in the Earth's orbit around the Sun might be a crucial factor in determining ice ages. It was not long before he had written a paper on the subject and had it published in the *Philosophical Magazine* in 1864.

Thus started 20 years of research on the astronomical causes of ice ages. James appreciated that each of the planets in the solar system induces a pull on the Earth that drags it out of its otherwise normal orbit around the Sun. Because each planet rotates around the Sun at a different speed, the combined pull by the planets on Earth changes in an irregular way over long periods of time. James used his knowledge of physics and astronomy to calculate these changes backwards in time – he published three more influential papers on the subject in 1865 and 1867. James believed that long, cold winters together with the effect of albedo represented the key processes responsible for triggering an ice age. His detailed studies culminated in a now classic text entitled *Climate and Time* in 1875.

The publications of James Croll came at a time when the causes of ice ages were being hotly debated, and when Louis Agassiz, a Swiss geologist, had shown that much of Europe, including Britain, has been covered by ice during the relatively recent geological past. The theories of James Croll provided the scientific community with a well-argued explanation of why and how such an ice age had taken place. By this time James was world famous and in 1876 he was made a Fellow of the Royal Society of London. He passed away in 1890.

Controversy does exist, however, on how ice ages start. One view is that since most of the world's land masses are located in the northern hemisphere, then cold conditions might begin as a result of widespread and prolonged winter snowfall. Others argue that the key factor that allows ice ages to start is the amount of summer melting, the logic being that it doesn't matter how much snow falls during winter, since plenty of heat the following summer will cause all the snow to disappear. Milankovitch was very aware of the link between the Earth's seasonal cycle and winter snowfall/summer melting, and focused his attention on how changes in the nature of the Earth's orbit around the Sun may have changed over thousands, and hundreds of thousands, of years. In order to do this he delved deeply into textbooks on astronomy. An important assumption he made in his calculations was that there had been no absolute change in the past in the amount of heat the Earth received from the Sun. In this way, he could use his knowledge of mathematics, physics and astronomy to investigate how long-term changes in the Earth's orbit may have caused changes in the redistribution of heat across the surface of the Earth.

Milankovitch recognised that over long time periods the nature of the Earth's orbit around the Sun had changed in three important ways. The first is based on the fact that the shape of the orbit of the Earth around the Sun varies over time from elliptical to circular and back again every 95,800 years (known as changes in *orbital eccentricity*). During times in the past when the orbit was highly elliptical, seasonal contrasts in climate would have been great, as would the climatic differences between the northern and southern hemispheres. In stark contrast, a circular orbit brings a blurring of the distinctiveness of spring, summer, autumn and winter. Back in the 1860s, James Croll proposed that at times in the past when the Earth's orbit was highly elliptical, winter snowfall is likely to have increased drastically in the northern hemisphere and may have led to the initiation of ice ages.

Milutin Milankovitch

Milutin Milankovitch was born in Serbia. As a student he completed his PhD at the Institute of Technology in Vienna and, having worked for a few years as an engineer, he managed to get a job as Professor of Applied Mathematics back home in his native Belgrade. One afternoon, over a few glasses of wine in a coffee house in Belgrade in 1909, he resolved to write a book. Talking with his friend and slightly the worse for drink, he made up his mind that he would 'grasp the entire universe and spread light into its furthest corners'. At the university he taught courses in physics, mechanics and astronomy. Soon he came up with the idea of developing a mathematical theory that could account for long-term changes in the climate of the Earth, as well as of the neighbouring planets, Mars and Venus.

Milutin was very aware of the work of Croll, and felt that with his more formal training in astronomy and mathematics, he could make significant improvements. It is said that he worked on the problem every day and that even on holidays with his wife and son he would take many of his books with him and spend part of each day on his studies. Whereas Croll had concentrated his efforts on the mathematics of the Earth's orbital eccentricity, Milutin also explored the mathematics of the changes that affect the Earth's orbit. He then moved on to calculate the changes in solar radiation received at the Earth's surface for each season and each latitude. Although Milutin's objectives were straightforward in theory, the actual job of making the calculations was incredibly difficult, since he had to take into account the spinning properties of each planet, as well as changes in wobbling and tilt in 'a crazy celestial dance'.

Apart from facing mathematical and astronomical barriers in the development of his theories, Milutin was also hindered by periods of time when he was enlisted as a soldier in the First War of the Balkans, which started in 1912. After the war ended he wrote up his initial findings in a series of papers between 1912 and 1914. He continued to work and write throughout this time of great political turmoil. In 1914 the First World War started and soon Milutin was taken prisoner by the Austro-Hungarian Army. Even as a prisoner of war he took the opportunity to use his period of captivity as a time when he could think. Then at Christmas in 1914 he was released and taken to Budapest, where he very quickly gained access to the library of the Hungarian Academy of Science. For the rest of the war, Milutin worked tirelessly on his calculations in Budapest. When the war ended he headed back to Belgrade and soon after that he wrote a paper on his *Mathematical Theory of Heat Phenomena Produced by Solar Radiation*.

Soon, one of the world's leading climate scientists, Walter Koppen, learned of Milutin's work. He wrote to Milutin and they were soon exchanging notes, letters and ideas. Milutin was not quite convinced of Croll's idea that ice ages were started by the degree of winter snowfall in high latitudes. Koppen persuaded him that the key to initiating ice ages was not winter snowfall but the amount of summer heating. Here was a key parting of the ways between the ideas of Croll and Milankovitch, the latter strongly influenced by Koppen's notion that 'it is the diminution of heat during the summer half-year that is the decisive factor in glaciation'.

Koppen and Milankovitch combined forces to publish their ideas on ways in which changes in solar radiation due to orbital changes had had a profound influence on the timing of ice ages. By 1930 Milankovitch's papers were starting to reach a wide audience and in 1938 he published a booklet titled *Astronomical Methods for Investigating*

Earth's Historical Climate, which represented the culmination of many years of hard endeavour. He died in 1958, but his legacy lives on. His classic works received astonishing confirmation many years later when signs of changes in the Earth's climate were discovered preserved in fossils on the world's ocean floors. The fossils show patterns of past climate changes in clear phase with those predicted by this great man.

The second change was based on the notion that the angle of tilt of the Earth on its axis has changed over time (known as *changes in inclination or obliquity*). Croll calculated that the tilt angle has changed over time from maximum (24.36°) to minimum (21.39°) and back again every 41,000 years. Not surprisingly, the highest tilt angles result in the greatest rates of heat loss during winter in high latitudes, and when this happens, it leads to significant climate cooling.

The third process, outlined by Milankovitch, is how the Earth experiences a 'wobbling' in its axis of rotation as it rotates around the Sun, rather like the wobbling of a spinning gyroscope (known as the *precession of the equinoxes*). This conical swinging of the Earth's axis moves from one extreme to another and back again every 21,700 years. This means that, over time, the northern hemisphere becomes tilted towards the Sun at successively different points in the Earth's orbit. Whereas at present the northern hemisphere is tilted away from the Sun during winter, the precession of the equinoxes means that there have been times when the northern hemisphere has instead been tilted towards the Sun during winter. At present, the orbital path of the Earth takes it furthest from the Sun during the northern hemisphere summer. Fortunately, this is also the time when the northern hemisphere is tilted towards the Sun, allowing us our summers – there have been times in the past when the northern hemisphere was tilted away from the Sun at the very time when the Earth was furthest from it. Given that the majority of land areas on Earth are located in the northern hemisphere, such times would have been highly favourable for the growth of glaciers and ice sheets. Milankovitch calculated that this 'wobble' takes place over a time interval of 21,700 years. It is a difficult concept to grapple with, since it implies that, for each hemisphere, the period when the orbit currently coincides with winter may in the past have been summer. Equally, summers in ice ages may have coincided with the times in the Earth's orbit that we presently associate with winter!

From these calculations Milankovitch concluded that the growth of ice sheets took place when summer heating was at its lowest – and he proposed that this occurred when the orbital tilt was low and the Earth was positioned furthest from the Sun in the path of the ellipse of rotation and, finally, when the ellipse of rotation was most exaggerated. Sadly, Milankovitch died in 1958, and was never to learn what the response to his theory of ice ages would be.

Clues about our icy past in the deep ocean

When scientists were first able to take core samples of sediment from the floors of the world's oceans, the potential of ocean floor sediments as an archive of past climate changes began to be realised. Alongside accumulations of sand, silt and mud on the ocean bed were the remains of micro-organisms (particularly those known as *foraminifera*) whose calcium carbonate shells on death had fallen through the seawater to settle eventually on the ocean floor.

Cores of sediment from the ocean bed therefore had the potential to tell a story of the life and death history of *foraminifera* over thousands and millions of years. It was realised that each *foraminifera* shell contained isotopes of oxygen derived from the seawater in which they had lived. At first, it was thought that measurement of these oxygen isotopes told a story of past changes in the temperature of the world's oceans. Later it was appreciated that this was incorrect and that the pattern of oxygen isotope changes over time was simply a measure of absolute changes in the volume of water stored in the world's oceans. During ice ages, when the volume was reduced as a result of the build-up of ice sheets on the continents, the oxygen isotope values would change in one direction. During periods of global warmth, when the melting of ice sheets returned huge volumes of water to the oceans, the oxygen isotope values would trend in the opposite direction. A history of past environmental changes could thus be constructed from the whole of the ice ages, and even further back in time than that.

What was especially remarkable about these oxygen isotope measurements was that the graphs showing the patterns of change in the oxygen isotopes over time were more or less identical, regardless of which of the ocean floors of the world the cores of sediment were obtained from. Scientists soon realised that the ocean floor sediments were providing, through their record of ocean volume changes, a detailed calendar of the various ice ages and intervening periods of relative warmth that took place during the last 2 million years of the Quaternary ice age.

The oxygen isotope record from the various ocean sediment cores was hailed as confirmation of the Milankovitch theory of ice ages, since they matched his patterns remarkably closely. There were some minor differences, however. Whereas Milankovitch thought the main beat of ice ages was in response to his 41,000- and 21,000-year cycles, the ocean floor record appeared to indicate that the biggest Quaternary ice ages took place approximately in phase with the 100,000-year eccentricity cycle. The ocean-floor record of ice ages thus pointed to perhaps as many as 20 major ice ages within the Quaternary ice age – each around 100,000 years apart. However, the saw-tooth and complex nature of the graph of change from the oceans cautioned against any simple counting of past ice ages – after all, how deep does a trough on the graph have to be until it can be taken as a sure indicator of a past ice age?

Ice-core diary of past Greenland air temperatures

During the late 1960s, at Camp Century in Greenland, scientists made their first attempts to put a drilling rig on an ice sheet and recover cores of ice in a sequence from the top of the ice sheet to the bottom. For large ice sheets like those in Antarctica and Greenland, the reasoning was that the highest part of the ice sheet was the best place to drill, because here the ice has hardly moved over time. In such areas the ice tends to sink and be compressed over time and therefore such areas are likely to yield a continuous record of past ice history, since none of the ice beneath the surface of the ice sheet is likely to have slid laterally at any time in the past. This ice-core research was to dramatically alter our understanding of past climates.

Scientific teams have returned to Greenland on several occasions, usually for months at a time, to undertake new ice-drilling programmes. The most famous of these are two separate drilling efforts completed during the 1980s by American and European scientific teams in Central Greenland at two locations approximately 30km apart. The projects, known respectively by their acronyms GISP (USA) and GRIP (Europe), each managed to drill through from the ice-sheet surface to bedrock, with each recovering hundreds of ice cores, each one several metres in length.

Ice is preserved in the ice cores in annual layers. Dust that is deposited on the ice at the end of cold, dry, windy winters is buried by the snows of the following winter. In addition, snow that has fallen on the ice surface and then refreezes the following winter possesses distinctive ice-crystal structures that aid the identification of annual layers of ice. In such ways, annual layers of ice can be counted back in time. As the ice becomes more and more compressed with increasing depth, eventually the annual layers merge together and become almost indistinguishable from one another. In Greenland ice, where winter snowfall is typically high, the annual layers in the ice can be counted back over tens of thousands of years.

One of the most common methods of reconstructing past air temperatures using ice cores has been the measurement in individual ice samples of the amount of the heavy isotope of oxygen, O_{18}. This isotope is incorporated within snowflakes as they form in the lower troposphere above the ice-sheet surface. The concentration of O_{18} within such snow is thought to be a measure of the air temperature in which the snowflakes formed. So by measuring changes in the concentration of O_{18} sample by sample at progressively greater depths into the ice, scientists can also reconstruct a history of annual air-temperature changes over Greenland going back over the period of time revealed by the annual snowfall record.

Of course, in trying to understand the history of past weather and climate in Scotland at the end of the last ice age, we have to appreciate that past air-temperature changes over Greenland are not likely to be the same as past air-temperature changes over Scotland. However, there is reason to be optimistic that the generalised *trends* in annual air-temperature changes in the two areas are likely to be similar.

It is generally believed that Scotland was overwhelmed by a series of ice sheets during the last 2 million years and that each ice age was separated by an interval of relative warmth. Since almost all of Scotland was buried by the last ice sheet approximately 20,000 years ago, we know almost nothing about the previous ice ages, since the passage of the last ice sheet across Scotland's landscape removed virtually all traces of what had existed before. There are a few exceptions, however. For example, near Kilmaurs in Ayrshire several mammoth tusks, a mammoth tooth and some reindeer antlers were discovered beneath glacial deposits. Similarly, in Bishopbriggs, several bones and a tooth of a woolly rhinoceros were found beneath glacial deposits, while reindeer bones have been found beneath glacial sediments near Carluke and also near Queen's Park in Glasgow. Elsewhere, plant remains have been found beneath ice-age sediments in areas as diverse as Ayrshire, Lewis and Shetland. All these discoveries provide tantalising glimpses of Scotland's past before it was buried by ice in the big freeze.

Imagining an icy wasteland

In relative terms, the last ice sheet that covered Scotland was tiny. In North America at this time, a continuous barrier of ice extended from Newfoundland in the east as far as the Pacific waters bordering the west coast of the United States and Canada. This ice sheet, known as the Laurentide ice sheet, also extended from the Canadian Arctic in the north to the Great Lakes in the south. It reached almost 4,000m in thickness across central Canada, in other words, it represented a dome-shaped mountain of ice of continental-scale proportions. To the east was another enormous ice sheet extending from the west coast of Norway towards Siberia. This ice sheet was of a similar size and thickness to the Laurentide. During summers, rivers of glacial meltwaters drained from the ice. In North America much of this water flowed through what became known as the Mississippi drainage system into the Gulf of Mexico. In northern Europe and Russia, the rivers drained southwards, some believe even as far as the Black Sea and into the eastern Mediterranean.

During the winters of the last ice age, sea ice formed a sheet of white as far south as the latitudes of Spain and Portugal. In the summers, the sea ice would melt into drifting floes, and ice-free areas of ocean would occur. Winter freezing would follow summer melt for a seeming eternity of thousands of years. There was no escape from the icy blast. Scotland, as elsewhere, passed into a world of howling icy winds, blizzards and probably, in summer, days of calm, with sunlight glinting across an absolutely silent surface of ice.

Travelling in ice-age Scotland

Since the age of enlightenment, scientists have managed to build up a reasonably detailed picture of what Scotland looked like during the last ice age. We are guided by the maxim 'the more we know the more we know we don't know . . .' – it would be a mistake therefore not to consider that the scene presented overleaf is but one of several possible landscapes. In particular, there is some controversy regarding the spatial coverage of ice and its thickness. Most believe, however, that if it were possible to time travel, we might start our journey at the western edge of the ice sheet somewhere west of the Outer Hebrides. Here, the edge of the ice sheet would have terminated in the sea and would probably have possessed a floating ice shelf, similar in many respects to those that flank the margins of parts of Antarctica today. We would encounter a rising ice surface and a steady climb eastwards. By the time we reached the vicinity of Skye, the ice surface would be about the same altitude as the tops of the Cuillins, which would have protruded above the ice surface – and we would still be climbing. Somewhere over the northwest Highlands we would reach the top and a relatively flat plateau of ice stretching to the north and south for hundreds of kilometres. Looking around, we would see nothing but ice and sky, with perhaps the occasional mountain summit, such as An Teallach (950m high today), protruding above the ice. To the south, the ice would have extended out of sight beyond the horizon, possibly ending as far south as Yorkshire, South Wales and East Anglia. To the north there is more uncertainty, with some believing that the ice sheet only extended just beyond the northern mainland coast of Scotland, while others envisage the ice having extended considerable distances offshore. Some hold the view that the ice did not overwhelm parts of northern Lewis, Caithness and Buchan, while others

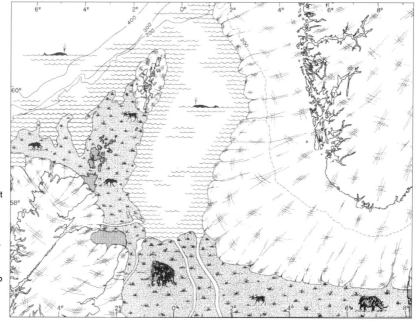

Example of a reconstruction of the extent of ice cover during the peak of the last ice age across northern Scotland, the North Sea and Norway. The areas of dry land are partly the result of lower sea levels and partly due to dry conditions caused by restricted snowfall. (Courtesy of H-P Sejrup.)

consider that most areas were overwhelmed by ice. Orkney may have been completely buried by ice, or the ice sheet might have been more restricted in size and left substantial areas of land uncovered. Likewise, some hold the view that Shetland was covered by a small ice cap of its own with some areas left clear of ice, while others propose a much more extensive ice cover.

The big disagreement concerns the east. The view of those who believe in a restricted ice cover maintain that the eastern edge of the last Scottish ice sheet was located in the eastern North Sea. They believe that *glacial moraines* resting on the sea floor 50–100km east of the present coastline would be at the edge of the ice sheet. Others maintain that the last Scottish ice sheet was much larger and that it extended across the area of the present North Sea to merge with ice in Scandinavia.

Scotland's on the rebound

Imagine the Earth as a gigantic, partially inflated balloon on which massive ice sheets lie over Scandinavia, much of Russia and North America, and smaller ice sheets lie elsewhere, like the one over Scotland. Let the skin of the balloon represent the Earth's crust. Let the air inside represent the molten viscous material underneath the crust. Each sheet causes changes in the pressures on the Earth, leading to bulges and deformations. As the sheets melt, the areas beneath them start to rebound back, while the peripheral areas start to subside. These processes of crustal depression and rebound took place over thousands of years.

The process of loading and unloading the Earth's crust by ice sheets is known as *glacial isostasy*. In general, since the density of glacier ice is slightly less than the density of water, and since the density of most rocks is much greater, as a general rule an ice sheet 900m in thickness will depress the Earth's crust by around 300m. So our mini Scottish ice sheet, dwarfed by the giant ice sheets over North America, Scandinavia and Russia, was nevertheless capable of causing significant depression of the Earth's crust underneath it. Of equal importance was that as the ice sheet expanded to its maximum dimensions, the Earth's crust around and beyond the edge of the ice sheet was deformed upwards. Once the ice sheet started to melt, become thinner and retreat inland, in the area where the ice was thickest the land rebounded at the greatest rate. However, the outer areas, such as Shetland, started to sink. The majority of these tremendous vertical changes in the Earth's crust across Scotland took place in the early stages as the ice was rapidly thinning and melting.

Isostasy and icy worlds

During the 1860s a scientist called Thomas Jamieson from Ellon had noticed that beneath the thick deposits of clay in the Forth Valley, known as *carse clay*, are layers of peat that were themselves underlain by marine deposits. Within the carse clay deposits, several people had found the remains of ancient whales and seals – clear evidence that the clay sediments had been laid down in a prehistoric estuary of the Forth. Jamieson appreciated that the peat deposits must have grown on an ancient marine surface that had been uplifted to a position above sea level some time after the end of the last ice age. On the face of it, the presence of the peat seemed to indicate that since it was laid down there must have been a rise in sea level to deposit the carse clay. Since these clay deposits occurred around Stirling over 40 feet above present sea level, this would seems to indicate, first, a relative lowering of sea level (to allow the peat to accumulate on the ancient marine sediments), followed by a high relative sea level (to deposit the carse clays), and finally a recent relative lowering of sea level (to explain the occurrence of the carse clays high above present sea level).

In 1865 Jamieson had a flash of inspiration. He wrote:

It has occurred to me that the enormous weight of ice thrown upon the land may have had something to do with this depression . . . and then the melting of the ice would account for the rising of the land, which seems to have followed upon the decrease of the glaciers . . .

Jamieson had provided the first explanation for the occurrence of the carse clays, the buried peat and the lowermost marine sediments that involved separate episodes of isostatic depression, each followed by a period of uplift. He had inadvertently found an explanation of the process of glacio-isostasy. He had reasoned that the weight of the ice would have resulted in a depression of the Earth's crust. Once melting started, however, the Earth's crust would have rebounded vertically. In this way, Jamieson thought, a land surface would have become exposed and peat could have formed on its surface. He imagined that as the rate of the uplift of the land slowed down it may have become progressively submerged by a rising ocean level caused by melting ice sheets worldwide. He thought that this would provide an explanation of how layers of peat could be buried beneath thick accumulations of marine clays in the Forth Valley.

Today, Jamieson's theory of glacio-isostasy is widely recognised, but has advanced in its sophistication. Geologists now envisage the Earth's crust, the *lithosphere*, as moving over a lower layer of molten rock known as the *asthenosphere*. In this way, our last Scottish ice sheet caused the lithosphere to sag down upon the underlying asthenosphere, with a converse process occurring when the ice finally melted. The concept of a lithosphere essentially 'floating' on a mobile asthenosphere under-pins the theory of *plate tectonics*.

These vertical movements, despite having continued for over 10,000 years, are not yet complete. Thus whereas the majority of mainland Scotland is still rising at rates up to 2mm per year, the outer regions continue to sink at similar rates. All this presupposes that the giant ice sheet in nearby Scandinavia had no effect on vertical land movements happening here. In all probability, it played a crucial role in determining patterns of crustal rebound in Scotland, but no one knows precisely what this influence was.

Disappearing ocean water

In terms of a worldwide ice age, Scotland's ice sheet was relatively tiny. Counted on its own, the volume of its ice was only sufficient to lower the average sea level around the world by no more than a few centimetres. By contrast, it is generally believed that the accumulation of ice in all of the ice sheets that formed during the last ice age was sufficient to lower average sea level worldwide by 120m. Such a lowering of sea level is immense. It implies, for example, that during the last ice age people could walk across a corridor of dry land (a *land bridge*) between northeast Siberia and Alaska. Similar land bridges would have connected Australia to many of the islands of southeast Asia. Closer to home, a land bridge would have joined northern France and southern England while, further east, those parts of the central and southern North Sea not covered by ice would have been converted to dry land.

What did this huge lowering of the sea level mean for Scotland? For most areas, the depression of the land caused by the weight of the ice was greater than the 120m lowering of sea level caused by the locking-up of ocean water in the world's biggest ice sheets. This implies that at the ice edge *relative* sea level may have been much higher than it is at present. Conceptually this is an awkward idea to grasp, since we are always told that sea level during the last ice age was much lower than it is at present. But it provides, for example, a simple and straightforward explanation of why, in the mid nineteenth century, the remains of a seal were discovered in glacial-age marine clays and silts in a brickpit in Cupar, Fife, at a height of around 25m above present sea level.

What goes down must come up

Once the climate started to warm and the ice sheets began to melt, some very remarkable changes took place across Scotland. First, the land surface, relieved of its ice cover, started to rebound. It did so at different rates in different places, the rebound rate being greatest where the ice was formerly thickest, over the western Highlands, and slowest where the ice was thin. As far as the ocean was concerned, the story was also one of rise. But this rise in sea level was *not* principally because of melting ice across Scotland. The rate of rise in sea level in the oceans was controlled by the rate of melting of ice in places such as North America, Russia, Scandinavia, Greenland and Antarctica. So changes along Scotland's coastline were dictated by the interaction of these two pro-cesses. To begin with the rate of the rise of the land was faster than the rate of the rise of sea level, but ironically much of the land-rise in the early stages took place while most of Scotland was still covered by ice. This was because the early stages of the melting of the ice sheet were associated with the thin-ning of its surface rather than through the uncovering of land areas.

So in many areas, when the land started to appear from beneath the ice, the sea initially flooded across coastal areas and then started to fall back. Relative to today's coastline, the highest levels reached by the sea as it flooded across coastal areas was in the order of 35–40m, and it is at these elevations that we find Scotland's highest raised beaches in the Inner Hebrides. From then on, the rate of land uplift outpaced the rate of rise in oceanic sea level, causing the relative sea level to fall. Thus we see raised beaches as common features around most of the mainland coastline of Scotland as well as in many of the Hebridean islands. By contrast, raised beaches do not occur in the outer areas such as the Outer Hebrides, Orkney and Shetland.

How do ice ages start?

Imagining an ice sheet covering most of Scotland is a long way from understanding how an ice age actually starts. No one really knows how an ice age starts. There are some interesting theories, however. As mentioned before, the orbital cycles of Milankovitch come close to the top of the list, with the key argument being that the Earth's orbit and tilt may have reached a critical state, say 25,000 years ago, when summer heating across the middle and high latitudes of the northern hemisphere may have been insufficient to melt the snows of the previous winter. If this pattern were repeated for several decades then an ice age may indeed begin. Another contributory factor may have been a dramatic drop in sunspot activity across the Sun's surface. This was certainly the case in respect of climate cooling between the fifteenth and nineteenth centuries, but it is another matter to envisage that such cooling may have started an ice age. Although there are no compelling arguments that the last ice age was triggered by a marked cooling of the Sun, neither can we argue that changes in the output of heat from the Sun had no effect in bringing about such changes. Another contender would be volcanic activity. It is well known that very large volcanic eruptions can result in significant cooling. Had such a huge eruption occurred somewhere on Earth at this time, it would undoubtedly have deposited ash over wide areas. One area that such ash deposits would have accumulated is on the ocean floor, yet studies of sediments from ocean cores have not turned up evidence for an enormous eruption capable of starting an ice age.

A giant volcanic eruption at the end of the last Ice Age

Buried in the seafloor sediments just east of Stornoway in around 50m depth of water lies a layer of very unusual sediment. Inspection of the sediment grains under a microscope shows that most are composed of a glassy type of material. Further analysis reveals that the grains are composed of thousands of tiny particles of volcanic ash. The occurrence of the same volcanic ash in the Greenland ice cores tells us that the Stornoway ash deposits started life as particles of volcanic ash that erupted from an ancient volcano in southern Iceland. Remarkably, by counting the ice layers in Greenland down to the ash layer we learn that the layer of ash (known as the Vedde ash) was erupted from Mt Hekla in southern Iceland approximately 12,180 years ago.

There must have been a day, or perhaps a few days at this time in

Scotland's icy past, when volcanic ash rained down over the Scottish landscape. While plumes of ash and sulphurous gases reached high into the troposphere above the noise and fire of an erupting Icelandic volcano, a huge spread of ash settled silently over Scotland's glaciers. In all probability, much of the ash was quickly washed off the ice by rivers. Beyond the ice, the ash settled in lochs, in the sea and across hills and glens. In recent years scientists taking cores of sediment from lochs as far apart as Lairg in the far north to the Borders in the south have found this ash layer buried deep beneath younger sediments. We may never know what the climatic effects in Scotland were of this huge volcanic eruption. It does remind us, however, that Scotland is not immune from the effects of erupting volcanoes in the Land of Fire and Ice far beyond our northern shores.

Some scientists believe that the key factor that triggered the beginning of the last ice age was a dramatic change in ocean circulation across the North Atlantic. Sediments deposited across the floor of the North Atlantic during the last ice age show widespread evidence of material having melted out from underneath floating icebergs. Within these sediments, the microfossils of *foraminifera* show an abundance of species than only survive in cold Arctic waters. Such indicators of a cold ice-age ocean can be traced as far south as the latitude of Portugal, thus showing that at this time the warm, salty waters of the Gulf Stream could not penetrate any further north. Thus we can start to build up a picture of an ice-age North Atlantic where icebergs were a common occurrence in the southern latitudes of Spain and Portugal. During winter and early spring most of the North Atlantic north of 45° North would have been covered by sea ice.

What did all this mean in terms of air circulation and temperatures? To begin with, we have to appreciate two very special influences of ice sheets on atmospheric circulation. The first is that they always cool overlying air from underneath. This makes the overlying air stable and liable to sink. The second factor is that ice sheets, once they are big enough, tend to generate their own weather. An air mass that is always stable and being cooled from underneath will always be characterised by high pressure. This pattern of air flow can be of continental proportions and may extend many hundreds of kilometres beyond the ice-sheet margin. In this respect, our little Scottish ice sheet can be considered, in atmospheric circulation terms, as the western part of the large ice sheet that covered Scandinavia and Russia (known as the Eurasian ice sheet). Thus the prevailing winds that blew along and beyond the southern edge of the ice sheet were from the east (easterlies). Such winds originated in European Russia and continued blowing from east to west throughout each year and would have continued to blow from the east as long as the ice sheet existed. So in Scotland, the prevailing winds would have been from the east. They would also have been cold, relatively dry winds blowing over an ice-age North Sea that was mostly dry land due to lowered sea levels.

What, then, happened to the North Atlantic storms with which we are familiar in our everyday lives? To understand this we need to look at the bigger picture. The Laurentide ice sheet still covered North America at this time, stretching all the way from the Pacific to the Atlantic and was nearly 4,000m thick in parts, as already mentioned. Such enormous ice masses as the Laurentide and Eurasian ice sheets represented a real obstacle to air flow in the troposphere – in effect, the prevailing winds would have had to be squeezed through the relatively narrow space between the top of the ice sheets and the top of the troposphere. Instead, the winds took a different course – they were steered to the south of the northern hemisphere ice sheets. So the North Atlantic storm track did exist during the last ice age, it even obeyed the same simple rule of occurring in the zone of turbulence where cold air came into contact with warm air. The difference was that this zone occurred at much lower latitudes than it does at present. The North Atlantic storm track during the last ice age therefore swept across the Mediterranean and North Africa, bringing its customary frequent and heavy rains.

Ice-age drought in Buchan and Caithness

There is a region in the north of Greenland today called Jameson Land. For Greenland it is a very unusual area since, unlike everywhere else, there is no glacier ice to be seen. It is, however, extremely cold, apart from during the very brief summer when the Sun sits just above the horizon. Why then is there no ice in Jameson Land? The reason is that the area is such a long way north of the North Atlantic storm track that there is no source of moisture in the atmosphere to provide the snowfall needed to enable the growth of glacier ice. In effect the region is a polar desert.

During the last ice age, when North Atlantic storms were tracking from west to east, beside and to the south of the southern edge of the ice sheets, the areas far to the north were located far away from the principal sources of moisture. So the last Scottish ice sheet may have been fed by snowfall along its southern flanks, with ice-free polar deserts in the north. In this case, during the maximum severity of the last ice age, Scotland may have had its own Jameson Land. Buchan may have been one such area, northeastern Caithness another, northern Lewis yet another – there may even also have been areas of dry land in parts of Orkney and Shetland. From this we can begin to understand how an ice sheet is dynamic in its behaviour, growing in one area while simultaneously contracting in another. We also learn how the development and growth of glacier ice depends on an intricate balance between air temperature, the amount of winter snowfall and summer melt.

Melting moments – the end of the freeze?

Even the last great ice sheets eventually came to an end. In Scotland, as elsewhere, the ice finally disappeared as raging waters in thousands of rivers drained the glacial meltwaters to the sea. What did Scotland's landscape look like then? Imagine the landscape we presently live in with no traces of human influence – no buildings, roads, fields and so on. Also no trees or vegetation. The land would have consisted of nothing but rock, gravel, sand, silt and clay, with ubiquitous rivers and streams. On the slopes there possibly may have been snowbeds, while the winds may have made it quite a dusty landscape.

No one is quite sure when the ice sheet started to melt or how it was that the reflectivity (albedo) of such huge areas of glacier ice across the northern hemisphere was insufficient to counteract the overall warming. Climate scientists have pointed out the strange fact that according to the Milankovitch cycles, the amount of summer heating and winter cooling in the northern hemisphere at the peak of the last ice age was similar to what it is today.

The millennia that followed the ice melt bore witness to two hugely significant changes. First, there was a progressive increase in the tilt of the Earth on its axis, which had the effect of increasing the amount of summer heating across the northern hemisphere. Second, the precessional cycle as described by Milankovitch played its part by causing the northern hemisphere summer to occur when the Earth was closest to the Sun and the corresponding winters to occur when the Earth was furthest from the Sun in its orbit. The combined effect of these changes was to induce a progressive increase in the amount of summer heating from the Sun across the northern hemisphere. It is thought that this change was a key factor in causing the great northern hemisphere ice sheets to melt.

An additional factor that is somewhat surprising is that during the last ice age the concentration of greenhouse gases in the atmosphere was incredibly low. Compared with today, carbon dioxide concentration values of around 370 parts per million by volume (ppm), the concentrations during the last ice age were very low – around 250 ppm. In other words, the greenhouse effect was operating only to a very limited extent during the last ice age, helping to keep the troposphere cooler than it otherwise would have been. As the melting of the ice sheets accelerated there was a corresponding increase in the amount of carbon dioxide in the atmosphere and a more efficient greenhouse effect. Where did the surplus carbon dioxide disappear to during the ice age? No one knows for sure, but it seems most likely that the world's oceans absorbed most of it. As the ice sheets started to melt the oceans appear to have been ventilated, and started releasing carbon dioxide into the atmosphere as temperatures warmed. By 10–11,000 years ago, summer heating of the northern hemisphere had reached its maximum – in fact, it has been declining ever since. It is not a surprise then that in the face of such sustained summer heating, the last great ice sheets in North America and Eurasia had substantially shrunk in size by then.

Whatever the processes of warming were, its effects were first felt between about 16,000 and 17,000 years ago. Scientists who have studied the melting histories of the Laurentide ice sheet in North America and the Eurasian ice sheet envisage that the ice sheets underwent significant thinning and contraction of their margins. Because the amount of heating in any year was finite, it was to take many thousands of years to melt these big ice sheets. For example, the Laurentide ice sheet did not disappear entirely until around 8,000 years ago. Similarly, the Eurasian ice sheet did not melt away until around 9,000 years ago. We can estimate that it took around 7,000–9,000 years for each ice sheet to melt.

Unfortunately we do not know for sure how long it took for Scotland's relatively tiny ice sheet to melt away. Some are of the opinion that the last vestiges of ice had gone by around 13,000 years ago – others hold the view that the ice may have lasted much longer. Whatever opinion is correct, it cannot be disputed that during the thousands of years when such widespread melting of ice took place, the climate must have been relatively mild. Studies of vegetation and insects that existed in the landscape at this time point to a relatively mild climate across Scotland, similar to that of today. By any stretch of the imagination, this was the time when the big freeze had come to an end.

One might imagine from the above that the melting and final disappearance of the great ice sheets represented the end of our ice-age world and the onset of warmth. But nature had a trick in store. Just at the time when the warming had become well established, the world was plunged into a brief period of severe cold and the renewed growth of glaciers and ice sheets. The difference was that this time the ice age was to last only 1,200 years.

The 1,200 year big freeze

According to the Greenland ice-core record, the prolonged period of warmth that was associated with the melting of the ice sheets came to a dramatic and shuddering end some time around 12,900 years ago. The ice cores appear to indicate that at this time the prevailing temperatures (both summer and winter) dropped by around 10°C over a matter of a few decades.

In Scotland, as elsewhere across the northern hemisphere, the response was a renewed growth and expansion of glacier ice, generally referred to as the Younger Dryas period. The biggest area of glacier ice developed across the western Highlands, but the ice cap was of a sufficient size to enable outlet glaciers to extend down into the lowlands. The largest such tongue of ice was over Loch Lomond, reaching as far south as Balloch and Drymen. Another lobe of ice extended along the upper Forth valley, terminating at the Lake of Menteith. Along the northern edge of the ice field the ice reached as far north as Torridon and Applecross. The ice crossed the Great Glen, with the ice front close to Fort Augustus and meltwaters draining northwards into Loch Ness. To the west, separate, smaller ice fields developed in Skye, Mull and

Trekking on the Skye glaciers

In many instances the last glaciers to cover Scotland left very distinctive traces on the landscape. Typically, the extent of former glaciers is marked by different types of glacial *moraine*. End moraines show the former position of the edge of the ice at the base of valleys while the margins of many glaciers coincide with linear moraine ridges known as *lateral moraines*. The study of sediments also provides clues to the former extent of glaciers. Scientists are able to distinguish sediments deposited underneath individual glaciers from those laid down initially on top of the ice and ultimately deposited on the land surface as the ice melted. Glacial sediments are also quite distinctive from sediments deposited on slopes and by rivers. Furthermore, the erosion and sculpting of bedrock due to the passage of ice over rock surfaces produces characteristic landforms described as *ice-moulded* bedrock, upon which occur linear grooves or striations that indicate the direction in which the ice formerly moved.

Doug Benn is an acknowledged expert in the study of landforms and sediments produced by glaciers and is an expert on the glacial history of the Isle of Skye. Over the years he has covered nearly every square metre of the Cuillins and surrounding areas, making highly detailed maps of all the glacial landforms and associated sediments. This work enabled him to produce a record of an ice field that developed in south-central Skye during the Younger Dryas. Several of the Cuillin peaks protruded as mountain summits above the ice field, while a series of glaciers extended beyond the ice field into low-lying valleys. One glacier, for example, moved down through Loch Coruisk and terminated in the sea, another flowed downslope into Loch Sligachan, also ending in the sea. The very detailed reconstruction of the Skye glaciers enabled Doug to produce an amazingly detailed map of how the Skye Cuillins looked at this time (below).

Glaciers on Skye during the Younger Dryas (courtesy of D. Benn)

even the mountains of Harris. To the east, the Cairngorms had a relatively restricted ice cover – demonstrating that eastern Scotland was relatively dry at this time, despite being phenomenally cold. Estimates have been made of air temperatures for this time – July temperatures at sea level are thought to have been around 9°C, while January temperatures may have been below -20°C.

Those who have examined sediments of this age in ocean cores paint a similarly bleak picture. The southern extent of sea ice at the end of winter is thought to have reached the latitude of southern Ireland at this time, in effect telling a story of all ocean areas north of 50° North enveloped in ice during winter. Nor must we forget that large areas of the North Sea were dry land at this time, and that to the east a substantial ice sheet still remained over most of Scandinavia, sending cold easterly winds across Scotland. With so much glacier ice and a frozen ocean, the North Atlantic storm track was again displaced considerably further south, causing trains of cyclones to move from west to east across southern England and France. So, in many respects, all the hallmarks of the last great ice age had repeated themselves – the main difference was that this particular ice age only lasted just in excess of a thousand years, leaving insufficient time to create anything like the enormous ice sheets that had developed 20,000 years earlier.

How can we be so sure about the extent of the ice at this time? The answer is that these were the last glaciers that existed in Scotland and, as such,

Scotland's biggest flood

Travel east from Spean Bridge to the tiny village of Roybridge. Turn left and head up the narrow winding road up Glen Roy. After a few miles turn a bend, park your car, step out into the chilling winter winds and look north. Ahead on both sides of the glen is an amazing sight. It looks as if the hillsides have been etched with sets of parallel lines as far as the eye can see. Legend has it that the lines are trackways put there by an Irish giant. In the nineteenth century the most popular view was that they were shorelines of an ancient sea. The height of the shorelines above sea level (up to 365m) was used by some as evidence for a biblical flood. By the late nineteenth century, people realised that the shorelines were produced in a huge lake that was ponded up against the ice of the Younger Dryas ice cap. Like an overflowing bath full of water, the overflow of water from the lake in Glen Roy drained out at its northern end into the Spey valley.

The problem with such glacier-dammed lakes is that they leak. Lake waters often find tunnels within the adjacent ice. If water occupies such tunnels, the heat of the water tends to melt the ice and make the tunnels larger. If such a conduit of water underneath the ice can extend to the opposite side of the glacier, the lake waters can drain through such routes and escape from the ice somewhere else as a catastrophic flood.

Some time during the closing stages of the Younger Dryas, the ice retreated southwards out of Glen Roy towards an area just east of Spean Bridge. A huge lake was dammed by the ice that extended eastwards from Spean Bridge to the eastern end of Loch Laggan. The lake also spread north up Glen Roy and occupied an area approximately twice that of Loch Lomond today. After some time a tunnel was opened up underneath the ice and extended from Spean Bridge westwards into the Great Glen and then north through the ice to Fort Augustus. On one cold day, the tunnel was complete and the lake waters started to drain out of glens Roy and Spean. As more and more water poured through the ice, the tunnels became bigger and bigger. The result was a huge flood of water that emerged from the ice at Fort Augustus and poured into Loch Ness.

According to the calculations of Brian Sissons, one of Scotland's foremost Quaternary scientists, the water poured into Loch Ness at a faster rate than it could drain from the loch at its northern end. The consequence was that at the peak of the flood, the level of Loch Ness may have been temporarily raised by over 8m. At the northern end of Loch Ness there was also a great flood – only this time the escaping waters flowed as an immense torrent of water finally reaching the sea at Inverness. The floodwaters also carried huge amounts of sediment. When the waters reached the sea a huge fan of sediment was laid across the ground surface and across the sea bed. Much of Inverness is believed to be built on the sediments laid down by this flood, while the foundations of the Kessock Bridge are built on the sediments and rocks laid down by Scotland's biggest flood.

the landforms that they left behind are for the most part easy to recognise. For example, scores of hillsides and valley floors are mantled by glacial moraines, while the frost-shattered rocks occur on mountain summits located above the ice surface. During the latter part of the twentieth century a team of research students at Edinburgh University, led by Quaternary expert Brian Sissons, undertook the painstaking task of making highly detailed maps of many of these former glaciers. Today, nearly all of the glaciers and ice caps that formed at this time in Scotland have been mapped. We now even know that the snowline at this time over Mull was around 300m, rising to 800–900m over the Cairngorms.

Ice and the Loch Ness Monster

Of all the millions of pages that have been written about the Loch Ness monster, very few consider the constraints placed by the last great ice sheets on the existence, evolution or otherwise of a monster. Clearly no monster of an age equivalent to the dinosaurs could possibly survive at least 20 separate ice ages, when on each occasion a gigantic ice sheet removed all vestiges of Loch Ness from its path. There may have been times at the ends of ice ages when the retreat of the ice was accompanied by the filling of the loch basin with fresh water.

We can be pretty sure that this was the case when the last Scottish ice sheet melted. We can also be fairly certain that it filled with fresh water derived from the melting ice. We also know from the assemblages of glacial landforms and sediments that make up the landscape between the northern end of Loch Ness and Inverness that after the ice melted the sea was never high enough to be able to enter Loch Ness from the Moray Firth (nor did the sea ever enter Loch Ness from the south).

Loch Ness therefore filled with fresh water during the melting of the last ice sheet. The freshwater loch was still there during the last expansion of glacier ice during the Younger Dryas. We know that the northern limit of the Younger Dryas ice cap reached only as far north as Fort Augustus. So during the 1,200-year period of cold climate, the loch received a continual influx of fresh water draining from the ice edge at Fort Augustus. Equally, large volumes of fresh water continued to drain northwards out of Loch Ness at its northern end.

Then, towards the close of this period of cold climate, came the big flood originating from the drainage of the ice-dammed lakes in glens Roy and Spean. After the flood came the final melting of the Younger Dryas ice cap, part of which also drained into Loch Ness. When the ice finally melted away, the amounts of water draining into the Loch reduced by at least an order of magnitude.

So where does this leave Nessie? It is clearly impossible for it to have ever entered the loch from the sea. Also, any creature would have to have evolved independently within the loch starting from the time when the last Scottish ice sheet melted. That gives it maybe 13,000 years – 16,000 years at best – to weave its mysterious and magical spells.

And then, almost as soon in geological terms as it had begun, the period of severe cold ended. Again, the Greenland ice cores tell us the story of how, after around 1,200 years of freezing conditions, the temperatures suddenly rose again around 11,700 years ago. Only this time they rose for good. Never again did glaciers form in Scotland. And with the rising temperatures came our first ancestors, approximately 300 generations ago.

CHAPTER 3
THE TAMING OF THE ANGRY BEAST

Scotland exists as a distillation of the accumulated debris left over
from its long and supposedly tormented past.

Fiona Watson, *Scotland: A History, 8000* BC–AD *2000*.

INTRODUCTION

The end of the Younger Dryas period and the start of the subsequent period
of climate warming in which we live (known as the Holocene) marked a time
when the amount of tilt of the Earth on its axis was at a maximum. It also
coincided with a time when the orbit of the Earth around the Sun was such
that (unlike now) the Earth was closest to the Sun during midsummer and
furthest from it at midwinter. The combined effect of these influences on
Scotland's climate at this time was to maximise the amount of heat received
from the Sun during summertime and make the winters particularly cold.
Curiously, the seasonal amounts of heat received from the Sun at this time
were similar to those that prevailed during the peak of the ice age. So why
should it have been that the severe cold of the Younger Dryas period took
place when it did? The answer, it would seem, had a lot to do with melting
ice sheets over North America and the discharge of huge volumes of fresh
water into the western North Atlantic Ocean. The amount of meltwater that
was draining into the North Atlantic Ocean at that time was so high that the
thermohaline conveyor may have switched off – thus causing Europe to
plunge into another, albeit brief, ice age. The ice cores from Greenland tell us
that the switch from a mild climate into severe cold at the start of the Younger
Dryas period took place very quickly – perhaps over a matter of years or a
few decades.

Such periods of cold climate, which appear to have started rapidly and
which lasted, by comparison, only a short period of time (in this case just over

1,000 years) then ended as quickly as they started, remind us of that 'angry beast' of climate. The lesson for us all is that if such dramatic climate changes have happened in the past, then similar rapid changes could happen in the future. This message is the one that, above everything else, demands that we understand the mechanisms by which climate can change rapidly – over decades or even years – from one climatic extreme to the other.

THE START OF THE PRESENT INTERGLACIAL

The end of the Younger Dryas period of cold climate and the start of the warming associated with the period of interglacial climate in which we presently live, may have been partly due to long-term changes in the Earth's orbit that, by this time, were leading to exceptionally warm summers and long, cold winters. It may also have been due to the Atlantic Ocean thermohaline conveyor switching itself back from off to on. Once the switch was on, the scene was set for global warming on a grand scale.

As the centuries progressed at the start of our present interglacial period, gradual changes in the Earth's orbit around the Sun led to a progressive decrease in the amount of summer heating and increasingly mild winters. In addition, there was a steady increase in the concentration of greenhouse gases in the troposphere – thus helping the Earth to warm up. Moreover, by decreasing the albedo of the Earth's surface, the melting of the ice sheets that had covered vast swathes of the northern hemisphere also played an important part in the warming up of the Earth's atmosphere.

The end of the Younger Dryas period of exceptional cold heralded a new age of relative warmth that started quickly. As far as we can tell from the ice cores, air temperatures soared in a matter of decades around 11,700 years ago. Although the climate had begun to become much milder, there were still factors that make any analogy with our present climate impossible. For one thing, a substantial ice sheet still existed over Canada and another over Scandinavia, even though ice had already disappeared from Scotland. As far as Scotland's weather and climate were concerned, each ice sheet exerted important influences. The ice sheet in North America had the effect of steering the west to east-moving cyclones well to the south as they crossed the Atlantic. Second, the ice sheet over Scandinavia was associated with a permanent cell of high pressure. Along its southern flank, therefore, came persistent cold easterly winds blowing over a North Sea substantially shrunken

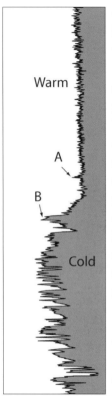

Warm

A

B

Cold

The angry beast of climate change as reconstructed from Greenland ice cores. The diagram shows the pattern of air temperature changes over the last 100,000 years. The saw-tooth lower half of the graph depicts the huge fluctuations in temperature that took place during the last ice age. By contrast, the upper part depicts the relative stability of climate during the last 10,000 years of the present inter-glacial period. The spikes at A and B represent the last two major periods of extreme cold to have affected Scotland. Spike A represents the cold period centred on 8,200 years ago. Spike B, known as the Younger Dryas period, lasted around 1,200 years.

due to the worldwide lowering of sea level. This meant that whereas eastern Scotland may have been dominated by cold, relatively dry easterly winds, the west coast was still quite wet.

The ice sheets over Canada and Scandinavia were not to disappear until around 8,000–9,000 years ago. Thus, the first 3,000 years after the disappearance of the ice was, in climate terms, a period of transition across Scotland. Thereafter Scotland's climate started to resemble that of the present more closely. The Greenland ice-core records of past climates send us a clear message of how our climate changed after the end of the Younger Dryas. In striking contrast to the cold periods that preceded it, the period of Holocene warmth was characterised by relatively minor switches between warm and cold. By modern standards, some of these small-scale changes (such as the Little Ice Age) were in themselves quite severe. But in comparison with those that took place during the ice ages they were nothing significant. We can learn a great deal about these relatively small-scale changes in climate from the cores from the Greenland ice.

TALES FROM GREENLAND ICE

The 'Angry Beast of Climate'

Study of the reconstructions of past climate from the Greenland ice cores shows us the fury of the 'angry beast of climate' that Wally Broecker described as existing throughout the last ice age. At the end of the last ice age, things changed for the better, with the Earth's climate becoming more quiescent. Two of the most useful ice-core records of past climate change in this respect are those of dust and sea salt. Changes over time in the concentration of dust within the Greenland ice tell a story of the transport of dust across the northern hemisphere between continental land masses. During times when large areas were covered by ice sheets, the surrounding land areas were devoid of vegetation and sediment resting on the bare land surfaces was easily whipped up by the winds and transported downwind. Some of this dust ended up deposited on Greenland ice.

Chemical analysis of sea salt deposits within the layers of Greenland ice tell us a story of past storms across the North Atlantic Ocean. During periods of increased storminess greater quantities of sea salt were deposited on the ice, while intervals of decreased storminess resulted in decreased concentrations of sea salt within the surface ice and snow. Since such storms invariably track across the ocean towards and across Scotland, we can be reasonably confident that changes in sea salt concentration within Greenland ice will serve as a good approximation of past storminess.

The calm after the storm

By any stretch of the imagination, the magnitude of the climate changes that have taken place during the last 10,000 years (before present) is tiny compared with those that went before. Despite this, many of the climate changes that have taken place during this period of interglacial warmth are in themselves not inconsiderable. Again, we can turn to the Greenland ice cores to provide glimpses into the past. When we do this, we see fluctuations that show periods of time when it was stormier and dustier and other times when conditions were significantly warmer or colder. There appears to have been a sustained decrease in storminess over the last 10,000 years, upon which are superimposed times when climate was more extreme. For example, the most recent increase in storminess took place soon after AD 1420, and has continued up to the present. Similarly, there seems to have been a period of minimum storminess prior to this time, including most of the last 2,000–2,500 years.

Approximately 5,000–6,000 years ago, we may guess that our ancestors were having a hard time of it. If the figures are to be believed, this was probably a period of storminess similar to the Little Ice Age. Similar, though less marked, periods of increased storminess appear to have occurred around 3,000 and 8,000 years ago. By the same token, the first 4,000 years of the Holocene (between around 6,000 and 10,000 years ago) appear to have been characterised by lower than average storminess (with the exception of the brief interlude centred around 8,200 years ago). The peaks and troughs shown

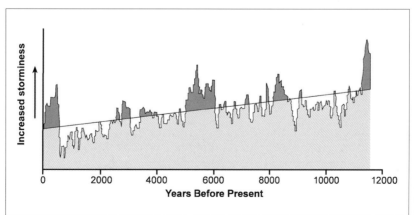

Graph showing the long-term pattern of changes in winter storminess across the North Atlantic over the last 10,000 years. The graph is based on variations in the concentration of sea salt in Greenland ice cores. Note that there has been an overall long-term decrease in storminess over time, with one of the stormiest episodes having charac-terised the last 600 years. (Courtesy of P. Mayewski.)

on the record of storminess for the last 10,000 years tell a story of changes in the pace or vigour of northern hemisphere circulation. No one is quite sure why such changes took place, although a popular view is that they are in some way related to differences in the amount of heat that the Earth receives from the Sun.

The sea ice

Studies of Greenland ice cores have also provided fascinating information on past changes in the extent of sea ice across the Arctic Ocean and Greenland Sea. Why should this be important to understanding Scotland's past climate? The answer is that many studies have shown that periods of increased storminess in the past have coincided with periods of time when the extent of the sea ice cover was at its greatest. For example, it was a marked increase in the extent of sea ice during the fourteenth and fifteenth centuries that obstructed movement of shipping across the northern North Atlantic and contributed to the demise of the Viking settlements in southwest Greenland. Ironically, it was the substantial decrease in sea ice cover during the preceding period of medieval warmth, coupled with decreased storminess, especially between the ninth and eleventh centuries that enabled the Vikings to explore and settle in places such as Iceland, Greenland and possibly also North America.

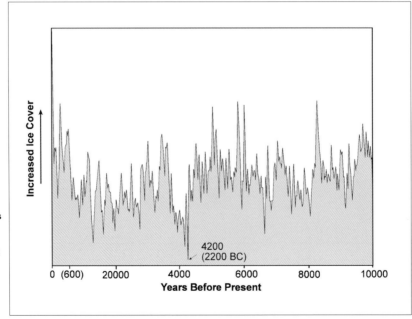

Graph showing the long-term pattern of changes in the extent of sea ice across high latitudes over the last 10,000 years. Note the remarkable period centred on 4,200 years ago that represents the period of most benign climate since the end of the last ice age. (Courtesy of P. Mayewski.)

The graph of changes in sea ice extent in the northern North Atlantic, Greenland Sea and Davis Strait is truly remarkable. We see as a striking feature the marked expansion in sea ice cover that was a feature of the Little Ice Age. Further back in time we see other periods of exceptional sea ice cover – most notably between 5,000 and 6,000 years ago. Going further back in time, we see another prominent spike of cold around 8,400–8,500 years ago. There have also been times when sea ice cover has been substantially reduced. Most prominent amongst these is a period of time between approximately 3,700 and 4,400 years ago, when Scotland's weather must have been wonderful. We can almost imagine Scotland at this time to have been a place where winters would have been mild and storms a rare occurrence. Summers, by contrast, would probably have been warm, dry and sunny, with many of our ancestors suffering from sunburn.

It is not difficult to understand why increased sea ice extent and increased winter storminess go hand in hand. An extensive sea ice cover effectively puts a 'lid' over the northern ocean, preventing the escape of moisture from the ocean surface into the troposphere. Furthermore, the cold ice surface chills the overlying air, causing this air to sink. Such circumstances favour the development of high surface air pressure and anticyclonic circulation. During such periods, cold polar air generally extends further south than normal, to collide with warmer moist air in the south and create storms. So, as with the sea salt history also obtained from Greenland ice, the account of changes in sea ice extent provides an indirect history of changes in Scotland's weather.

The fire and ash

It is well known that volcanic eruptions affect climate. Sufficient quantities of ash circulating in the atmosphere will reflect some of the incoming radiation from the Sun back into space – thus causing cooling of the Earth's surface. It is relatively straightforward to make a list of the largest volcanic eruptions that have happened during recent history, since all we have to do is consult written accounts. However, trying to work out which of these eruptions have induced cooling of the Earth's climate is much more difficult. Estimating which eruptions have had an impact specifically on Scotland's climate is even more problematic. Trying to determine what major eruptions have taken place during prehistory is, on the face of it, the toughest task of all. Fortunately, however, the Greenland ice cores help us out yet again, in two ways. First, if the eruption resulted in the deposition of volcanic ash on the surface of the Greenland ice sheet, any traces of ash preserved within the ice cores will tell

Graph showing long-term changes in volcanic activity. The spikes show changes in the concentration of volcanic sulphate ions in Greenland ice. Note the occurrence of the very largest volcanic eruptions that took place between 7,000 and 12,000 years ago. The most recent large spike (left) is the unknown eruption of ad 1258.

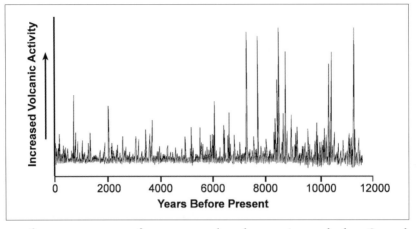

us, often to an accuracy of a year or so, when the eruption took place. Second, most eruptions are associated with the release of huge volumes of sulphate aerosols into the atmosphere. In the atmosphere, the sulphates combine with hydrogen to make a very dilute sulphuric acid. Thus most volcanic eruptions are associated with acid rain.

Chemical analysis of the ice cores reveals peaks of sulphate acidity in snowfall preserved in the ice. Volcanic eruptions, if sufficiently distant from northern Europe (in the tropics, for instance), can be associated with acidity peaks in Greenland ice cores, but an absence of ash. So changes in sulphate concentrations within the ice give us a very good indication of how many major volcanic eruptions have taken place beyond northern Europe in the past, and which ones were the biggest. When we look at the graph of sulphate concentrations indicative of volcanic eruptions for the Holocene (last 10,000 years) we see large numbers of minor sulphate peaks but only seven or eight very large ones, most of which took place between 7,000 and 10,000 years ago, as well as one enormous one that appears to have taken place around AD 1258 (see Chapter 4).

The peaks evident in the sulphate graph are all the more remarkable when we think of some of the largest volcanic eruptions that we know have taken place during recent human history. For example, in the Greenland ice cores there is a clear sulphate peak coincident with the eruption of Vesuvius in AD 87 and of the famous eruption of Santorini in the Aegean Sea approximately 3,500 years ago. Not surprisingly, many of the sulphate peaks and ash deposits preserved within Greenland ice derive from Iceland, the land of Fire and Ice. Traces of several of the largest eruptions from Iceland are also preserved as ash deposits in Scottish peat bogs.

Hard rains falling

Several years ago, scientists who were taking core samples of peat from some of Scotland's bogs made an amazing discovery. In some cores, clusters of small grains appeared as if they were simply grains of sand, However, when the samples were put under the microscope in the laboratory it soon became clear that the grains were composed of glass-like material with very sharp edges. Many of them appeared to have unusual fracture marks, as well as tiny bubble-shaped structures. The team of scientists soon realised that they were looking at small pieces of volcanic ash (known as tephra) produced as a result of a large volcanic eruption. Further studies revealed that the chemical composition of the volcanic ash corresponded with that of a volcano in Iceland. Today, after many more studies, we now know of at least five major volcanic eruptions in Iceland during the last several thousand years, which on each occasion led to falls of ash across Scotland. In addition to these five major events, there have been many other eruptions of volcanoes in Iceland that have affected Scotland, with a significant numbers of these coming from Mt Hekla.

Mt Hekla is one of Iceland's most active volcanoes, having erupted 18 times in recent history as well as having produced some of its biggest eruptions during the Holocene. It even signalled the arrival of the new millennium with a big eruption during February 2000. It is thought that the three largest eruptions took place around 8,500, 6,500 and 4,900 years ago, on each occasion covering most of Iceland with ash and pumice. One of the biggest eruptions during historical times was in 1104. Even as recently as 1693 an eruption caused many across northern Scotland to observe dense sulphurous fogs that caused the crops to wither. As has often been the case, the most immediate consequence of such eruptions was the withering of crops, rising food prices and hunger.

From the evidence for past volcanic eruptions in the Greenland ice cores, we can be almost certain that no eruption anywhere on Earth over the last 10,000 years has led to sufficient cooling of the atmosphere to have caused an ice age, or even a mini ice age. As far as we can tell, the largest eruptions may have led to some cooling over a few years, or perhaps several decades at the most extreme. As we shall see later, some of the largest Icelandic eruptions known to have taken place during the last several hundred years have resulted in a variety of complex effects on Scotland's climate. Instead of strong climate cooling, some have resulted in extensive crop failures due to the production of acid rainfall.

Swings in Scotland's temperature

The final story that ice cores can tell us is that of air temperature. Measurements of changes in the amounts of the isotopes of oxygen preserved in the ice provide a history of past changes in air temperatures across Greenland. The pattern of inferred changes in past air temperature also show remarkable features. Firstly, they show that in contrast to the very large swings in temperature that were a feature of ice ages, the temperature swings that took place for most of the last 10,000 years were much less pronounced. Even the cold temperatures normally associated with the so-called 'Little Ice Age' of the fifteenth to nineteenth centuries do not show up on the ice core 'temperature' graphs as a big change. There is one amazing period of time, however, where a big downturn in air temperatures is very clear. This is for a period of several hundred years centred on approximately 8,200 years ago (see p. 70). Around this time something very unusual happened to the Earth's climate. Scientists attempting to reconstruct past climate for different parts of the world have independently identified a period of dramatic cooling across northwest Europe, while drought conditions appear to have affected North America and Africa at this time. The popular view is that the period of cooling lasted around 400 years – in effect a small-scale version of the Younger Dryas period of cold climate.

The cause of this remarkable episode of cooling is still being debated, but general opinion points to one key theory. This is that the cooling was brought about by the sudden draining of enormous volumes of fresh water into the North Atlantic as a result of the emptying of one of the Earth's largest ever lakes. The lake is known as Glacial Lake Agassiz-Ojibway, which owed its existence to the damming of glacial meltwaters along the southern edge of the large great ice sheet that existed at this time in North America. The lake was around 3,500km in length from east to west, with its eastern margin located over eastern Canada and its western shoreline located far to the west at the foot of the Canadian Rockies. As the ice over Canada continued to become thinner and shrink in size due to global warming, a point was reached

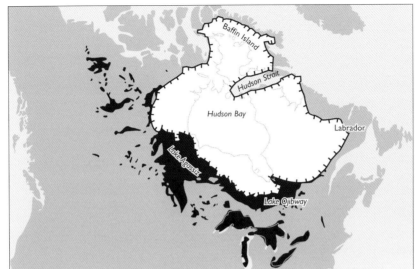

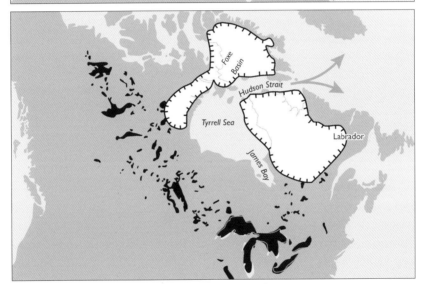

The world's biggest flood took place around 8,200 years ago where a huge area of lake water impounded by the last major remnant of the North American ice sheet located over the Hudson Bay area, suddenly burst through and underneath the ice. The water escaped through the Hudson Strait into the North Atlantic. Many believe that this event led to a disruption of oceanic thermohaline circulation in the North Atlantic and the onset of a short period (200 years) of extremely cold climate.

around 8,400 years ago when the waters started to penetrate northwards through tunnels underneath the ice.

Eventually the network of tunnels found an outlet in Hudson Bay. The northward flow of water started off as a trickle, developed into a raging torrent and finally became one of the Earth's largest floods. The escaping waters emerged from beneath the ice sheet in Hudson Bay and flowed eastward into the North Atlantic through the Hudson Strait. Estimates place the volume of water that poured into the North Atlantic as near 150,000km^3, a volume sufficient to raise sea level around the world by, on average, about half a metre. No one is quite sure how long it took for all this water to drain into the ocean. It may have happened very quickly indeed – perhaps even over a few days or weeks. After the water had emptied from the lake, the ice sheet over Hudson Bay started to disintegrate. This may have rung the death knell for the last North American ice sheet, since a few hundred years later the whole of the ice sheet had finally melted away. Glacial Lake Agassiz-Ojibway was gone forever. No one knows why, given such dramatic changes, the subsequent period of severe cold climate did not last longer than just a few hundred years.

TALES FROM SCOTLAND'S LANDSCAPE

Voices in a changing landscape

The changes that accompanied the onset of the Holocene must have come as something of a shock to a landscape previously overwhelmed by glacier ice. The rapid warming of the climate and the readjustment from glacial-age conditions was paralleled by the vertical rebound of the land surface due to the removal of the mass of ice that had previously buried large parts of Scotland's landscape. Climatic conditions and rebound of the land combined to cause a multiplicity of landslips and rockfalls in the hills and glens. Some may even have been triggered by earthquakes – also caused by the release of stresses as the land continued to adjust to the disappearance of the weight of ice.

As winter rains continued to fall during the first few thousand years of the Holocene, sediments were repeatedly washed down hillsides into rivers. To begin with, a sparse cover of vegetation facilitated the processes of sediment erosion, transport and deposition. Later on, as vegetation became more established, the rate of landscape change may have slowed down, although the undoubted occurrence of extreme storms and floods from time to time may have had the same destructive effects on the landscape as they do today.

It was in this context of a changing landscape that Scotland's first settlers arrived. Although there is fragmentary archaeological evidence for the presence of people in Scotland during the Younger Dryas cold period, it is abundantly clear that people began to arrive in significant numbers as soon as the climate started to improve. Within areas previously covered by glaciers the landscape, to begin with, was barren, but was starting to be colonised by vegetation. It was thus a virgin landscape of silent rocks, raging rivers and bare, dusty ground. Outside the area covered by the Younger Dryas glaciers, the landscape had already been uncovered from the ice for a long time, and had started to develop a more mature cover of vegetation. With relative warmth and some degree of climatic stability, tree colonisation gradually took place. At the coast, the beaches were later to disappear in different ways: in the far-flung isles of the west, as well as across the north and south of Scotland, the beaches were later to be drowned by rising sea levels as the big ice sheets in North America and Scandinavia continued to melt, causing sea levels to rise, but in areas closer to the Western Highlands, where the land was rebounding at a faster rate than the sea was rising, the ancient shorelines were later to be elevated and preserved as raised beaches.

Holocene waterworlds

Compared with the present debate regarding the speed at which the sea level is rising, sea-level rise during the Mesolithic took place at astonishing rates. Even in areas where the rate of land uplift (due to the unloading of the earlier ice cover) was at its greatest, the rate of sea-level rise was even higher still. Because the rate of land uplift was different across Scotland, it is not possible to ascribe a single figure to the rate of relative sea-level rise that took place at any point in time. However, typical figures range from between 10mm per year to 30mm per year. Such figures are between 10 and 30 times greater than the present rate of relative sea-level rise across much of Scotland (1mm per year). Indeed, the rates of rise were so great that Mesolithic people could scarcely have failed to notice the relentless rise of the sea.

The culprits causing such fast rates of rise in relative sea level were far away from Scotland. They were the large ice sheets in North America, Russia and Scandinavia, which were in their final stages of melting. As the pace of ice melting accelerated, so did the rate at which glacial meltwaters entered the world's oceans. Probably one of the most detailed and complete records of sea-level rise covering the last 17,000 years comes from studies of submerged coral reefs thousands of miles away in Barbados. Dating of the ages of submerged coral reefs at different water depths around Barbados gives us a clear idea of what the pattern of sea-level rise was on the other side of the Atlantic in an area largely unaffected by vertical land movements.

What we see from the Barbados record of sea-level rise provides some important insights into what life was like for Mesolithic coastal communities in Scotland. The most important issue is that the very high rates of sea-level rise continued uninterrupted for over 2,000 years, from approximately 9,000 to 7,000 years ago. It was not the case that this astonishing rise occurred over a handful of generations of Mesolithic people. Instead, it may have been that, by the time Scotland's first settlers had started to inhabit the coast, the rapid rise was already underway and then became a characteristic of the entire history of the Mesolithic period.

Map showing the likely distribution of dry land in the Outer Hebrides at the start of the Holocene interglacial around 10,000 years ago. Drowned landscapes such as these may have been available to Scotland's first settlers.

Archaeologists have found many locations in Scotland containing evidence of Scotland's first settlers. The term 'Mesolithic' is generally used to refer to this period, when most people were hunter-gatherers – until the start of the Neolithic period, when people started to farm the land. As with all such simple divisions, there were almost certainly places and times in history when Mesolithic hunter-gatherers and Neolithic farmers must have co-existed. In respect of the Mesolithic, the traces of the very earliest settlers are in the form of scatters of crudely shaped implements, often fragments of flint. Opinion is divided on what the tiny pieces of chipped flint were used for. Perhaps many were tools, while others may have been arrowheads. There are so few pieces of archaeological evidence that can be put together to tell a story of how our first ancestors lived that much is speculative. Later in the Holocene, however, we start to find evidence in certain locations of groups of people living together in camps for lengths of time. One of the most famous locations is at Kinloch on the Isle of Rum, where remarkable discoveries have enabled us to build a picture of what life was like for these, our oldest ancestors. On the shores of Colonsay and Oronsay also, ancient middens containing thousands of limpet shells and fish bones tell a story of some of the earliest coastal communities in Scotland. Yet, curiously, no traces of the boats they must have used have ever been found.

The archaeological story of Scotland's first settlers is a long and complex one. We can learn some important things about the climatic conditions in which they lived from a number of indirect sources. Part of the story again comes from the Greenland ice cores, another from geological reconstructions of past changes in relative sea level, while studies of sediment cores taken from peat bogs and lochs tell us how vegetation responded to climate change.

Stories from the bogs

The stories from the peat bogs are complex. Many water-filled hollows created after the ice disappeared were gradually infilled with lake sediments and peat deposits within which, due to the oxygen-starved conditions, are preserved a rich variety of plant remains, including those of fruits, seeds, wood and other parts of plants such as leaves, buds, scales and spines. Within such deposits are also to be found grains of pollen and spores that were released into the atmosphere from plants. The remains of insects, including beetles and midges, have also provided important sources of information on past climatic conditions. In fact, during recent years, study of the remains of non-biting midges (known as *chironomids*) preserved within peat have proved invaluable in reconstructing past climates.

Reconstruction of changes in Scotland's past climate has also been made through studies of peat in blanket bogs. These are areas of bog that have evolved as a result of heavy rainfall – usually in areas where the annual rainfall is in excess of around 1m per year. In Scotland, since it is a well-known fact that heavy and sustained rainfall is a normal feature of daily life, it should not raise eyebrows that blanket bogs are quite common features of the landscape. Remarkably, waterlogged tree stumps occur underneath many areas of blanket bog, telling us that the areas where such bogs presently occur used to be characterised by woodland. No one knows precisely why or when this change from woodland to blanket bog occurred, although many areas of blanket bog

The highest seas

No one is quite sure when the sea reached its highest level. Intuitively, one might imagine that sea level around the Scottish coast reached its highest point once all the large ice sheets that had existed during the last ice age had finally melted. If this was the case then we might envisage that the highest seas occurred once the last ice sheet to disintegrate had finally done so. This ice sheet was the gigantic Laurentide ice sheet in North America. We know that the last vestiges of this ice sheet disappeared around 7,000–7,500 years ago. Inspection of the pattern of sea-level rise for Barbados shows that the rise in sea level starts to slow down markedly around about the time that this ice sheet finally disapppeared. So we might imagine that it was about this time that sea levels around the Scottish coast were at their highest. The problem is that this estimate might not be correct.

A number of scientists have shown from geological studies that the highest sea levels may have occurred much later – perhaps even as late as around 4,000 years ago. If this was the case then we have to search for some other explanation as to how this could have happened. A simple explanation may be that this was the time where there was less ice locked up in the world's ice sheets and glaciers than at any time before or after. A key clue comes from our understanding of the extent of North Atlantic sea ice which, if correct, is a good indicator of past changes in North Atlantic climate. From this, we see a dramatic decrease in sea ice cover between approximately 4,400 and 3,700 years ago – hinting that this time interval may possibly have been the warmest of the last 10,000

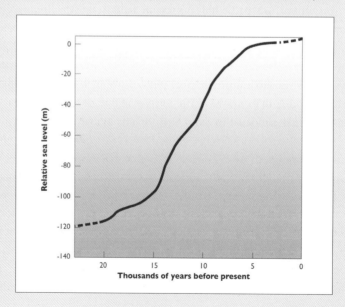

Curve of the rise in sea level over the last 20,000 years for Barbados. Note that the most rapid rate of rise corresponds with the time when the last great ice sheets were melting.

years. If the climate was as warm at this time as the sea-ice record would appear to indicate, could it be that there was a bout of global warming at this time, together with a shrinking of alpine glaciers and thinning of ice sheets in Greenland, Antarctica and elsewhere, with all this melting ice leading to additional sea-level rise?

Whatever the pros and cons of the arguments regarding precisely when the sea reached its highest level, the effects of rising seas on Scotland were remarkable. Marine waters were sufficiently high to flood into Loch Lomond, turning the loch into an arm of the sea. Eleswhere on the west coast, the sea flooded into Loch Sheil and Loch Morar. In Loch Sheil the sea waters reached a level several metres higher than the present level of the loch. At Loch Morar, the sea reached a maximum level only half a metre or so higher than the present loch level. Huge changes also occurred in eastern Scotland, nowhere more so than in the Forth valley. Here the sea extended as far west as the Lake of Menteith. When the sea was at its highest levels, Scotland was nearly separated in two, with only a short strip of land, extending from the Lake of Menteith to Drymen, preventing the land in the north from becoming an island.

In valleys like the Forth and Tay, the areas flooded at this time by the sea are represented by the 'carselands' – huge flat areas of land that today represent some of the finest agricultural land in Scotland, but which then were enormous mudflats. From the foot of the Ochils on the route from Stirling to Tillicoutry the ancient level of this sea and its cliff line can be seen stretching for miles today. Equally, the view of fields (carselands) from the villages of Airth and Bannockburn towards Grange-mouth represents part of the former mudflats of an ancient estuary.

appear to have started to form around two separate times during the Holocene – the first around 7,000 years ago and the second around 3,000 years ago. Since both of these periods of time appear to have been characterised by increased wetness, there may be a case for linking times of blanket bog formation to episodes of climate change. But such a simple explanation is made more complex by the possibility that the clearance of woodland may have been caused by people. The discussion is made even more obscure by the observation that some areas of blanket bog in the Highlands and Islands may have begun to form before the arrival of people in the landscape. As with most things, both explanations are probably true for different areas, although there is a persuasive argument that blanket-bog development may have accelerated later during the Holocene, as human activity became much more widespread. The studies that have been made of past changes in vegetation are remarkable.

They show that the rapid warming that characterised the start of the Holocene provided optimum conditions for the arrival of broad-leaved, warmth-loving trees. The first waves of woodland expansion appear to have been mostly associated with the arrival of birch, mainly in central and eastern areas, and then hazel starting in the west and spreading east and south. This was followed soon after by the arrival of elm and oak. Later still came lime, ash and alder. Most authorities agree that it was not climatic conditions alone that led to these waves of plant and tree colonisation. Just as important were the soil conditions, the airborne spread of seeds as well as vegetation competition. Some have observed from studies of tree pollen preserved in peat that the woodland appears to have remained approximately stable until around 5,000 years ago. Thereafter, the influence of people on the development of vegetation seems to have become a dominant factor.

Stories of heather and moor

Much of Scotland's heather slopes and moorland areas was covered by trees at some time during the Holocene interglacial. Today they have been replaced by extensive moorland areas characterised by poor soils and a very restricted range of tree species. To a large extent we can regard this dramatic change in the Scottish landscape as an extension of the blanket-bog debate, although as far as Scotland is concerned some of the moorland areas had already started their transformation from the earlier tree cover during the Neolithic period, while others may owe their origins to clearance of land during the Bronze Age. One study has even shown that areas of the Outer Isles and Shetland maintained a cover of trees down to sea level from around 8,000 years ago until at least 5,000 years ago. Observations such as these send the clear message that even though the angry beast was relatively tame during the Holocene, the scale of climate change, linked in many instances to the impact of humans on the landscape, was sufficient to lead to spectacular changes in our landscape.

By contrast, across Scotland's moors the areas of heathland dominated by heather generally occur at lower elevations and in areas of lower rainfall than those associated with blanket bog. Studies of heathland vegetation have shown that not all areas of Scotland were covered by woodland during the early millennia of the Holocene. Some parts of Scotland, such as areas of Shetland, Orkney, the Inner and Outer Hebrides and Caithness, appear to have been characterised by treeless conditions, with grass and heathland communities, through nearly all of the Holocene. As in the case of woodland, the activities of people appear to have been crucial in the development of heathland.

Carselands stranded high and dry

Climb up the hummocky mounds on the eastern edge of the Lake of Menteith and look eastwards down the valley of the Forth. The present river winds its course through fields of carse clay that reach out to the horizon. The river in the upper Forth is everywhere cut deeply into the clay sediments. Part of the reason for this is that between Menteith and Stirling the fields of carse clay lie between 12 and 15m above present sea level. How can this be? Does this tell us that when the waters and currents of this ancient sea surface rose and fell with the tide the sea level was actually as high as this? And does this mean some kind of global warming was taking place several thousand years ago, sufficient to raise sea level by this amount? The answer is – absolutely not!

The reason that the fields of carse occur at such relatively high altitudes in places like the Tay and Forth valleys is that the Scottish land mass has continued to rebound vertically as a result of the disappearance of the last ice sheet across the country. The rates of land uplift across central Scotland have continued to decelerate over time (although it is still rising – today in the Forth and Tay areas the rate of land uplift is in the order of 1mm per year). When the carse clay mudlats of the Forth and Tay were being washed by the tide several thousand years ago, sea level was approximately at the same level as it is today. Since then, however, land uplift has continued uninterrupted (although gradually slowing down over time) and today has resulted in the occurrence of the carse clay sediments at their present levels.

The Forth and Tay valleys are not the only places where carse clays are widespread. Other examples include the low fields between Troon, Irvine and Dundonald in Ayrshire, as well as much of the low, flat area bordering the Beauly Firth and on part of which Inverness is built. Large areas of carse clay extend inland from the present coastline of the Solway in areas as far apart as Annan, Newbie and Newton Stewart.

Comparing clocks

As everybody knows, a clock that is not working properly is not much use. Often when we are uncertain of the time we compare watches. As in our modern lives, it is also necessary to compare timepieces that measure past time. This is particularly necessary for the various attempts that have been made to determine when the most significant climate changes took place during the Holocene. It will come as no great surprise to learn that the different methods used to measure at what times the most important changes took place tell different stories.

The established view, long held, is that a characteristic of Holocene climate across Scotland was a prolonged period of maximum warmth between about 8,000 and 4,500 years ago, described in many quarters as the 'Climatic Optimum'. This conclusion is in broad agreement with the reconstructions of temperature based on the studies of Greenland ice cores – these show that the culmination of this period of warmth took place between around 6,000 and 5,000 years ago. Mean annual temperatures across Scotland at this time may have been slightly warmer than at present, but by no more than 1–2°C. During this time, the drier conditions may also have resulted in lower loch levels, a lowering of water tables and the drying out of bogs.

At some time in the Holocene it started to become wetter. Some have maintained that climate may have fluctuated quite strongly between around 5,000 and 3,000 years ago, with a progressive deterioration in climate between 3,000 and 2,500 years ago and a particularly marked downturn between 2,800 and 2,500 years ago. Throughout these complex episodes of climatic cooling, the 1–2°C of warming mentioned earlier may have been entirely reversed.

Apart from changes in past air temperature, many other important elements of the climate system have changed during the Holocene. Prominent among these are changes in North Atlantic sea surface temperature, changes in storminess, changes in regional sea ice cover across northern ocean areas and, of course, changes in the behaviour of the North Atlantic oceanic thermohaline conveyor – all of these have exerted profound influences on Scotland's climate. Inspection of the Greenland ice-core record of changes in regional sea ice extent reveals a fascinating tale, with a massive reduction in sea ice cover between around 4,400 and 3,500 years ago. In terms of archaeology, this time interval broadly corresponds with the Bronze Age and late Neolithic period. Ordinarily, such a change would indicate a period of prolonged and exceptional warmth, yet according to peat-bog records of climate change, this was a time of climatic deterioration. The ice cores point to the period around 2,500 years ago as a time of increased North Atlantic storminess, an observation consistent with the results of peat-bog research. The story becomes further complicated by studies that point to a decrease in the temperatures of surface waters across the North Atlantic, starting from around 4,400 years ago, a viewpoint inconsistent with the Greenland ice-core record of reduced sea ice cover at this time.

All this begs the question – ought we to expect that all parts of the ocean-atmosphere system march in phase with long-term increases or decreases in air temperature? For example, should one expect that as soon as air temperatures start to fall, there should be a decline in ocean surface temperatures, an increase in sea ice cover, an increase in regional storminess and a slowdown in the North Atlantic oceanic conveyor? Similarly, should we expect a rise in air temperatures to be followed by a rise in ocean temperatures etc? The simple fact is that, even now at the start of the twenty-first century, we do not fully understand how the ocean and atmosphere interact during periods of climate change.

Sandstorms at the coast

As with the present coast, we ought not to imagine such ancient seas forming mudflats everywhere along the coast. Where the rising seas encountered sandy coastal areas, water and wind combined to transport large quantities of sand inland which were later covered by vegetation to produce strips of land at the coast that we now know as 'links'. Often, as areas of links were produced, periods of sand-blow during Holocene windstorms resulted in the creation of sandhills. To these winds we therefore owe a debt since they created the coastal landscapes now described as 'links' golf courses. Famous courses such as Royal Troon, Carnoustie and St Andrews were formed in exactly this way.

Bronze, iron and the elements

Archaeologists normally refer to the Bronze Age as broadly extending between 7000 BC and AD 2500. This period is thought to correspond with an age starting with the first metalwork, normally involving copper, and ending with the replacement of copper by iron as the principal metal used in everyday life. As with all terms used to describe past societies, the term 'Bronze Age' can only identify a period when people's way of life was distinct from that which came before and after.

We have already seen that this time interval is complex from a climatic point of view, with extremes of temperature (both warming and cooling), storminess and rainfall. Scientists seeking to understand the nature of the environmental changes that took place during this period always face the difficulty of not being to tell which changes in the landscape were due to climate change and which were attributable directly to the activities of people. We know that clearance of woodland was extensive during this period and that soil erosion was becoming a significant agent of landscape change. Added to this is the fact that some time around 4,300 years ago, a large eruption from Mt Hekla in Iceland showered volcanic ash across nearly the whole of Scotland as well as much of Ireland and northern England. Although its effects

When the storms abated

In the descriptions of the archaeology of St Kilda there are accounts of a former settlement in the north of the island. But who would ever be crazy enough to live on the north side of St Kilda? Living on the island is tough enough at the best of times, but the hostile north-facing slopes would be by far the worst site to choose. The answer to this puzzle lies in the Greenland ice cores that show that there have been times in the past when winter storminess across the North Atlantic may have been exceptionally low. For anyone living in Scotland, such an observation borders on the incredible. After all, the lives of all of us, plus those of our parents, grandparents and great-grandparents, have been dominated by the annual repetition of winters characterised by howling winds and rain. Horrible winters are so deeply entrenched in our psyche that it is almost impossible to imagine that conditions were ever any different in the past. But different they were, and in the not too distant past.

The Greenland ice cores tell us that the stormy winters with which we are familiar only extend back as far as the early 1400s. Prior to this, there was a period of mild climate extending back to the eighth century AD, when winter storms were infrequent. Similarly, as revealed by the ice cores' account of the extent of sea ice, the period between approximately 3,700 and 4,400 years ago could have been another time when our ancestors could have considered the vast expanse of the North Atlantic Ocean as a benign rather than a hostile environment.

on Scotland's climate are unknown, it was clearly one of the largest such eruptions to have affected the country over the last 5,000 years.

Although it isn't certain that the first half of the Bronze Age was characterised by benign climatic conditions, both warm and free of storms, there is more certainty that the latter part of the Bronze Age was quite different. Many have described a climatic deterioration that took place around the seventh to eighth centuries BC, and some have argued that this return to cool, wet conditions was triggered by a cooling of the Sun around this time. The coincidence between the beginning of the Iron Age and the climatic deterioration of the seventh to eighth centuries BC may be fortuitous. Whatever the human impact on climate at this time, lifestyles had certainly changed. The start of the Iron Age witnessed the introduction of metal smelting and increased use of iron materials. It ended with the Roman invasion. Of course, since the effects of the Roman armies were not felt everywhere in Britain, we can envisage that the development of Iron Age society across the Highlands and Islands was quite different from that in the Southern Uplands and across the Central Lowlands. Our sketchy knowledge of climatic conditions for this time gives hints that rainfall and winter storminess were much greater than the long-term average, while summers were slightly cooler. No doubt the builders of the Iron Age brochs were well aware of the vagaries of Scottish weather!

POSTSCRIPT

In the following chapters some of the most important weather and climate changes that have taken place since Roman times will be explored in detail. The various historical documents recording weather in the past that are available for this period provide many fascinating glimpses into the past, and it may be possible to make sense of the patterns of climate change that these snapshots of history indicate. Many of these scraps of information have been lying hidden for years in dusty volumes in libraries and estate papers. Until now, most have not seen the light of day.

PART 3
HISTORY

CHAPTER 4
PEN TO PAPER:
FROM THE ROMANS TO BEYOND THE SPANISH ARMADA
(AD 200–1599)

So greit ane wynd and storme upone the se
That schippis all war drevin to the north land,
And sum on craig, and other sum on sand,
War brokin all.

Anon. 1328

INTRODUCTION

The story of Scotland's weather and climate is a complicated one, and most of it has gone unrecorded. There are, of course, a number of ways in which one can reconstruct Scotland's past climate prior to the availability of written records. However, as soon as pen was put to paper, very accurate glimpses of what past weather and climate were like began to be revealed. In many ways the written story is a frustrating one to read, since the various available accounts each only cover very short periods of time. This story of written records therefore begins with fragmentary scraps of information, starting at a tumultuous period of Scotland's history, when the Roman empire almost reached into Scotland's icy winter wasteland.

The last Roman soldiers left Scotland around AD 211. As they kept their winter sentry duties they must have watched the rain clouds scudding across the Border hills and longed for summers in the heat and the dust of Rome. Scotland may not have had had quite the same appeal.

By the middle of the first millennium the peoples of Scotland included the Britons in the southwest, the Gododdin in the southeast and the Picts in the east and northeast. By the fourth century St Ninian had already established his church near Whithorn. Then, by AD 500 the Scotti had arrived in Argyll from Ireland and during the seventh century groups of Germanic-speaking Angles started to settle in the borderlands. With the complexities of various languages associated with these various groups, we are left with mere fragments of information with which we can piece together information on the weather and climate they experienced. For this reason, the Greenland ice-core record of past climate continues to provide a priceless chronology of what climate may have been like in Scotland during this time. In using this climate record, we have always to remember that past climate changes in Greenland need not correspond exactly with patterns of change in Scotland. However, Greenland's ice-core records do tell us how climate is likely to have changed across the North Atlantic region as a whole. We know, for example, how the changing concentrations of sea salt preserved in Greenland ice reveal past changes in North Atlantic storminess. So we can be fairly sure that this change also reflects changes in Scotland at the same time.

With the fragments of historical information available for the first half of the first millennium AD, we learn, for example, of damaging floods in the Tweed during 218, severe rains across Scotland in 233 and ten months of almost continuous rain in Scotland during 470 – so nothing changes! We learn also from accounts of the life of St Columba that some time between 665 and 669 there was 'a very great, continuous and severe drought in the spring time'. At other times there are indications of the effects of distant volcanic eruptions. For example, 685 is quoted as the year when there were bloody rains in Britain and when milk and butter were turned into blood. Some maintain that the 'bloody rains' refer to eruptions of Vesuvius and Etna. During the fifteenth century the chronicler Walter Bower, continuing the work begun by John of Fordun a century earlier, recorded accounts of this earlier time in the *Scotichronicon*. He describes a 'bloody rain that fell for seven days in Scotland', while accounts from Northern Ireland allude to Lough Neagh turning the 'colour of blood'. Yet other records illustrate how easy it is to misinterpret historical information. For example, there are descriptions of how the sky across Scotland was darkened for six months after the death of Duff of Scotland in 967–968. While at first sight this might be considered indicative of darkened skies following a volcanic eruption, it should also be remembered that this period also coincided with a number of prominent solar eclipses.

The Greenland ice cores tell us that marked changes in weather and climate took place during the latter part of the first millennium and culminated in a period of exceptional warmth during the eleventh and twelfth centuries. This time, generally known as the period of medieval warmth, was preceded by a well-defined period of cooling during the ninth and tenth centuries. Some of the most stupendous volcanic eruptions in Iceland took place some time between 934 and 940. The eruptions happened in the district

The Eldgja fires

The Eldgja volcanic vents stretch along a 75km length of southern Iceland between Mt Katla and the Vatnajökull ice cap. The early settlers of Iceland must have been amazed by what was happening. Hundreds of square kilometres were covered by lava flows associated with fifteen separate eruptions taking place over a six-year period. Some of the columns of ash are thought to have been in the order of 14km high. The sagas tell of the destruction of farmland, the abandonment of land. Some families are even described in the sagas as having attempted to rake the cover of volcanic ash from the fields. No one knows for sure what the effects were on the weather of northern Europe. Some information can be gained from a similar, though less extensive, eruption of Laki in Iceland during 1783–84 (see Chapter 10). It is well known, for example, that the years following this eruption were associated with a lowering of air temperatures across northern Europe, the occurrence of dry sulphurous fogs and damage to crops and vegetation. From what we know, the Eldgja eruptions were twice as big as those of Laki. Thus we may expect that the effects on society were at least as severe as those associated with the Laki eruptions, which took place throughout the summer of 1783. Although hardly any historical accounts exist for this period, there are descriptions of a drought in Ireland at this time, when the mountains of Connaught were 'burnt with celestial fire, and the lakes and rivers were dried up' (C.E. Britton 1937). There is also an account for 941 of a great frost across Ireland and the freezing of rivers and lakes, but no information is available for Scotland.

of Eldgja in southern Iceland and nearly 220 million tonnes of sulphate aerosols were injected into the northern hemisphere atmosphere, which combined with water vapour to produce around 450 million tonnes of dilute sulphuric acid that were dispersed worldwide into the troposphere. The violent eruption of Mt Pinatubo in the Philippines during 1991 produced a mere 10 million tonnes of sulphate, yet the 'aerosol cloud' that formed as a result led to significantly reduced global temperatures for at least two years. We can only speculate what effects these earlier, more severe eruptions had on Scotland's climate. One likelihood is that is that the country experienced one or several decades of climate instability – perhaps more severe winters. Another effect may have been the withering of crops due to acid rains caused by the huge volumes of volcanic sulphur in the atmosphere.

Viking longships

It is against the background of changing climate that we find the first Vikings stepping ashore on Iceland during the latter part of the ninth century. Their later exploits in Scotland are well known, as is their establishment of a settlement in southern Greenland during the tenth century. What is less well known are the climatic conditions that existed during Viking times. The years of the longships belonged to a time when atmospheric circulation across the North Atlantic region was quite unlike present patterns. The key difference was that storms were infrequent during winter while those that did occur were generally less intense than those with which we are familiar today. An additional factor of considerable importance was that the sea ice cover across high-latitude oceans during winter and spring was greatly restricted. Thus, not only were the sailors on the longships the recipients of benign weather but also the routeways across the ocean to the west were relatively free from the obstruction of ice floes. The Vikings undoubtedly must have taken advantage of the relatively calm waters to journey south to our shores and beyond. They would also have benefited from the fact that the frequency and intensity of cold easterly winds blowing off the continent were considerably diminished. Surviving winters in medieval Scotland was thus not fraught with the perishing cold of blizzard and snow. Doubtless, it must have snowed sometimes, but with nothing like the severity of the centuries that followed.

A far cry from the vineyards

According to most chronicles, the eleventh and twelfth centuries were times when climatic conditions were so wonderful that vineyards were a common sight across southern England. We can be fairly sure that this period of time, coincident with the so-called 'Medieval Warm Period', was not as warm in Scotland. The Greenland ice cores tell us that it *should* have been relatively mild but there is insufficient contemporaray information in the available references to weather in Scotland to tell us either way. Those pieces of information that are available are limited to descriptions of occasional storms and sea floods.

We read, for example, one of the earliest written accounts of a Scottish storm in the 1067 account of Edgar Atheling, a claimant to the English throne, when he found his ship driven by a storm into Scotland:

Thair passage maid than out of Thamis mouth,
The wind it blew so stark out of the south,
Ay be ane bird it draif thame to the north,
Quhill tha tuke land richt far vp into Forth,
Into ane place, as my author did sa,
Sanct Margaretis-hoip is callit at this da'.

(quoted in C.E. Britton, *A Meteorological Chronology to AD 1450*,
Meteorological Office, London, 1937)

Severe winters are recorded across Britain in 1074 and 1077, drought in the summer of 1084, sea floods in 1087 – the latter related on one occasion to a great storm in the North Sea in 1091, when in late September, according to Walter de Hemingburgh, 'before they arrived in Scotland, a great tempest arose about the feast of St Michael, and almost the whole fleet was sunk, many of the horsemen of the army perishing with hunger and cold . . .'

After the terrible winters and the great frosts and snows recorded in Ireland at this period, drought again followed in the summer of 1095. The extremes of climate that marked the close of the eleventh century continued into the twelfth so that for the year 1100 there are various reports of coastal flooding in Moray. By 1110 we hear of a very long, sad, severe winter with '. . . the earth fruits greatly injured' (quoted in Britton's *Meteorological Chronology to AD 1450*) that was to be repeated in 1114.

The cold winters continued throughout much of the early twelfth century. One vivid account of how things were in 1143 in the Scottish Borders comes from Simeon of Durham who, in giving an account of the atrocities committed by the soldiers of the violent bandit, William Cumin, records how:

> other of them they plunged into the bed of the river in the depth of winter, after having broken the ice with which it was covered: and, having tied ropes about them, they alternately dragged them out of it and thrust them back again . . . The feet of some they thrust through holes made in the wall, and thus exposed their naked bodies to the extremity of the cold, leaving them in this misery all the night long
>
> (Quoted in Britton, 1937).

Reports for the late 1100s in Scotland are patchy. Walter Bower describes how 1196 was a year of severe famine in Scotland, and we know also that 1200 in Ireland was 'a cold, foodless year, the like of which no one of these times has seen'. As always, the state of sea ice off Greenland is a useful indicator of conditions. For 1203 we find reports that sea ice was very extensive around the Greenland coast. In 1205 there was another famine in Scotland. In fact the early months of 1205 coincided with one of the severest winters in medieval history. Hector Boece, more than 200 years later, describes how:

All this wes done, as I haf said zow heir,
So strang ane storme doun fra the hevin fell
Of frost and snaw, as my author did tell
Continewallie all winter throw and throw,
That neuir ane ox wes zokkit into bow,
Bot lay full still into thair stall wnsteird
Quhill that mid Merche come neuir pleuche in eird.
So furious ouir all part wes that frost,
Of bestiall that thair wes mony lost;
The starkest aill of malt thay mychy be browin,
Thocht it war keipit neuir so clois and lowin,
It wald congeill and freis into hard yis,
The thing of all men thocht wes than most nys,
That this be weycht, and nocht mesour, wes sauld,
That tyme for drink, as that my author tald'.

In 1209 famine and floods again returned to Scotland. This year is well-known also for the first descriptions of river-flooding in Perth attributed in part to high tides and also to heavy rainfall. According to Boece:

Off ane greit Spait and Tempest of Weit
that did greit Skayth in Bartha Toun,
and sindrie Pepill thairin did droun
be the Efflux of Amond and Tay.
Off Barta toun quhilk in that samin da
At Amond mouth stude on the water of Ta,
Weil wallit wes with stone and lyme about.
Out of the hillis thair come sic ane spait,
With so greit force als fast as it mycht flow;
Quhilk causit hes the tua fluidis to grown,
Amond and Tay, into sic quantitie,
That throw the greit impetuositie

Of tha fluidis it brak the wallid doun,
Syne with greit force it enterit in the toun

By 1233 Scotland had returned to successions of severely cold winters and
great frosts. The first of a series of bad winters started in late December 1233
and continued almost without cease until February, 1234. In Greenland it was
a severe winter also, with sea ice widespread and lasting until late summer. In
Ireland, according to the Annals of Boyle, there was 'a great frost in this year
so that the lakes were bound up and people, horses and flocks went upon Lake
Eradin, Lake Ce, and Lake Tus and upon many other lakes'. The bad weather
continued for several years, and in 1248 the Vikings were to lose their king in
stormy seas near Shetland.

The 1250s – droughts, storms and floods

The 1250s represent a time of great change in medieval climate and weather.
It started in 1252 with a major drought across the British Isles. Robert of
Gloucester even wrote a poem about it, stylistic enough to rival Mac-
Gonagall:

In the year of grace twelve hundred and fifty and two,
In this year was the summer so dry and so hot,
That even until this day there has been none hotter

In Ireland, the drought was associated with the drying-up of the Shannon,
trees burning and a great heat. Although there are reports of sea floods in 1253
and another drought in 1255, the biggest change was in 1258, but it is
shrouded in mystery. The Greenland ice cores show that the concentration of
volcanic sulphates for this year was higher than at any other time in 'recent'
history.

The problem was that no one knew of any volcanic eruption that had
occurred at this time. First it was speculated that the volcano concerned was
El Chichón in Mexico, then this was discounted. The presence of a similar
sulphate 'spike' in ice cores recovered from Antarctica indicated that the
volcano was located somewhere in the low latitudes. Whatever its source, the
occurrence of such a huge volcanic eruption strongly suggests that climate
cooling took place in the months, years and possibly decades that followed.

The first hint that climate change was taking place closer to home comes
from Greenland, where there was a marked increase in the extent of sea ice

off the coast. In Scotland we learn from the diary of Walter Bower that the early 1260s represented the start of a decade of famine that was also experienced in Ireland. Sharp, wintry weather is described for the start of 1261 – in fact this is one of the first descriptions of a winter when the Thames froze over. The following year, 'the watteris of Forth and Tay rais with sic inundation of spait, that many tounis wer drounit, to the gret dammag'.

Some have argued that this period of famine was used by King Haakon of Norway as an opportunity to invade Scotland in 1263. However, as reports from the ensuing Battle of Largs reveal, there were severe storms and flooding that year, and in fact the stormy weather helped defend the country, as it scattered and destroyed Haakon's ships while he was forced to overwinter in Orkney (where he died).

The bitter, severe winters continued into the 1270s. We know very little about the details of the climate of this time, although there are occasional glimpses. For example, more floods are known to have taken place in the Tay in 1266 and in the Nith in 1268. Walter Bower describes famines across Scotland in 1271 and there are a variety of accounts for this time of hard snowy winters, river flooding and storms. One of the most famous took place in 1271 when a dreadful storm destroyed a large part of St Andrews Cathedral as it was being built. Then in the following year the church at Arbroath was destroyed by fire caused by lightning.

Distant echoes from Greenland tell of conditions that were continuing to deteriorate. The killing, for example, in Iceland in 1274 of 22 polar bears that had wandered dangerously close to populated settlements points to a huge expansion of sea ice off the East Greenland coast. By 1275 there are reports of sea ice surrounding the entire coastline of Iceland and the killing of even more polar bears that had wandered over the ice. The shortest distance from East Greenland to Iceland is around 175 miles – this alone gives an impression of the extent of the expanse of ocean covered by drift ice. This huge growth of sea ice marked the start of several centuries when sea ice was widespread across northern waters. Prior to this, during medieval times, sea ice cover around Icelandic waters was rare, if not absent entirely.

As far as we can tell, the 1280s were characterised by cold snowy winters but also by hot dry summers, with those of 1284, 1285 and 1286 approaching drought conditions. Some have attributed such contrasts to the occurrence of anticylonic circulation, in others words, long periods of high pressure during winter, lengthy frosts and late-lying snows. By contrast during summer, high air pressure meant high temperatures, a lack of rain and plenty of sunshine.

Such extreme conditions were unfavourable for crops. Long winters led to late harvests. Often the crops were blasted by unseasonable rains or damaged by drought. Rainy autumns often tipped the scales towards shortages of hay and forage. Under such circumstances, people found it hard to survive. Dearth and sometimes famine ensued – the year 1293 being particularly severe.

The end of one century and a new beginning

And so ended the thirteenth century. Although many hoped and prayed for an improvement in the weather, none was forthcoming. The first omen that things were not well occurred in 1308. Due to bad weather, in particular autumn rains, the harvest was poor across Scotland. In Ireland the autumn was very wet with accounts of widespread cattle mortality.

Most Scots are hardy enough to cope with the extreme cold and blizzard conditions that winter can throw at us. In many respects it was little different during historical times. As long as the harvest was in and there was enough provision for winter, people could cope. But when it was so stormy and wet during summer and autumn that the crops were irreparably damaged and the harvest could not be gathered in, nor peat for fuel, things were very different. Much depended on the oats and bere (barley). If they failed then a hard winter was in prospect, and if failure occurred again the following year things became critical. With soaring food and grain prices most could not afford to eat or provide for their children.

After poor harvests in 1308 and 1309, followed by a famine during 1310, there was a short respite till more poor harvests again returned in 1313 and 1314. In 1315, famine struck again across Scotland, England and Ireland. The summer and autumn of 1315 were very wet, the crops failed yet again. Much of Scottish history for this time fails to mention these famines and instead concentrates on the political and socio-economic consequences of Bannockburn and the Bruce invasion of Ireland. For most Scots, however, it was a time when society received some powerful jolts, when there was a decline in population and abandonment of farmland. After the Battle of Bannockburn in 1314, Robert Bruce and his brother embarked on a military campaign in Ireland in 1315. Their expedition coincided with one of the worst periods of hardship, which affected nearly the whole of northwest Europe. The years 1315–18 are known as the 'Great Rains'. If Robert Bruce had indeed sat huddled in a cave watching his spider, he might well have felt he was living through one of the worst, if not the very worst, period of climate deterioration in history – and he would have been right. A near incredible story comes from 1317. While the Scots under Bruce were fighting their campaign, a garrison of Irish soldiers were besieged in Carrickfergus Castle. A number of reports describe how several Scots prisoners were held in the castle. Food was in such short supply that eight prisoners are thought to have been eaten.

Greenland ice cores explain the 'Great Rains'

A remarkable explanation for the 'Great Rains' of the early fourteenth century comes from study of the Greenland ice cores. Scientists studying changes over time in the temperature of the surface of the North Atlantic Ocean have discovered that the Great Rains appears to have coincided with a time when the ocean overheated. Ocean temperatures during summer were higher than average. Then in the following winter, the ocean surface remained much warmer than it otherwise would have been. With the same pattern repeated for two to three years in a row it turned into a disaster, with no end to rain in sight for months on end. Summer and autumn rains put paid to the harvest and very quickly, by 1318, Scotland was brought to its knees.

The Annals of Kilronan tell of the destruction of people in great multitudes in the war and famine and various fatal distempers, and an intolerable and damaging inclemency of weather also. From Berwick there are reports from the English army garrison of many dying from hunger at this time. The year 1316 showed no improvement. After an inclement winter (1315–16) the summer is known to have again been very wet and cold across both Scotland and Ireland. There was yet another harvest failure in England. It will come as no surprise that famine struck again across Scotland in 1318 after a wet autumn. Another famine followed in 1321, a year described by Walter Bower as having had a very grave winter which afflicted men and killed nearly all the animals.

And then, the climate changed dramatically. First, in 1325, there was a very dry summer. Then another drought in 1326, in fact some referred to the summer of 1326 as the driest year in living memory. It was a time in Scotland when rivalries between Robert Bruce and John Balliol, and disputes involving Edward III of England, were the political intrigues of the day. For those working in the fields, the summers of drought were beginning to become a memory as the harvests started to deteriorate again. There were signs of this in 1330, with a scarcity of corn, oats, peas, beans and barley due to a return of excessive summer rains. The summer was so rainy and stormy that summer and autumn were followed without a break by winter winds and rains. Famine returned in 1331 after a stormy winter and dry summer.

By the time that war had broken out again in 1337 the weather had not improved much. In many respects, conditions prevailed that were analogous to those of the Great Rains of 1315–18. There was a general famine in Ireland in 1339, there may have been a famine in Scotland this year also; there was certainly a famine across Scotland in 1340 following the siege of Perth.

Change in the Greenland air

By the mid fourteenth century there was a change in the air. Greenland experienced its coldest winter in 1352–53; temperatures plunged to depths rarely equalled since. Archaeologists and historians tell us that the period of Norse settlement in southwest Greenland came to an end some time between 1341 and 1363. We also know that a ship, the *Knarren*, belonging to the King of Norway, was wrecked in a storm around this time and that any form of regular communication with Greenland after this seems to have stopped. Sea ice spread across the Greenland Sea, with periods of significant expansion between 1341 and 1351. And with this change came the southward movement of cold polar waters to lower latitudes. A dramatic increase in North Atlantic storminess was to follow at the turn of the century. In the meantime, the latter decades of the fourteenth century were characterised by pulses of change leading inexorably towards yet more deterioration in climate.

The wars continued, only to be followed by the horrors of the Black Death, which arrived in Scotland in 1349. There were significant changes in the weather and climate afoot. Far to the north, many of the old sailing routes to Greenland were being abandoned. Tales from Greenland describe frosts so severe that the sea froze up to such an extent that it was possible to ride on horseback from all the outermost capes and on all the fjords and bays. Winters were becoming colder in Scotland too. The cold winter of 1349–50 could not have helped as many struggled to cope with the plague. In Greenland, the winter of 1352–53 was one of the coldest in history.

And with the winter cold came storms across Scotland. Walter Bower, for example, described how, in 1355, 'a great wind came out of the desert regions, that is, from the north, driving . . . ships into danger, and submerging them in the deep'.

Floods arrived too. Bower gives a vivid account for September 1358 when:

> such a great inundation of rain burst forth in parts of Lothian, that from the time of Noah until the present day the like had not been known in the realm of Scotland, whereby the waters swelled up and overflowed their channels and banks, and spread over fields, villages, towns and monasteries: it overturned from their foundations, and destroyed in its rush, stone walls in villages and houses and very strong bridges. Also great oaks and stout trees standing near the rivers were torn up by the roots whence they were violently carried down to the edge of the sea.

Occasionally other disasters happened along the way. For example, we learn from the *Book of Pluscarden* that during a remarkable storm on 6 December, 'in the year 1372 a wind called that of St Nicholas burst upon Scotland, and

Everything changes

So what did the deterioration in northern hemisphere climate during the early 1400s signify? For one thing it meant that as from this time the North Atlantic Ocean suddenly became a place where winter storms started to take place on a much more regular basis and where many storms became much more violent and longer lasting. It led to changes in ocean currents with a general southward expansion of cold polar water. Together, wind, ocean and atmosphere conspired to push the North Atlantic storm track further south. Thus the winter storms, many of which today track across Iceland and the Faroes, were displaced so that most tracked across the British Isles. Scotland's climate thus became unrecognisable from that of, say, the ninth and tenth centuries, when Viking longships had ploughed through northern waters with ease.

overturned and blew down houses and churches and everything else fixed in the ground, such as trees, towers, the pinnacles of the temple, causing inestimable damage'.

But by the early 1400s things were to change drastically, due to a radical change in the atmospheric circulation of the northern hemisphere. Prior to the 1400s circulation was slack. After the early 1400s the main elements of northern hemisphere circulation became much more entrenched. For example, the Icelandic low-pressure cell during winter became much more strongly developed (in other words, there was an increase in stormy, wet weather during winter). Similarly, the winter high-pressure cells over the Russian and Canadian land masses became much more prominent features. For Scotland, this meant an increase in the frequency and intensity of cold easterly winds blowing off the European continent. And with the easterly winds moving over a cold North Sea came snow.

A hostile ocean

What then of the effects of this marked change in climate? One of the main areas to suffer from a sharp increase in the frequency and severity of storms was the Outer Hebrides. Near Udal in North Uist, the storms of the early 1400s led to the burial of large expanses of machair by drifting sand. Archaeological evidence at Udal of a Viking settlement now lies buried beneath metres of sand. The winter of 1407–08 is known as one of the 'great winters' in history. Bitterly cold from December until March, snow lay for weeks on end in the fields. Unmistakeable signs of deteriorating climate in the north come from Greenland in 1408, with the last recorded wedding in the Viking settlements – in fact after 1410 there was no regular communication between Europe and any part of Greenland until the 1720s. With the changing climate came the end of the Viking settlements in Greenland. Stormier seas and great expanses of sea ice in northern waters made it impossible for Viking longships to ply between mainland Scandinavia, Iceland and Greenland.

Hunger and cold winter nights

Cold winters also became more frequent around this time with, for example, those of 1422–23 and 1432–33 being particularly horrendous. In fact Boece, describing the latter winter tells us that, 'in the time of King James the First . . . a vehement frost was in the winter afore, that wine and ail was sauld be pound wechtis and meltit agane be the fire'.

For most, the thought of being able to melt bottles of wine and beer for consumption may have been akin to paradise. The reality of daily life was more depressing. Some accounts hint at the summer of 1433 as another time of famine. This summer was known in Ireland as the *samhra na mearaithne* (the summer of slight acquaintance), because no one could recognise friend or relative, as a result of the greatness of the famine.

Another severely cold winter took place in 1434–35 and lasted from around St Andrew's Day until the following February. Another followed in 1437–38 so that Walter Bower's account again reports famine across Scotland in 1438. Accounts are sketchy for the years leading up to the middle of the fifteenth century, but there are signs that things were not good. For example, the 1450s are well known to have been famine years, with contemporary documents from the Scottish parliament hinting at widespread crop failures and poverty.

The period between 1460 and *c.* 1600 is another during which there was further expansion of sea ice around the coast of Iceland. We know that there was a succession of cold winters between 1460 and the late 1470s. In 1479 there was a large eruption of Mt St Helens in Washington State (thereafter it lay dormant for over 500 years until it erupted again in spectacular fashion in 1980). The cold returned again in the 1490s when people were treated to the cold, dry winters and dry summers typical of pervasive high pressure across northern Europe.

The summer and autumn rains returned in 1491, causing the withering of the crops in the fields. This happened again in 1501 and also in 1505 – and on each occasion the price of grain soared and the poor suffered dreadfully. Sometimes the rains came in summer, as in 1523, and soaked the fields; in other years they came in autumn, as in 1525. But the effect was always the same – sufficient to leave the plates on the table close to empty the following winter and spring. When the staple crops of oats and barley failed, hungry eyes often turned to cattle – but it was always in desperation, since loss of cattle meant loss of livelihood.

So, time and time again, we find accounts of Scots struggling to find enough food to survive. The years 1541–51 appear to have been particularly tough with prolonged storms, for example, in 1541 from New Year through to early April. It was one of many periods of bad storms at this time. In North Uist the year 1542 marked the culmination of a series of ferocious storms and floods causing loss of land to the sea. The storms continued for the next few years and some of them appear to have been exceptionally severe – for

Disappearing coastlines

The city of St Andrews is characterised by a high, steep cliff that fronts the town as far as the famous golf links. Perched high on the cliffs is St Andrews Castle, the outer walls of which overlook a sheer drop to the sea below. Yet it may not always have been thus. George Martine of Clermont, thought to have been secretary to Archbishop Sharpe during the latter decades of the seventeenth century, describes in August 1683 how:

> there goes a tradition in this place, that the Culdees of old, at least Regulus and his companions, had a cell dedicated to the blessed virgin, about a bow-flight east of the shore of St Andrews, a little without the end of the pier (now within the sea) upon a rock, called at this day our Ladies Craig; the rock is well known, and seen everyday at low water: and that upon the sea's encroaching, they built another house at, or near the place where the house of the Kirkheugh now stands, called Santa Maria de Rupe, with St Rewel's chapel. To examine the tradition it must be granted that the first part of it may be possible; for in my time there lived people in St Andrews who remembered to have seen men play at bowls upon the east and north sides of the castle of St Andrews, which now the sea covers on every tide; so it may be that the sea of old came not so much up to our east coast as it now doeth.

This appears to tell us that the coastline at St Andrews used to be further out to sea. It suggests that storms over the recent centuries have led to considerable coastline retreat (and put an end to any thoughts of playing bowls east of the famous castle).

Coastal erosion was also a serious problem in other areas of Scotland. In the Outer Isles, decades and centuries of damaging winter storms saw the ocean encroach on the land. Nowhere is this more vividly demonstrated than off the coast of North Uist and Benbecula. Here there is an island called Heisgeir that lies just over four miles off the coast of North Uist. Gaelic speakers refer to the island as *h-Eisgeir* meaning 'rock of the isthmus'. Tradition describes how Heisgeir used to be connected to both Benbecula and North Uist, and how, in ancient times, people tried to construct embankments to keep the sea out, but that eventually the ocean broke through, creating *heisgeir* as an island. There are descriptions of iron bolts sunk into certain low-water rocks between Benbecula and Heisgeir, while the remains of buildings are presently visible offshore just beneath the water when the tide is low. Some submerged reefs have retained their Gaelic names, testifying to their former presence on land. For example, one reef is known as *Sgeir a Choidhean* ('the barrier rock', the site of the flood gate) and another as *Ceardach Ruadh* ('the red smithy'). When all the available fragmentary evidence is put together it points to an acceleration of winters storms and loss of coastal land along the machair coastline of the Outer Isles during the first half of the fifteenth century.

example, during January 1553 when great wind storms accompanied by tidal surges caused considerable damage throughout the Hebrides. Apart from a brief period between 1575 and 1582 when there were near drought conditions and in Edinburgh there was such scarcity of water that the magistrates prohibited all brewers from drawing any out of the town well, cold and stormy conditions marked the remainder of the sixteenth century.

The Armada

Of all the storms at the end of the century, by far the most famous was in August 1588. Two cyclones crossed the British Isles and North Sea region broadly from west to east. Winds were reaching around 80–85 knots, with southwesterly winds followed by the passage of the cold front and winds from the northwest. One of the ships' logs of the Spanish Armada described how, 'there sprang up so great a storm on our beam with a sea up to the heavens so that the cables could not hold nor the sails serve us and we were driven ashore with all three ships upon a beach covered with fine sand, shut in on one side and the other by great rocks' (quoted in H.H. Lamb's 1991 book, *Historic Storms of the North Sea, British Isles and Northwest Europe*).

The cyclone centre moved northeast from the region of the Azores to lie off the Hebrides on the 21st and off western Norway on 23 August. Remarkably, the flagship of the Armada was wrecked on the Fair Isle with the survivors reaching the relative safety of the pounding surf at the base of the cliffs. The captain of the flagship plus some of his crew later managed to sail by other means from the Fair Isle to Shetland, landing in the south at Quendale Bay.

CHAPTER 5
FROM THE UNION TO THE JACOBITE REBELLION (1600–1749)

Sometimes about this Country, are seen these men they call Finn-men. In the year 1682, one was seen in his little boat at the south end of the Isle of Eday.

Rev. J. Wallace, *An account of the islands of Orkney*, London, 1700

INTRODUCTION

When people talk of the seventeenth century they frequently refer to the Little Ice Age and how harsh the climate must have been. Images are conjured up of frost fairs on the Thames – leaving us with the feeling that if it was that bad in London then it surely must have been incredibly severe throughout the rest of the British Isles. The period covered in this chapter was a tumultuous time in Scotland's history, starting at 1600 (just before the Union) and ending at 1749 (just after the Jacobite rebellion). At the beginning of the seventeenth century, contemporary accounts are dominated by the proposals of King James VI for a union between Scotland and England. For this time, there are only a few scraps of information about the nature of weather and climate but there is enough to reveal that the weather was as changeable as the political climate.

THE PERUVIAN VOLCANO

The seventeenth century literally started with a bang. Between 16 February and 5 March 1600, a spectacular eruption engulfed the 4,800m-high Huay-naputina volcano 70km east of Arequipa in southern Peru. The effects were felt across the globe. Traces of volcanic dust recovered from Greenland ice cores show that the sulphate levels ejected into the atmosphere were twice that of the 1991 eruption of Mt Pinatubo and about 75% of the vast Mt Tambora eruption of 1815. As a result, the summer of 1601 was one of the

TOP. Winter land and seascape from Harris reminding us of the vulnerability of Scotland to extremes of weather and climate (photograph courtesy of J Jordan).

LEFT. This old fountain in the market square at Falkland, Fife, reminds us of the vital importance of water over the centuries to Scottish weather and climate.

ABOVE. Mother and child on frozen Loch Leven during February 1959 (photograph courtesy of the Trustees of the National Museums of Scotland).

TOP. In high-latitude oceans, for example here near Spitsbergen, the low air temperatures often result in the freezing of the ocean surface that leads to the development of sea ice. The sea ice is usually no more than 1–2 metres thick although it can be much thicker in areas where sections of pack ice are driven against each other by wind and tide. When sea ice forms it expels salt from the freezing ice. This extra salt results in an increase in the density of the surrounding water causing it to sink to the ocean floor. In this way the descending salty water helps to create strong return currents in the depths of the ocean (photograph courtesy J Mangerud).

ABOVE. Storms have ravaged Scotland's coast for centuries and are certainly not a phenomena linked to 'global warming' – this recent scene shows storm waves breaking over the harbour wall in Kirkwall, Orkney (photograph courtesy C Rendall).

Some recent winters in Scotland give us an indication that 'global warming' is not such a straightforward concept (photograph courtesy *The Scotsman*).

ABOVE LEFT. This swirling mass of cloud represents the passage across NW Europe of a classical cyclone (photograph courtesy of NASA).

ABOVE RIGHT. The media has played its part in providing spectacular eye-catching headlines warning us of imminent peril due to trends in recent climate change (photograph courtesy *The Scotsman*).

LEFT. The Great Snowstorm of December 1906 here affecting the Skye Line of the Highland railway near Dingwall (photograph courtesy of the Trustees of the National Museums of Scotland).

BELOW. Skeletons composed of calcium carbonate of microscopic marine protozoa known as foraminifera. Sediment cores collected from the world's oceans contain thousands of foraminifera and information gained from their analysis has provided valuable clues regarding the Earth's ice age climate (photograph courtesy of R Gehrels).

TOP. The complex movements of land and sea at the end of the last ice age left some beaches stranded high above present – as here in northern Islay.

ABOVE LEFT. Reconstructing past changes in climate has been revolutionised by the study of ice cores. This set of ice core samples are taken in a frozen state to the laboratory for further analysis. During the late 1980s a programme of drilling through the Greenland ice sheet produced a set of ice cores that provided a detailed record of past climate change covering the last *c.* 100,000 years (photograph courtesy of P Mayewski).

ABOVE RIGHT. Explosive volcanic eruptions (such as Mount Etna here), if sufficiently violent, can pump volcanic ash and gases through the troposphere into the stratosphere causing climate change (photograph courtesy of NASA).

LEFT. Archaeological evidence for Scotland's first settlers often occurs in places that one might not expect. This site at Kinloch in Rum is one of the best known. People appear to have settled here around 8–9000 years ago. At this time the population of Scotland may have been no more than a few thousand (photograph courtesy of C Wickham-Jones).

ABOVE. Archaeologist showing children the remains of a Pictish house uncovered from beneath sand dunes at Sandwick Bay in Unst, Shetland Isles (photograph courtesy of T Dawson).

BELOW. Reconstructing past changes in the position of relative sea level around Scotland's coast is complex. In some areas, relative sea level was much lower than present. For example, in Raasay, peat deposits located close to present low tide and formed around 9,000 years ago represent part of a landscape inhabited by some of Scotland's earliest settlers (photo courtesy S Dawson).

These sand dunes at Luskentyre, Harris, were mostly formed during a period of greatly increased winter storminess over the last 600 years (photograph courtesy J Jordan).

Perched on the edge of the Atlantic the Neolithic settlement at Skara Brae is continually exposed to the threat of destructive storms. The settlement dates from around 5000 years ago when North Atlantic climate may have been more benign. Some scientists believe that where people lived at Skara Brae the position of the coastline was located several hundred metres farther out to sea, this stretch of coastal edge having been subsequently lost to nature (photograph courtesy S Towrie).

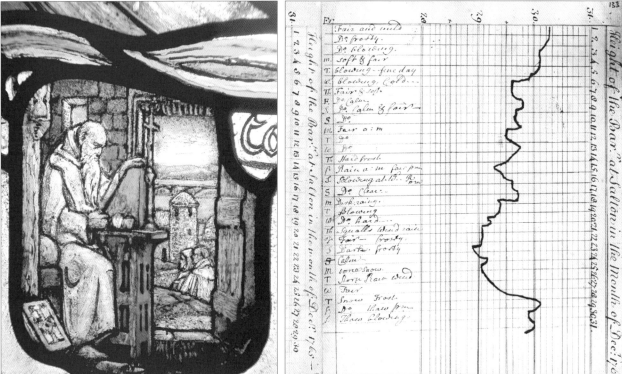

TOP LEFT. When St Columba reflected on Scotland after the Dark Ages he would not have known of the prolonged interval of fine weather and climate that was to follow during Medieval times (this stained glass image from St Margaret's Chapel, Edinburgh Castle).

TOP RIGHT. This table and chart of daily air pressure for Saltoun for December 1769 is one of the first instrumentally measured records of weather for Scotland. The values are in inches of mercury and they show the passage of a low pressure cell across Scotland over the Christmas period.

ABOVE. Wreck of *The Sun* that has lain on St Fergus beach at Rattray Head since a violent storm on 17 January 1728. The ship was driven north by a fierce SSE gale and driven 300 miles off course from the Dogger Bank. Three days later, and the winds having swung to northerly the *St Nicholas* of Stockholm was wrecked nearby with heavy loss of life.

LEFT. The sign above the Bell Rock Tavern in Tayport reminds us of the famous Bell Rock lighthouse located in the North Sea east of Arbroath. Robert Stevenson and his team of builders encountered tremendous storms while constructing the lighthouse between 1807–1811. The lighthouse was opened on February 1 1811 and was eventually automated in 1988.

BELOW. Cartoon from the *Northern Looking Glass* of 9 January 1826, depicting foul weather in Glasgow at Hogmanay. Entitled 'Scene First' it depicts would-be revellers fighting their ways through the busy and rain-lashed streets. The dandy in brown is in danger of losing his teeth owing to the careless handling of a ladder by a drunken 'leary' (lamplighter). The dandy's lady friend has her clothes set alight by the leary's torch. Drunken coachmen quarrel in the driving sleet and snow (photograph courtesy of the Trustees of the National Museums of Scotland).

BOTTOM. Scene of desolation due to the Moray Floods of 3 and 4 August 1829 (from *Nairne* 1895).

ABOVE. Extreme flooding of the River Ness at Inverness during the great floods of 1849 (from *Nairne* 1895).

LEFT. Weather diary for Dalkeith for January 1784. Against the spectre of widespread hunger across Scotland, the scientific revolution had inspired Henry, Duke of Buccleuch and first president of the Royal Society of Edinburgh, to start the detailed recording of weather.

BELOW. The Krakatoa eruption of 1883 had a profound impact on weather and climate across the world (after Judd, 1888).

TOP. The Uig Flood of October 14th 1877 came to take an important place in the cultural history of Skye. On that day, floodwaters poured through the ravine (top right), spreading out across the low ground and destroying the estate house. Most of the graveyard, shown at the base of the ravine, was washed away. As a result, dozens of corpses were deposited in the fields while others were washed out to the sea. The disaster was attributed by many to the wrath of God against Captain Fraser, the estate owner (from *Nairne* 1895).

ABOVE. The remote Monach Isles lighthouse, located out in the North Atlantic west of North Uist in the Outer Isles, was opened in 1864 and continued to remain operational until 1942. Over the years the keepers of the lighthouse faithfully kept a record of daily weather (photograph courtesy of S Angus).

The aftermath of the Tay Rail Bridge collapse (photograph courtesy of the St Andrews Preservation Trust).

Even as recently as just over 100 years ago, Scotland endured great weather extremes such as the Great Frost of 1895 (from *Nairne* 1895).

TOP. The memorial on an isolated hill above Gloup on the Isle of Yell, Shetland, shows a woman and child in mourning for the souls lost at sea in the storm of 1881 (photograph courtesy Shetland Museum and Archive).

ABOVE. The Ben Nevis Observatory officially opened in 1883. The purpose of the Observatory was to help scientists understand the relationships between weather at low and high altitudes and thus to improve understanding of weather as a whole. Despite valiant efforts the money finally ran out and the station was closed for good in 1904 (photograph courtesy of D Herd).

ABOVE. Image from the early 20th century of the wreck of the *Wilhelmina* stranded on West Sands beach, St Andrews (photograph courtesy of the St Andrews Preservation Trust).

BELOW. Fisherman enjoying Amy McLean's ice cream in Mallaig during one of the fine summers of the 1930s (photograph courtesy of the Trustees of the National Museums of Scotland).

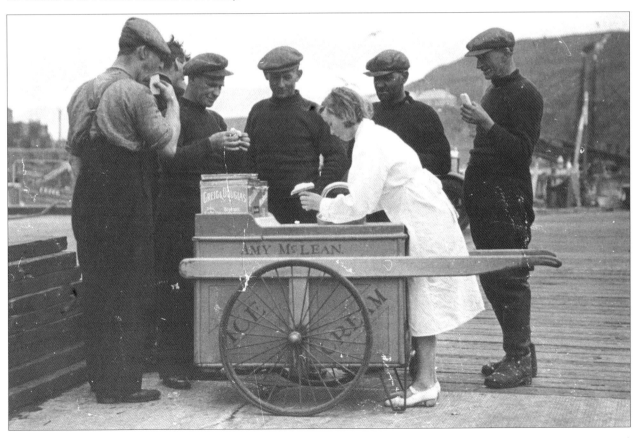

ABOVE LEFT. An old school building at Heugh Loan, North Berwick during the desolation of the 1947 winter (photograph courtesy the Trustees of the National Museums of Scotland).

ABOVE RIGHT. The great storm of January 11 2005 that devastated the Outer Isles and that led to the tragic loss of life of five people is a reminder of the power of the elements. This boat was wrecked on the rocks at Pollochar, South Uist.

BELOW. Extremes of climate change may mean that it will be difficult to make par on the Old Course.

ABOVE LEFT. Climate change may also imply an increase in the risk posed by river flooding such as here in Forres during the summer of 1997 (photograph courtesy of A Black).

ABOVE RIGHT. The running aground of the *Braer* in Shetland on January 5 1993 during a ferocious storm led to one of Scotland's worst oil spill tragedies (photograph courtesy P Fisher).

BELOW. Mrs Mitchell of *Dundee Ladies* in the *Grand Curling Match* on Loch Leven in February 1959. Rising air temperatures most probably will mean that we will never see the likes of such a scene again (photo courtesy of the Trustees of the National Museums of Scotland).

RIGHT. Close shave to
ferry passengers caused
by dense fog or 'haar'
(*The Sunday Post*).

FAR RIGHT. Pub sign
at the Kinneuchar Inn
in Fife showing curling
on Kilconquar Loch.

2   The Sunday Post, August 17, 1947.

Scare For Clyde Steamer Passengers

Passengers aboard the L.M.S. steamer Duchess of Hamilton, held up at Dunoon Pier by fog yesterday morning, were startled when suddenly the bows of the big, three-funnelled MacBrayne turbine St Columba loomed into view.

As she made straight for the stern of the moored steamer, officers and men on her fo'c'sle called to the Duchess passengers to run to safety. There was a hurried scramble.

The St Columba's engines were going full astern, but still it came on. The men aboard her stood ready with fenders to lighten the shock of the impact.

But it didn't come. By superb seamanship and in the nick of time, the Saint Columba lost headway and started to draw astern.

There were sighs of relief from hundreds of people as she slowly stopped, then moved astern out of sight into the fog.

Shortly after, when the Duchess of Hamilton had discharged her passengers and cleared the pier, the Saint Columba came alongside the Waverley, also held up by fog.

All scheduled sailings of Clyde steamers were upset yesterday morning by the heavy fog which lay over the Firth of Clyde. Hundreds of returning holiday-makers lost their train connections, but the railway companies arranged special trains to meet the incoming boats.

The Waverley, due to leave Dunoon at 7.25 a.m., left at 11.30 a.m.

The Jupiter was two hours late in sailing. The Marchioness of Lorne from Holy Loch piers was held up for some time at Kilcreggan.

Later in the day fog lifted, and services were restored.

FOG INTERRUPTS ORKNEY SERVICES

Dense fog, which has lasted for over 40 hours, yesterday interrupted sea and air communications with Orkney.

The passenger steamer Stola arrived at Scrabster on the mainland several hours late and was unable to make the return passage.

North-bound planes to Orkney could not proceed farther than Wick where passengers and mails remained overnight.

Warm Again in Edinburgh

Weather in Edinburgh yesterday reverted to something like last week's warm although temperatures did not reach the same high level. After morning mist, the sky cleared, and there were 8.9 hours of sunshine. The maximum temperature for the day was

ABOVE. Destruction of part of Lerwick Harbour in the aftermath of the great
storm of February 16 1900. People said that they had never known in living
memory such a fearsome sea as occurred on that day (photograph courtesy
Shetland Museum and Archive).

RIGHT. The ship *Hessonite* wrecked on the cliffs of Birsay, Orkney during
October 1924 (photograph courtesy of Orkney Museum).

coldest since records began. The Sun was dimmed by a constant haze and acid rainfall washed over the land. Most crops withered and food was scarce. The year was known as the 'year of the seeds', owing to the failure of the corn to provide a harvest. Climatic deterioration at this time is also indicated by numerous reports of European ships facing difficulties trying to pass through a barrier of extensive sea ice off the southwest coast of Greenland.

AN EARLY REPORT OF FROST

By late 1607 a severe frost across the whole of Scotland continued from November till 20 February 1608. Rivers and springs froze over while the Forth was frozen to the extent that in the area near Airth and Alloa people were able to walk from one side of the estuary to the other. This winter is often referred to as one of Europe's 'great winters', when the severity of the frost split the trunks of many great trees. Perhaps it is no more than chance, but this winter also coincided with one of the strongest El Niño events in recorded history. Travellers in Scotland reported permanent snow cover on the Cairngorms, which requires temperatures 2–2.5°C cooler than those we've been accustomed to since the mid twentieth century. John Taylor of Deeside wrote around 1610 that, 'the oldest men alive never saw but snow on the tops of divers of these hills, both in summer as well as in winter'.

The poor weather continued throughout the first two decades of the century. In 1613 some of the highest spring tides in the first half of the seventeenth century caused severe damage at Findhorn. The bad weather was taking its toll on the people. The rains were so persistent and heavy during summer and autumn that the harvests rotted in the fields while people struggled to find food. The year 1620 was one of the worst. Snow lay in the fields and many sheep died from the cold.

The harsh conditions continued, with ferocious hurricane-force winds striking the Hebrides in 1623. That Easter Monday, a fierce storm led to the drowning of the chief of the Clan MacLeod of Raasay (Iain Garbh MacIlle Chaluim). On Skye this storm was associated with the deposition of thick banks of beach shingle opposite Stenscholl at Moll Staiseall Staphin, near Staffin. Elsewhere, huge numbers of boulders were deposited by storm waves near Monkstadt. The drowning of the Macleod chief is still vividly remembered in song and story.

Ten years later, in Orkney, harvests were still terrible. In his 1987 *History of Orkney*, William Thomson describes how:

Bitterly cold gales had destroyed the corn before it ripened, great numbers of people died in the open fields . . . some were so desperate that they threw themselves into the sea . . . The 1634 harvest was also a disaster, where 3,000–4,000 people perished . . . such corn that had been sown was utterly broken and blasted.

The following winter of 1633–34 was one of the stormiest, with snow lying in the fields in many areas from December until March.

Brief respite

The two decades spanning 1640–60 witnessed the rise of the Covenanters in Scotland and conflict with Charles I. Except for the four years between 1648 and 1651, this time was one of climatic improvement across northern Europe. The *Chronicles of the Frasers* of 1674 report that across Scotland, 1642:

was a wonderfull fruit yeare, and aboundance of all kinds, field and garden fruits, berries and cherries, summer peares, and pipens, such varieties and plenty, that the Laudian and Fife gentlemen declared they came not to visit the rude Highlands, but the cultivat Canaan. They admired the orchards of Lovat and Beuly, the fishing of the river and linn was charming; hunting, fishing, fouleing, arching, good divertisements; nor was tilting, riding, jumping, combating, wanting; for men

The four weather diarists

The decade of 1650–59 is very special in the history of Scottish weather for a number of reasons. For the first time, detailed records of the weather were made in diaries. Alex Brodie near Elgin was one diarist, John Lamont and John Nicoll in Fife were two others and Alex Hay in Biggar was the fourth. The diary entries of Lamont, Nicoll and Brodie all summarised each month of weather for each year. Then, at the end of the decade, Alex Hay starts to provide us with additional daily weather records. For these reasons, we can say without fear of contradiction that Scotland's weather during the 1650s is described in more detail than any succeeding decade until the early 1800s.

began now to learn the use of armes, and, alas, soon after they got sad triall of such. The Earl of Sutherland, Balnigown, and Fowles, came here to visit the Lords; and, as there was good fare and cheere, so there was merry, joviall, facetious society.

THE SETBACK

The years 1648 and 1651 represented a reversal to this warming trend, however, as the Fraser chronicles continue:

> for dearth and scercity succeeding one another, and next to a famin, a just punishment with which God scurges our disloyal Sectarian schism. The poor suffers sadly, the bole of victuall at a high rate at 10 libs Scots, 12 libs this summer, and could hardly be hade, so much of it transported beyond seas; the country oppresed with quartering, especially the loyalists, termed malignants. The Highlanders were well on it, had store of milk, their cattell thriving, all manner of store grass in plenty, their pastures in glens fertil beyond beleefe, such aboundance of sea and fresh water fish that almost men lived by, such sholes of hering in our firths that a 100 was sold for two farthings.

John Nicoll, writing from his estate near Musselburgh, completed a weather diary for the period between 1650 and 1667. In 1651, for example, he described how 'much pepill killed this yeir in Scotland, and the riches of this natioun robbed and spoyled out of the toun of Dundie, eftir the storming, quahairin the famin wer hid for saiftie. Great dearth this yeir, the boll of beir being at twentie pund Scottis the boll in mony pairtes of the cuntrey.'

Fine weather returned to Scotland during the three remarkable long, hot summers of 1652, 1653 and 1654. Each one was almost totally dry, with early harvests. But at the end of each year, with the ground baked hard, the winter rains brought floods. Nicoll continues to describe how, in December 1653:

> the greatest tide and overflowing was of the sea these 40 years . . . [which] went over the works in Inverness, and the highway there, almost to the top of the bridge, and in Findhorn took away some houses. In the end of August, and many dayis of September 1653, thair wer great windis, stormes, and tempestis, almoist throw all Ewrop, both be sea and land, be ressoun quhairof mony schips, barkes, and veschellis

did perische. This yeir 1653 haid plenty of cornes and very chaip . . . the harvest and winter very dry, so that fra October 1653, till the 15 of Marche thaireftir, in anno 1654, thair wes not full sevin schouris, as salbe declairit in the awin place: besyde, this harvest and winter wes exceiding hett; sa that in effect thair wes no winter, the season being both warme and dry.

The three long, hot summers of 1652–54

According to the textbooks, the years 1652–54 lie slap bang in the middle of the Little Ice Age. Yet the diaries of John Lamont (living in Newton, Fife) and John Nicoll (in Musselburgh) show that the three summers of those years were some of the warmest and driest Scotland has experienced. The summer of 1652, for example, had, says Nicoll, a 'plentiful harvest . . . with corn shorn in June and harvest finished in August without rain, storm or tempest.' He continues:

> all this summer ther was ane extraordinary great drought throw-out the wholle kingdome, with great heate, fewe rains; the corns generallie both short and thin, the best grounds worst cornes. (ther be none liveing that remembers a dryer summer); the grasse brunt up, the blowms of the pease wallowed [withered] a fourtnight before Lammis, wheras some years they continowe till Michelmisse.

And later, during November and December:

> the wheat, after it was sowen, did spring againe in severall places in the shyre of Fyfe, betuixt 9 and 12 dayes; about this tyme also, the greatest pairt of all the tries, whither fruit tries of other tries, begane to bud againe. The whine generallie did blome, and some brome also, in some places. The veilet also had its floure (which is not ordinar till March); the fege trie young feggs; the crawes also, in some places, begane to gather sticks to ther old nests; strawberries leaves blomed the first of January 1653 . . . this harvest of 1652 was such as never man can remember the lyke, all the corne being gottin in without rayne, and land befoir the

usuall tyme. The lyke harvest was in our nychtbour natioun of
England.

Nicoll adds that:

I can not omitt the remembrance of this rair and singular yeir
1652, quihilk not onlie producit ane airlie harvest, sum cornes
being ryped and schorne in Junij (yit not much), yit in mony
pairtes in Julij, and all in August, without weit, storme, and
tempest; bot also yeir producit rype wyneberries and graps, and
abundance of Scottis chestanes oppinlie fauld at the mercat
croce of Edinburgh, and bakin in paistes at bankettis . . . This
yeir, be ressoun of the continuall heattis all the monethis till the
end of December, and eftir that to the 3 of Januar 1653, and of
the extraordiner fair weather during that tyme, was the
occasioun that the fruit treyis to bud and floorische, and sum of
thame to bring furth fruitt, albeit not in perfectioun; foulles
began to big thair nestis, and lay eggis evin at or neir Martymes;
swa that this yeir in effect producit twa someris.

Much micht be spokin of the heat and fair weather of this
yeir 1652, quhich producit mony rarities as is befoir mentionat.
Amongis utheris, I can not forget to set doun heir that, upone
the 27 of November this yeir, sellettis and sybees wer oppinlie
cryed and sauld in Edinburgh; and sicklyke fresche hering,
indured, and wer oppinlie sauld in November 1652, December,
and a great pairt of Januar thaireftir, in anno 1653, abundantlie
plentifull and chaip.

Life also seemed fine for John Lamont in 1653:

[T]his summer, generally through all Scotland, the corns were
att a great rate: beare, oatts, and pease being 11, 12, 13 lib. the
bolle; wheate 14 and 15 lib. the bolle; bot after the crope was
brought in to the corne yeards, (this crope being more plentifull
and large, both in corne and stra, blissed be God, than hath
beine for severall yeares preceiding), the prices fell strangelie, to

the admiration of many, so that from Michelmis 1653 till the
end of the yeare, beare, oatts, and pease, was at 4 lib. and 4 lib.
10s. att most; wheat 7 and 8 the bolle; cheese, this summer, at
30s. the stone, and the best at 40s. the stone, wooll at 7 and 8 lib.
the stone, and the darrest at 12 lib. and 20 marke the stone.
Things continued at the cheapnesse, or rather cheaper, oatts
being at 5 marke the bolle, and 12 bolls for 10; till Mairtimis
1655.

The good weather continued through the summer of 1654 with Nicoll
describing how:

this former 1654 producit much abundance of cornes, and
much abundance of fruitt, in all the corneris of the land, and
exceiding chaip, as the lyke was nevir sene in this natioun. All
this somer and harvest, anno 1654, thair fell out ane exceiding
great drouth throw all the pairtes of Lothiane, and from Berwik
to Glasgow, bot speciallie about Edinburgh, quhairin all the
wellis wer dryed up, sa that the inhabitantes could not get
sufficient for ordoring thair meatt, and watter could not be
fund. Notwithstanding all the west cuntrey, from Glasgow to
the Rynes of Galloway, haid moir nor ordiner abundance of
rayne and weitt. All this tyme, and sensyne, thair continued
great drouth in all the wellis in Edinburgh, and throgh all the
land of Lothiane, so that the pepill in Edinburgh wer
constrayned to go abroad the space of ane myle, befoir thai
could get ony cleane watter, ather for brewing of aill or beir, or
for thair pott meitt.

To most, such tales of wells drying up and abundant fruit on the
branches might seem out of place in the middle of the climatic severity
of the Little Ice Age. But such was indeed the case. For some reason,
Scotland was bathed in warmth throughout most of the 1650s.
Whatever the explanation for this occurrence, it cautions us to steer
well clear of the sweeping generalisations often made – and of
describing such times as of unending extremes of cold.

END OF THE DROUGHT?

The good weather broke in November 1654. Nicoll relates how:

> thair wes great stormes both by sea and land, quhairin sindry schipes
> and barkis, cuming and going to and fra France, Spayne, England,
> Yreland, Flanderis, Swaydin, and uther pairtes in Europ, wer cast away
> and perisched; much skaith also done be land both to man and beast.

Another big storm took place across eastern Scotland on 10 December when,
Nicoll says, 'all that night there blew a great wynd that caused the flooding of
several salt pans in Fife, caused damage to many piers and loss of ships'. There
are also descriptions of trees and houses having been blown down during this
storm. The stormy weather was accompanied by ferocious Christmas blizzards

Edinburgh's drought and the draining of the South Loch in 1657

By 1657 Edinburgh had more or less run out of water, with all the
wells dried up. Nicoll describes how:

> the Toun, taking this to thair consideratioun, they concludit to
> dry the South loche, and to essay, if the drying up of that loch
> micht help this evill. And for this end, they delt with the English
> sodgeris to cast trinsches about this loch, for gaddering the
> wattter thairto for the use of the Toun; quhilkes Englische
> sodgeris began thair wark upone the 3 day of August being
> Monday, the yeir of God 1657; and endit upone both sydes of
> the loch, befoir the twentie day of September, except a lytill
> parcell not above the lenth of a pair of buttes, quhilk wes left to
> be finiched and outred by fyve pure Scottis misterfull men for
> thair livelhood . . . The harvest was exceiding pleasant, and the
> cornes throw the haill natioun win and brocht in to the berne
> and berne yarid long befoir Michaelmes, and sum befoir the last
> of August, this yeir 1657 . . . The victuell this yeir wes verrie
> guid, weill win, and very chaip. The somer being het and dry,
> and the harvest exceeding pleasant and airlie.

and high seas. In Fife, for example, many boats were wrecked while anchored in the harbours of Dysart and Craill, and sections of piers were washed away in St Andrews, Wemmys and Leith.

GOOD WEATHER CONTINUES THROUGH THE 1660S

By and large, the weather between the 1660s and 1680s represented a continuation of the good weather of the 1650s, as indicated by only four seasons between 1660 and 1695 with high grain prices. There were bad times, however. Sometimes there were single years or pairs of years that were inclement; at other times fine summers were countered by wet and cold winters. Also, there were individual catastrophic events. One severe storm, for example, took place during 1661, when a damaging sea flood washed away the stone pier at St Andrews. Another happened in 1663, when sand drift accompanied by northerly winds nearly led to the town of Nairn being lost to the ravages of sand and water. A further sea flood took place during 29 and 30 April 1663, when two ships from Newcastle were wrecked with the loss of 36 lives near St Andrews.

Francis Masterton of Parkmilne, Clackmannanshire, wrote of a great frost at the end of 1663, which continued till 20 March 1664; on 5 March 'ye ploughes went, and others and I curled the same day'. Nicoll described the same severe winter:

> It is formerlie recordit, that the frost and snow began on the 25 of December 1664, and now, on the 14 of Marche 1665, the snow, for the maist pairt, began to dissolve – a storme, indeid, worthie of observation; the lyke hes not bene in mony yeiris of befoir, and doutles will be keipt in memory for mony yeiris to cum by these that did sie it. Yet the year again was a good one. This yeir being now at ane end, the qualification thairof wald be remembred, for this yeir was very fruitfull and plentifull in cornes, and abundant in fruitis. The monethis of Januar and Februar being very fair and plesant weather; Marche, Apryll, and Maij sumquhat cold, bot guid rayne to thefull; Junij and Julij pleasant, het, and warme weather, bringand on the cornes to a full maturitie; August het weather and pleasant, and much cornes cuttit doun and schorne in the moneth of Julij preceding. Much stane frute this yeir, so that the chyrreis we sauld at twelf pennyes Scottis the hundreth, and much les. The victuell this yeir wes very chaip and fyne; helthsum cornes of all soirtes of grayne.

Andrew Hay – Scotland's first weather diarist

Andrew Hay deserves a place in history. He was the first person to complete a daily record of weather in Scotland. He lived at the house of Stane, three quarters of a mile east of Biggar and 700 feet above sea level. He is known to have completed at least five diaries, but only one, covering the period May 1659 to January 1600, has so far been discovered. Quoted here is the first month recorded by him – May 1659:

Su 1   A very filthie raine all day.

M   2   Snow and raine till 4 hors, then fair.

Tu 3   A gray dawkie [misty, drizzling] day.

W   4   A fair gray day.

Th 5   A gray mistie day.

F   6   A foule day till neer night.

Sa 7   A gray louring [gloomy, overcast] cloudie day, some raine.

Su 8   A gray cloudie day.

M   9   Warme with clouds of raine.

Tu 10   A gray morning and fair afternoone.

W   11   A warme day with 2 great showers.

Th 12   A very fair warme day.

F   13   A dustling [drizzly?] gray day.

Sa 14   A prettie fair seasonable day.

Su 15   A prettie fair sharp day.

M   16   A raine and mist all day.

Tu 17   Raine till noone, thereafter fair.

W   18   A very hot seasonable day.

Th 19   A fair seasonable day.

F   20   A very fair caller [cool] day.

Sa 21   A very great raine.

Su 22   A fair caller day.

M   23   Fair befor noone, and raine after.

Tu 24   A sharp, louring day with raine.

W 25 A fair, windie day.

Th 26 A prettie, fair day.

F   27 A gurle [bleak and windy] day of blinks ['sunny periods']
          and showers.

Sa 28 Foule in the morning and windie y after.

Su 29 A fair, windie day.

M 30 Some shouers of raine but warme.

Tu 31 A fair day and drying wind.

The year 1665, by contrast, was a tough one for all. The spring was so unseasonal that many were fearful of being able to turn the frozen soil and till the ground. The winter storms continued till late March. In Strathspey, Badenoch, Atholl and Stratharick, many deer died of starvation, with many cattle lost to the bad weather. In Gairloch one man had 60 of his cows die in one night.

Nicoll's accounts of the weather of this year, the backdrop to the expeditions of Cromwell and the Covenanter uprisings, are juxtaposed with descriptions of the horrors of invasion and warfare. So we read, for example, that this year was, 'ane dangerous, crewell, and bluidie yeir, by sea, both by sword and stormes, and tempests, namelie, among the Hollanderis, quha had great experience of it. Notwithstanding, this yeir was a verrie fertill yeir, plentifull of cornes, and exceiding cheip.'

The fine summers continued through 1666 and 1667. The summers of 1669 and 1670 were also warm, causing a scarcity of grain. There were some tragedies, however, as a result of occasional yet severe storms. The most notable, reported in Lamb's *Historic Storms of the North Sea, British Isles and Northwest Europe*, may have been on 13 October 1669, when a great storm of wind, rain and thunder arose in the night and caused great losses both on land and at sea: 'In divers harbours . . . vessels were broken and clattered; as in Dundee, where they sustained, as some affirm, above ten thousand marks' worth of losse; St Andraes, Crail, Enster, Pittenwyne, Ferry, Wemyss, where a vessel of Kirkcaldie brake loose out of the harbour and spitted herself on the rocks.'

In the Firth of Tay some of the islands used for grazing cattle were submerged by the sea and all the beasts were drowned. Trees were uprooted in many places. This was probably an easterly or northeasterly gale, which raised water levels in both the Firths of Forth and Tay possibly up to a metre or two above normal high-tide level. Scots living in Covenanter times were thus experienced in coping with climate warming – although whether the warming was global or not is another question!

There followed a brief deterioration and, according to Fraser, 1670:

> was a very afflicting yeare in many places; great losse by raines, winds, frosts, the Spring too drye, snow and hard frost, the seed time cold and wett, the summer and fore-Harvest constant rain; then ensued tempestuous winds, that all our costs south and north had incredible losse by shakeing; and many parts in our Highlands rotting, blasting, and mildew destroyed corns.

THE END OF THE WARMTH

By the early 1670s the accounts from the various Scots diarists come to an end. Reconstruction of weather for the decades that followed is mostly based on scraps of information, with some years having no information of any kind. For example, we know of the shipwrecking of the *Hope* off Fraserburgh in April 1673 with considerable loss of life. We know also of legislation made in the Scottish Parliament at this time, addressing the issue of crop failure and famine. There was also a lengthy spell of blizzard-like conditions during 1674 that was especially severe in the Southern Uplands (Hawick, Eskdale and Lauderdale were some of the places affected). December 1675 was exceptionally severe, with extreme cold. Perhaps of greater regional significance are accounts that the cod fisheries off Greenland seem to have ended around 1675. The kidneys of cod do not tolerate water temperatures of less than 2°C, hence their disappearance off Greenland and their presumed movement hints at a southward extension of cold polar waters at this time.

D.A. Maclean's *The Weather in North Skye* describes how, by 1688, the Reverend Martin of Kilmuir in Skye was writing of raging storms and destructive rains and that, 'the seas were so eminently unfavourable and the corn so deficient in quantity and quality that the poor actually perished in the Highways for the want of food.' We also know from contemporaray reports that Shetland experienced great suffering between 1684–88 due to successions of devastating storms that ruined harvests and led to the loss of many lives due to famine.

LIVING IN A FREEZER

After another cold winter in 1689 to 1690 we enter the 1690s, associated by many with the lowest air temperatures throughout the period 1350–1700. Across northern Europe it was once again a time of dislocated society, population decline and abandonment of farmland. Scotland's climate was already in shock from freezing winter temperatures and wet summers when a series of volcanic eruptions took place. Mt Hekla, in Iceland, erupted in 1693, depositing ash across much of Iceland and as far afield as Scotland and Norway. It is also well known that a major southward extension of sea ice took place at this time across the northern North Atlantic. Whenever this happened, the tracks of storms were displaced further south than normal, leading to bitter winter winds and exceptionally high rainfall across Scotland.

The Glencoe massacre

On 12 December 1691, the exiled King James VII and II gave permission for the Jacobite chiefs to submit to King William by the end of the year. The news arrived in Glencoe in mid December, thus leaving the chiefs of the MacDonalds of Glengarry and the MacIains of Glencoe to face the near-impossible task of braving west Highland blizzards and reaching Inveraray in sufficient time. Their journey through snow, ice and atrocious weather conditions took them first to Inverlochy and then to Inveraray, and they finally arrived a day late. They were not able to meet with Campbell of Ardkinglas until well after the deadline, on 5 January 1692. This was seen as an opportunity to make an example of the MacDonalds and simultaneously eliminate some enemies, and led to the infamous massacre at Glencoe in February 1692.

The year 1694 was particularly disastrous, since it was the first of seven years of famine across Scotland known as 'King William's Dear Years'. The famine took place prior to widespread potato cultivation in Scotland and hence there was a great dependence on grain. The famine is said to have begun with a cold east wind and sulphurous fog (from the Icelandic volcanic eruptions) over the whole country. Hugh Miller from Cromarty, a self-taught geologist and natural historian, one of Scotland's great figures from the nineteenth century, tells us in the only known written account of this remarkable event:

one night in the month of August 1694, a cold east wind, accompanied by a dense sulphurous fog, passed over the country, and the half-filled corn was struck with mildew. It shrank and whitened in the sun, till the fields seemed as if sprinkled with flour, and where the fog had remained longest – for in some places it stood up like a chain of hills during the greater part of the night – the more disastrous were its effects. From the unfortunate year till 1701, the land seemed as if struck with barrenness, and such was the change on the climate, that the seasons of summer and winter were cold and gloomy in nearly the same degree. The wanted heat of the sun was withholden, the very cattle became stunted and meagre. November and December, and in some places January and February, became the months of harvest, and labouring people contracted diseases which terminated in death when employed in cutting down the corn among ice and snow.

By 1695 Iceland was almost completely surrounded by sea ice. In most areas, open water could not be seen from the highest mountains and merchant vessels could not make their way to the harbours. In a letter from Kirkwall, dated 20 September 1695, a Mr Binning wrote, 'this harvest is lyk to prove very bad and late here and much rains. The mercates is now very high.' Even the cod fisheries off Shetland began to collapse as a result of the southward incursion of cold polar waters. The magnitude of the disaster was exemplified in Orkney in 1696, when the harvest of that year was said to have yielded 'not one twentieth of the normal crop'. Masterton describes 1696 as having had 'a cold bad summer, a rainy late harvest, a great frost in August that mutch of ye vitail was frosted, and mutch to shear at Christmas. The bear 12 lib ye boll, meal 10 lib, pease and beans 20 mrks ye boll.'

There are few contemporary accounts of conditions in Scotland during the last years of the 1690s, when cold conditions were most severe and deprivation most widespread. One account, dated August 1696, is a letter by a Mr Umphray on behalf of the people of Shetland to the Lords of 'His Majestie's Council'. In it, he describes how:

the sad and miserable conditione of the inhabitants is such that many hundred families have not soe much as sein bread for this three or four moneths bygone, and soe lamentable is their conditione that they are not able to buy any for want of money, although it were at ther doors, and sent some small fishes about the shoare, which they have catched and lived upon hitherto . . . more as ane third pairt of the arrible land within the said cuntray now ley for want of seed, and that quich is laboured by the coldness and unseasonableness of the summar and great rains is lickly not to rypin

The year 1697 saw a continuation of the severe cold winters and wet summers while the famine continued. During the third week of September, however, a storm took place that surpassed most others in its magnitude and intensity. A very great gale in the autumn of 1697 buried a township at Udal, North Uist, in up to 6m of sand nearly 300 years after storms had last buried settlements there. There is reason to believe that the Udal storm was the same as that which went on to cause the highest North Sea tidal surge of the seventeenth century in the German Bight. Elsewhere in the Outer Isles great damage was done in the south of Pabbay, Harris, where the farm of Middleton disappeared from the rent rolls, while on Berneray the farm of Sheapie was overblown to a depth of several feet.

In his history of Lindores Abbey and Newburgh, Alexander Laing describes entries in the Session Books for Fife that record the abbey's purchase of meal for distribution among the poor. There are also entries for payments 'for mort-chists [coffins] for the poor', proving that Newburgh did not escape the terrible famine which prevailed for several successive years towards the end of the seventeenth century. He also quotes a contemporary writer, speaking of the scarcity of food who wrote:

these unheard-of-manifold judgements continued seven years, not always alike, but the seasons, summer and winter, so cold and barren, and the wonted heat of the sun so much withholden that it was discernible upon the cattle, flying birds and insects decaying, that seldom a fly or cleg was to be seen. Our harvests not in ordinary months, many shearing in November and December, yea some in January and February, many contracting their deaths, and losing the use of their feet and hands, shearing and working in frost and snow, and after all some of it standing still, and rotting upon the ground, much of it for little use either to man or beast, and which had no taste or colour of meal . . . through the long continuance of these manifold judge-ments, deaths and burials were so many and common that the living were wearied with burying the dead. I have seen corpses drawn in sleds. Many got neither coffin nor winding-sheet. I was one of four who carried the corpse of a young woman a mile of way, and when we came to the grave, an honest poor man came and said, 'you must go and help me to bury my son, he has lain dead these two days, otherwise I shall be obliged to bury him in my yard'.

Great sandstorms and the onset of cold north winds

The marked increase in winter storminess that the Greenland ice cores tell us started around the 1420s was in full swing during the last decades of the seventeenth century. One characteristic of these storms was the development of sandstorms at the coast. During the late 1600s there were many reports of sand drift at Culbin in Moray. For example, during December 1674 violent windstorms caused extensive sand drift across the Culbin area. Some believed that the sand drift was due to the grazing of areas of marram grass by sheep and cattle. In 1676, a rich grain harvest on western farms of the Culbin estate, a few kilometres east of Nairn, was waiting to be reaped when a northwesterly gale carrying clouds of sand before it covered the fields to a depth of over two feet. The occurrence of northerly and northwesterly winds at this time supports a variety of reports that all the winters between 1676–77 and 1682–83 were consistently cold, with prevailing winds from the north. The following winter of 1683–84 was so cold that the ground froze to a depth of more than a metre in parts of southwestern England and belts of sea ice appeared along the coasts of southeastern England and northern France. The ice lay 30–40km offshore along parts of the Dutch coast. Many harbours were so choked with ice that shipping was halted throughout the North Sea .

Similar difficulties were experienced in Shetland. For example, at Quendale a series of storms resulted on several occasions between 1660 and 1710 in the burial of fields, including the old church. The Reverend James Kay, who was the minister for Dunrossness between 1682 and 1716 wrote that previously:

> it was all Cornland and pleasant Meadows. It is a white sand, so admirably light, but an ordinary gust of wind it flies so thick that (like mist) it darkens ye horizon . . . Here lay the estate of Brew once worth 300 Merks a year, now a mere wilderness,

> occasioned by the blowing of a small dusty kind of sand, which never possibly can rest, as the least puff of wind sets it all in motion, in the same manner as the drifting snows in winter.
>
> In 1695 the government passed an act forbidding pulling up of bent, juniper and broom bushes by the roots because 'many lands, meadows and pasturages lying on sea coasts have been ruined and overspread in many places by sand driven over from adjacent sandhills'. Bent had many uses for the people of the Hebrides, and at least one of the stabilising plants, lady's bedstraw, was used for dyeing; a pound of the roots of this small plant was needed to dye a single pound of wool. It came to be an offence on many estates to pull bent or to collect the roots of bedstraw. However, during these hard times the lack of provision of winter fodder for the cattle led to them being driven to eat the bent shoots, thus preventing it from establishing itself on the dunes. Overstocking of cattle must have played a major part in maintaining the blow and reducing the arable acres.

The sufferings of these years must have been terrible, and the entry 'for mortchists' tells with certainty that the famine did its fearful work.

The year 1698 saw no improvement. It was an unkindly, cold and winterlike spring and there was a great want of food and seed; sheep and cattle died in great numbers. The dearth was associated with a very late harvest; corn in many places was not reaped till January 1699, and the snow beaten off it. Bread made of it fell in pieces and tasted sweet, like malt. The diary of the Reverend Turnbull for May reads, 'this was a severe season, a very bitter, cold Aprile, on Tuesday, May 3, a great showr of snow and frequent showrs of haill till Saturday, May 7th when the weather begane to mend'. In December, however, he writes that:

> the weather all this winter was very stormy, very high winds from the Martyaess till this time, chiefly on Saturday December 17th were extraordinary winds, a great deall of præjudice done thereby both by land and sea, yet our king having been since July last in Holland, arrived safely in England about the beginning of the moneth, and had

good passage. This also was a sad year among the commons and tradsmen the dearth continuing and encreasing.

By 1699, the progress of the famine had led the Commissioners of Supply, an early form of country administrators, to take matters of food supply and distribution in hand, such were the problems of starvation. Hints of changes in the weather come from the diary of Reverend Turnbull, who says of July: 'this moneth was violent hot weather, this evening came a pleasant rain,' and December: 'all this moneth extraordinary mild winter weather, yet much sickness still'.

The start of the eighteenth century – the recovery

The first people on the scene in the story of Scotland's weather in the new century were three 'finn-men' in waters off Orkney. A lone kayaker was observed off Stronsay and another off Westray in 1700. But the most famous was a kayaker whose canoe was driven into the River Don in Aberdeen around 1700. The man in it was described as all-over hairy and spoke a language which no person there could interpret. He died of natural causes after three days, though all care was taken to help him. Today, the kayak can be viewed in the Marischal Museum in Aberdeen. The appearance of the dying kayaker in Aberdeen at the time of maximum sea ice extent across the northern North Atlantic at the dawn of the new century may not have been coincidental.

The visits of the eskimos

The Reverend James Wallace, who lived in Orkney and graduated from Aberdeen University in 1659, wrote a book called *A Description of the Isles of Orkney*, which was posthumously published in 1700 by his son, James. The following amazing story appears in it:

> Sometimes about this Country, are seen these men they call Finn-men. In the year 1682, one was seen in his little boat, at the south end of the Isle of Eda(y), most of the people of the Isle flock'd to see him, and when they adventured to put out a boat with men to see if they could apprehend him, he presently fled away most swiftly. And in the year 1684, another was seen

from Westra(y); I must acknowledge it seems a little unaccount-
able, how these Finn-men could have come on this coast, but
they must probably be driven by storms from home, and cannot
tell when they are any way at sea, how to make their way home
again; they have this advantage, that be the seas never so
boisterous, their boat being made of fish skins, are so contrived
that he can never sink, but is like a seagull swimming on the top
of the water. His shirt he has is so fastened to the boat, that no
water can come into his boat to do him damage, except when
he pleases to unty it, which he never does but to ease nature, or
when he comes ashore.

There has been some discussion about the Finn-men: where they came
from and why. The prevailing view is that they were Eskimos (Inuit)
from southwest Greenland. Many reasons have been advanced to
explain why and how they reached Orkney. The most likely, however,
is that the extent of sea ice across the northern North Atlantic may
have been vastly greater than it is now. In other words, they were
caught in an ice floe that kept taking them further and further south
until it was impossible for them to return home.

By 1700 Masterton is describing how 'this year we had an early spring, a cold
summer, and a late harvest'. The early spring is confirmed by Reverend
Turnbull, who describes February as having 'very high winds about this time,
the countrey begane to sow pise about the middle of January, the season being
very dry'. In July he notes very windy, dry weather, and by November how
the harvest was late in many places and that it was not 'got in' till Martinmass.
In 1701 he writes that the harvest was finished by September, with all the
corns in. All things considered, the weather seemed to have improved drastically from the horrors of the 1690s.

Yet there are signs that the recovery from the 1690s was incomplete. The
year 1703 started with storms. According to Reverend Turnbull, 'all this
moneth of January was exceeding windy blowing weather, the sea was
observed to flow very high in some places as at Barrostounness and Leith . . .
cold, dry conditions occurred across eastern Scotland during spring and early

summer when there was still a violent drought and easterly wind'. The year also drew to a close with storms, in particular on 11 October, 'this Lord's day was most stormy and rainy, all our saltgreens att Tyningham covered with water, much late corn destroyed, the like not seen for 40 years. This inundation was generally through all East Lothian, the confusion was such that there was no sermon in severall churches, as Aberlady and Ormiston'. The storm was strongly felt along the Moray Firth coastline where the wind, apparently from about west-southwest, but shifting later to northwest, caused further severe drifting of sand across the Culbin estates, extending the devastated area so that the River Findhorn was forced to change its course to the east, to reach its present mouth. Some reports describe how the old town of Findhorn, at the mouth of the river, was destroyed by the sea at this time. A few building remains of this old village salvaged from the sea sit in Findhorn museum today.

By 1704 the return to good weather had resumed, with a warm summer and early harvest, a pattern repeated in 1706 and 1707. Frost and snowstorms returned during the winter of 1707–08 but this was nothing compared with the blizzards that started at the end of 1708 and continued well into 1709. This was to become another of the 'great winters' across Europe, and it is no surprise that across Scotland the harvest of 1709 was very poor, with a widespread dearth of food.

A popular view is that strong warming took place in northwest Europe during the decades between 1710 and 1730. Reports for Scotland are scarce for the start of this period, although those available point to severe winters during parts of this time interval. For example, in Shetland the winter of 1710–11 was a bad one, the latter part of the 1711–12 winter was very stormy, with a great gale on 7–8 November, and the spring of 1713 is described as having been very rough. The year 1717 in Shetland was also described by Bruce, the Shetland archivist, as having been 'a very bad corn year, a stormy winter, and altogether an exceedingly tempestuous year . . . very little butter could be exported, and there was practically no white fishing, which has reduced the poor people to the utmost misery'. The year 1719 was also very stormy, and 'left the people very poor for the most part being turned disprat and indifferent about payment of any debt'.

Weather summaries for other areas of Scotland are rare. One account from Islay refers to bad harvests and poor weather on Islay throughout the period 1714–21. In particular bad and unseasonable weather in 1715 and 1716 resulted in such poor harvests that the landowners had some difficulty in collecting rents. For 1718 we read of another disastrous harvest. But the summer of 1723 was one of sunshine and drought conditions across Scotland. There is also an isolated report of continued sand drift for 1726 on the Isle of Coll, where two farms at Crossapol were buried by so much sand that they had to be abandoned.

The Cromarty herring and whales

The cold waters that marked the start of the eighteenth century were associated with the arrival of the herring in huge numbers, and with them came the whales. Historical documents for Shetland show a concentration of reports of whales for the two decades between 1720 and 1740. These reports include whales driven ashore in Unst in 1720, a shoal at Hillswick in July 1731 coincident with the arrival of the herring, a large whale at Bressay in 1734 (reduced to 'ten barrels of oil and some whalebone'), culminating with 276 whales at Urafirth during 1740–41.

During the 1710s, a spectacular sight was to be seen during summers in the Moray Firth. In the middle of the July every year huge numbers of herring could be seen swimming up the Moray Firth, often pursued by whales and porpoises. The herring would head to the many sandy banks, where they would spawn before leaving again at the start of September. This annual migration, linked to the southward push of cold polar water in the North Atlantic, became known as the *'har'st of the herring-drove'*. So great were the numbers of fish that some beaches were entirely covered, with not enough salt to cure all the fish. When this happened, people took the rest of the fish as manure for the fields, causing a vile stench. The whales attracted lots of attention and often local fishermen would take to their yawls to try to catch a whale – mostly unsuccessfully.

The winter of 1729–30 was another cold one across Scotland. Large amounts of sea ice had formed around Iceland. The climate was on the change again, with cold polar waters spreading much further south than normal. This change is well illustrated by information on annual changes in the export of fish from the Faroe Isles. Whereas the fish harvest was excellent in 1729, it dropped by half in 1730, and there was a further fall in 1731 until in 1732 there was a complete failure of the fisheries. The history of cod movements partly helps to explain the change. Cod are highly temperature sensitive, and poorly suited to extremely cold water. Their kidneys do not function well below about 2°C but they thrive in water between 2°C and 13°C, with temperatures between 4°C and 7°C optimal for reproduction. There is evidence that this southward movement of cold polar water was also accompanied by a southward migration of whales. A shoal of whales was observed at Hillswick in Shetland during July 1731, while in 1732, 50 small whales were seen at Weisdale, one large one at Walls, and a large whale of '14 barrels of oil' was seen at Northmavine. The changes in ocean currents may also explain why in Shetland 1731 was considered a very bad white fishing year, with the shoals of fish moving further south in search of warmer waters. Coupled with all of this, a large volcanic eruption took place in Lanzarote in 1730, contributing to even more cold weather. In 1732 the winter was so cold in Edinburgh that the ice in the lochs was thick enough in early May as to 'bear man and horse'.

By the time 1738 arrived, Scotland was deep in the grip of the cold. The Faroese fishing industry had totally collapsed during the mid 1730s and did not recover until between 1747 and 1749. There was a return to severe winter storms. One of the worst took place during January 1739. The *Caledonian Mercury* describes the devastating storm from the west-southwest that uprooted trees, tore many ships from their anchors and wrecked many others across both the western and eastern coasts of Scotland. The area worst hit stretched from Arran and Glasgow in the west to Berwick and Montrose in the east. At the start of November the wind shifted to the northeast and it became desperately cold. Scotland was about to face one of the worst winters in its history.

The winter started with a severe frost that began on 26 December 1739 and lasted till the end of January. It was long remembered for its severity. Rivers were frozen over. Even the Tay at Perth was frozen nearly to the bottom. All the mill wheels ground to a halt. Food rose to famine prices, and large contributions were required from the rich to keep the poor alive. People perished of cold in the fields. Then, in the middle of the cold, a storm with hurricane-force winds swept across southern Scotland. It started on 14 January 1740 from the southwest and was beyond parallel for its destructiveness. It tore sheet lead from churches and houses. Many houses were demolished, trees were uprooted and corn stacks scattered. Laing describes how 'at Loch Leven great shoals of perches and pikes were driven a great way into the fields, so that the country people got horse-loads of them, at one penny per hundred'.

Not surprisingly 1740 and 1741 are described as years when dearth reached famine proportions. Bruce describes how, across Shetland, 'it was a tempestuous spring, pretty good white fishing, but herrings and [whale] oil failed. There was smallpox in Zetland, many deaths, a great famine and a bad harvest with a great deal of ye corns rotted under ye snow. A shoal of whales were landed at Hillswick, where many of the people thankfully ate the whale beef'. Across the Highlands and Islands this year appears to have been the only time when the scale of the hunger and deprivation came close to famine proportions. In Edinburgh at this time, as a result of crop failure and the high price of provisions due to the bad harvest in 1739, a mob ran riot in Leith and at Bell's mills the military were called out, fired on the crowd, and wounded three, one of whom died.

Across northeast Scotland this trying calamity was followed by another failure of the crop in 1740, causing great distress. Many were reduced to absolute want, and starving men ravenously seized on any food within reach for themselves and their families. The magistrates, both in the towns and the country, made the most strenuous efforts to meet the fearful emergency, and the rich came forward to procure meal to sell to the poor at comparatively low prices. But still the fearful conditions prevailed.

Dramatic coastal changes

Scottish historical records abound with stories of storms, the retreat of coastlines and the loss of past villages to the sea. Just listen to Hugh Miller:

I am old enough to have conversed with men who remembered to have seen a piece of corn land, and a belt of planting below two properties in the eastern part of the town [probably Tain], that are now bounded by the sea. I reckon among my acquaintance an elderly person, who when sailing along the shore about half a century ago [c. 1780s] in the company of a very old man, heard the latter remark that he was now guiding the helm where, sixty years before, he had guided the plough. Of Elspat Hood, a native of Cromarty, who died in the year 1701, it is said that she attained to the extraordinary age of 120 years, and that in her recollection, which embraced the latter

part of the sixteenth century the Clach Malacha, a large stone
covered with seaweed, whose base only partially dries during
the ebb of Spring and Lammas tides, and which lies a full
quarter of a mile from the shore, was surrounded by corn fields
and clumps of wood. And it is a not less curious circumstance
than any of these, that about 90 years ago [the 1740s], after a
violent night's storm from the north-east, the beach below the
town was found in the morning strewed over with human
bones, which, with several blocks of hewn stone, had been
washed by the surf out of what had been formerly a burying-
place . . . it is not much more than 20 years since a series of
violent storms from the hostile north-east, which came on at
almost regular intervals for five successive winters [estimated as
1810–1815], seemed to threaten the modern town of Cromarty
with the fate of the ancient. The tides rose higher than tides had
ever been known to rise before; and as the soil exposed to the
action of the waves was gradually disappearing, instead of the
gentle slope with which the land formerly merged into the
beach, its boundaries were marked out by a dark line resembling
a turf wall. Some of the people whose houses bordered on the
sea looked exceedingly grave, and affirmed that there was no
danger whatever; those who lived higher up thought differently,
and pitied their poor neighbours from the bottom of their
hearts.

Burial of coastal townships by drifting was also a huge problem. As
recounted earlier, for example, in the south of Shetland at Quendale, a
series of storms on several occasions between 1660–1710 resulted in
the burial of fields, including the old church of Quendale.

In Gaelic, 1741 was described as the *Blaidhainn an Air* (the year of the
slaughter). Accounts from Shetland provide vivid images: 'thick rainy weather
in July, and very wet harvest-time, bad markets in Hamburg, but good price
for butter – which was scarce. Very little frost or snow in the early part of
winter, and fairly good weather until the latter part of the year, when there

was a very stormy, snowy time.' A Mr Gifford of Busta wrote in July that, 'most families in Zetland have not tasted bread for two months past, nor can expect to do till they get it off the ground, but Good Providence hath supplied them with plenty of small fish, upon which, with the milk they have, they live pretty well. But they can't go to the Great fishing without bread.' Smallpox was still raging, with nearly a quarter of those living on the islands 'cut off by Death'. The year 1742 saw no improvement, with a stormy spring and a poor harvest. By the following year we find descriptions of snow lying on the ground in Shetland till 2 May. Gales were commonplace across Scotland at this time, including one in Edinburgh on 19 February 1744 that was so severe that it took the roof off the Tron Church.

The change to better weather seems to have occurred around 1747–48. The summer of 1747 appears to have been fine and warm across many areas of Scotland. In Edinburgh and across the Lothians and Fife there was a summer and autumn drought, while the rivers were at the lowest in living memory. Similarly 1748 was exceptionally warm and dry and the fish harvest in the Faroes was the best that it had been for many years. But the weather loosed a parting shot. On 19 February 1749 hurricane-force winds struck Barra. The Reverend Walker describes how,

> on the 19th February 1749, a hurricane ... with a high tide, broke over for the first time, an isthmus which divides the island [of Barra] into two parts. The isthmus was very extensive and consisted of excellent land but ever since that inundation has been a blowing sand, though the sea has never again forced its way over it. The same tide made also great devastation in the Clyde, and at Greenock and Inveraray flowed into houses.

At the township of Baleshare on North Uist, drifting sand once again buried most of the buildings and covered much of the machair pasture.

POSTSCRIPT

So what conclusions can be drawn? Probably first and foremost is that it is naive to imagine that this time interval, conventionally falling within what most refer to as the Little Ice Age, must have been uniformly cold throughout. Although there are many reports of poor weather and famine (for instance in the 1620s), the cold was occasionally interrupted by spells of exceptionally fine weather (such as in the 1650s and 1660s). First-hand reports also show how a drastic climatic deterioration took place around 1675, culminating in King William's so-called 'Dear Years' of famine in the 1690s. Hugh Miller's accounts of a volcanic eruption in Iceland during 1694 that created sulphurous fogs across northern Scotland may help explain this spell of exceptionally cold climate. Hunger and starvation were features of extremely cold winters around 1720, followed soon after by a second phase during the late 1730s and early 1740s. Frequently, however, it appears not to have been the cold that caused the hunger, but summer and autumn periods of stormy weather and heavy rainfall. Such storms had the capability of entirely ruining crops of barley (bere) and oats – leaving people with nowhere to turn for food during winter. By 1745 and the Jacobite uprising, Scotland had been suffering from cold, stormy, wet weather with the destruction of a succession of harvests leaving many people hungry and causing intense suffering across the whole nation.

What were the causes of these changes? In truth no one knows. A popular explanation of the prolonged periods of cold is that the Sun itself was much colder, with very few sunspots across its surface. Equally, changes in ocean circulation have been advocated as a causal factor and linked to the southward expansion of cold polar waters. The complexity of such explanations is illustrated by the argument that changes in the circulation of North Atlantic waters were an effect of climate change rather than a cause.

CHAPTER 6
AFTER THE '45:
A COLD WIND DOTH BLOW (1750–99)

'There will soon be no remembrance in this poor miserable island, the best of its inhabitants are making ready to follow their friends to America, while they have anything to bring there, and among the rest we are to go, especially as we cannot promise ourselves but poverty and oppression, having last spring and this time two years lost almost our whole stock of cattle and horses.'

Letter from Flora MacDonald to John McKenzie, 12 August 1772

INTRODUCTION

As the second half of the eighteenth century began, the omens for an improvement in the weather were not good. The year 1750 was associated with a widespread cover of sea ice across the northern North Atlantic, with storm tracks pushed further south than usual. Not surprisingly widespread coastal sand drift continued to take place across the Outer Hebrides. Also, as the cold water pushed further south, so did the herring. Fish harvests were booming and in Shetland herring were reported as present in the northern waters in immense quantities. Despite this, there are descriptions of many people in Shetland starving at this time and having to resort to eating their own seed corn.

Between 1752 and 1756 (with the exception of the summer of 1753, described in some reports as beautiful), summers were cold, crop harvests were late, and winters were cold and stormy. From Orkney we hear of a hurricane which blasted the corn crop in August 1756. From the Outer Hebrides we learn of a severe storm and sea flood in 1756 that led to another burial by sand of the township of Baleshare in Benbecula. Walker describes the flood as:

such a tide . . . broke over an extensive isthmus and turned it into a heap of sand which before would have pastured 100 cows in summer for a fortnight or three weeks. By this iruption, the peninsula of Inchenish, which is two miles long and a mile and a half broad, was disunited from North Wist [Uist] and turned into an island, and by the breaking of the isthmus a deluge of sand has been poured in upon the farm town of Ballyshar. The houses in this village are now blown up to the roofs, so that there will soon be a necessity of having it removed further into the country. Near this place the sand drift has also choked up a canal, which had been dug 7 or 8 feet deep and half a mile long in order to drain two lakes.

The life and times of Patrick Fea

Patrick Fea was born in Stronsay, Orkney, around 1710. After Culloden, he had sided with the Jacobite cause and was pursued by government search parties. In later years he settled as an Orkney farmer and laird working from his home on the island of Sanday. He kept a record of his later life in a series of diaries, the first entry of which was on 1 January 1766. With the exception of a few missing years, the diaries extend until 19 August 1796. Stored in the Orkney Archive of the County Library in Kirkwall, they provide a rare glimpse into Orkney life during the eighteenth century. But they are also important for weather history, since every entry in the diary contains a description of the weather, as well as local events. Witness the following description of a gale and shipwreck that took place on 5 October 1767:

A very violent gale or rather a storm att NW & WNW wt severe haill and Snow no work done in the forenoon. Got ane Express from Westove advising a large Ship from Archangel bound for Amsterdam being wrecked upon Rive about 3 in the Morning the Capt & 12 men being drowned only one man Saved. Her loading consisting of 100 lasts of Rye, 100 lasts of Sink Lead, 50 lasts of matts & 49 large Casks tallow whereof saved only 13 Casks of Tallow. By his appointment I went there befor Dinner and Seed the Wreck & some of the dead men, a very mournful sight to See for never were there a Wreck in this Country so useless all made by the extraordinary Land Brees.

The 1760s seem to have been characterised by more of the same. In Shetland in 1761 during February and March there were long periods of prolonged snowfall and a very poor fishing catch led to many going hungry. During late December 1763 the *Caledonian Mercury* reported a 'hurricane' that swept across northern Scotland. Also in August of that year there were exceptionally high winds which led to further sand drift across coastal areas of the Outer Hebrides. Walker describes how:

> it was indeed melancholy in the beginning of last August, after a tract of high winds, to see some excellent fields of bear [barley] turned in a few days into fields of sand in some places a yard deep . . . the violent surge of the western ocean in this shallow water both forms and pushes on the sand to the shore. When it arrives there, the west winds being predominant, and of great strength, it is hurried forward upon the flat country . . . in South Wist [Uist] the foundations of stone walls are to be seen at the lowest ebb, above half a mile from the present floodmark.

In 1765 the difficulties caused by so many storms and sea floods were compounded by the volcanic eruption of Mt Hekla in Iceland. Ten years earlier, in 1755, the *Shetland Times* had reported quantities of black dust falling across Shetland. William Brown, then the master of Scalloway Grammar School, described in a letter dated 28 May 1756: 'there fell a black dust all over the country. It was very much like lamp black, but smelled strongly of sulphur. People had their faces, heads and linen blackened by it . . . some people assign the cause of it to some extraordinary eruption of Hekla.' (A fragment of pumice stone, found floating in the coastal waters, may also have derived from the same source but it did not, as said by some at the time, represent the head of a man who had fallen into the crater and was expelled in the eruption.)

Across Scotland, widespread ashfalls led the year 1765 to become known as the year of the 'black snow'. Perhaps for this reason, possibly combined with the continuing bad weather across the country, Scotland experienced a famine and a very poor harvest in 1766. In 1768 in Shetland the summer was very stormy. On 9 June two Shetland boats were lost with ten hands, and in the beginning of July, another boat with five hands went down.

For some, personal plight compounded by poor weather was too much to bear. In June of 1768 some 40–50 families left Jura for Cape Fear, North Carolina, sailing on the *Bell* from Port Glasgow.

Further famine and bad harvest followed in 1769. Across the Highlands and Islands the years 1769–78 were characterised by severe hunger and hardship. During 1770, for example, across the Highlands and Islands, there were severe storms in springtime that caused many cattle to starve to death. The price of cattle fell, disease was rife and sub-tenants were unable to pay their rents. Thomas Pennant, in his famous book of 1776, notes that the people were starving in July that year, with no corn to be had in areas which usually had a surplus. Many substantial farmers in the Highlands faced ruin and destitution. Snow lay late on the ground, in many areas until April and May. Against such horrendous weather and a background of social turmoil after the Jacobite uprising, we find accounts such as that of Governor Tyron of North Carolina, who wrote that 1,600 settlers from Arran, Jura, Islay and Gigha had arrived in the colony, mostly in Cumberland county, between 1767 and 1770.

With cold Arctic waters having been displaced southwards, there was a boom in fisheries. In Shetland during June 1771, as many as 350 Dutch buses rendezvoused in Bressay Sound with tales of amazing catches, while the *Edinburgh Advertiser* of 19 July 1771, announced reports from Hamburg describing how, 'more than 100 sail of Dutch buses have come from Brassa Sound to that port with large cargoes from the Shetland fishery'.

The emigration ships continued to fill as the people left to escape the poverty and hardship induced by the combination of poor harvests and the Highland Clearances.

The spring of 1771 was known in the Highlands as the *Bliadhna an Earraich Dhuibh* (the Year of the Black Spring). Skye was particularly badly hit, with much livestock lost. Dr Johnson, who visited the island in 1773, wrote that:

> in '71 they had a severe season, remembered by the name of the Black Spring, from which the island has not yet recovered. The snow lay long upon the ground, a calamity hardly known before. Part of their cattle died for want, part were unseasonably sold to buy sustenence for the owners; and, what I have not read or heard of before, the kine that survived were so emaciated and dispirited, that they did not require the male at the usual time. Many of the roebucks perished.

The Kintail poet Iain mac Mhurchaidh wrote:

> *This has been the black spring of destitution*
> *Many's the man who has been stripped bare by it*
> *Though we have lost the milch cows*
> *It's the ponies I have been mourning.*

Life was indeed grim across the Highlands and Islands. For example, a very poor harvest in South Uist during 1772 left many to perish during the spring of 1773. During the years 1772–75 there was an almost continuous movement of hundreds of people walking from various places in the Highlands to ports of embarkation on the start of their journeys to America. With the snow lying late and cattle dying by the dozen, William Tod, the factor on the Duke of Gordon's land of Badenoch and Lochaber, expected 'one third of the poor people to die of mere want before the new crop is available due to a shortage of meal, seed and provender, and still the weather is making it impossible to start labouring'.

For many living at or near the coast, one way to avert starvation was to eat fish. But this brought its own problems. For example, a report from Lewis quoted in D. Macdonald's *Lewis: a History of the Island,* describes how:

> the pestilential fever that has rag'd in this part of the country for some time past, is greatly abated. We were afflicted with this disorder much about the same time last year, but it did not prove so fatal. It is thought to be owing to the vast quantities of fish and herrings that are daily eat by the inhabitants, the greatest part of whom live entirely upon herrings and potatoes during the fishing months, owing to the scarcity of corn and the want of bread.

When Boswell and Johnson made their famous 'tour of the Hebrides' in 1773 they encountered similar tales of bad weather and human tragedy. When Boswell arrived in Coll, for example, he found 'a large extent of sand hills, I daresay two miles square . . . this sand has blown of late over a good deal of meadow . . . it is very alarming'. People on the island told them that their fathers described how they used to farm on large areas of pasture that are now covered with sand. In a letter from a father in Strathspey to his son in America in July 1773 came the words, 'we cannot entertain you with any news from this country, which is still in the same situation as when you left it excepting that it is much poorer. Our crop this last season was exceeding ruined and scanty. The whole nation is threatened with a general famine.'

The story of desperation for many Scots continued through the remainder of the 1770s. While the herring fisheries continued to prosper, winters were extremely cold, snow lay late on the ground and the spectre of famine haunted many while emigration ships often lay anchored in Hebridean bays. But for some, the colder conditions brought leisure and in Edinburgh in 1778 some of its wealthiest patrons founded the Edinburgh Skating Club.

The black year

And so the battle against the elements continued into the 1780s. The harvest of 1781 was very poor across Scotland. Across much of the country the summer was cold and too dry for the grass or corn to grow. As if conditions were not bad enough, they were soon to deteriorate even further. Famine returned in 1782, with the winter of 1782–83 being known in Scotland as the 'Black Year'. The famine was, however, mitigated to a certain degree as a result of the cultivation of potatoes and better communication and transport, which enabled government provisions to be supplied.

This time of want also coincided with the end of the American War of Independence, and peasemeal that had been intended for the navy was quickly released and distributed to those with empty bellies.

The conditions were aptly summarised in a letter written by Dr Nisbet, minister of Montrose, who noted:

> heavy rain and flooding in the spring of 1782 resulted in the late sowing of seed; the summer was so cold that the grain barely ripened, early and widespread frosts meant failure of the crops over much of the country . . . the farmer had no easy task in selecting his seed, for in 1782 two distinct oat crops had been harvested . . . that which had ripened, or nearly so, and harvested early, and the late-harvested, which had a poor, soft seed.

Flooding on the Clyde

The *Scots Magazine* of 14 March 1782 describes how bad weather led to serious flooding in Glasgow. We read that,

> On Tuesday last the river Clyde rose to a greater height than the oldest people in this city remember. It has sometimes over-flowed that part of the town which lies very low; but, upon this occasion, it rose about twenty feet of perpendicular height above the usual course of the river. This remarkable inundation was occasioned by a very heavy fall of rain and snow, which began on Sunday last, about three in the afternoon, and continued without intermission, all that night, and next day. Upon Monday night, about ten o'clock, some parts of the

Bridgegate were underwater, and the flood continued to increase. It was at the greatest height upon Tuesday morning about seven o'clock.

At that time the Bridgegate, the lower parts of Saltmarket, Stockwell, Maxwell Street, Jamaica Street, and the populous village of Gorbals, were all underwater. The inundation was sudden and unexpected. Hundreds of families were obliged to leave their beds and their houses. A particular account of the damage which individuals have sustained cannot be ascertained; but the loss in tobacco, sugar and other mechandise, carried away by the river, or spoiled by water, will amount to a very large sum. A young woman in the Gorbals was drowned; and a woman in Partick, thinking herself in safety, refused to leave her house; and, being afterwards removed from it by her neighbours, expired in half an hour. A great number of horses and cows, which could not be removed from the stables and byres, were drowned.

In Kintyre and Gigha there was a bumper season for the herring fishery in August 1782, and then, because of a shortage of salt, the herrings were used as manure instead of being salted down for the winter.

At sea during 1782, destructive winter storms were wreaking havoc. Several fierce storms crippled both the naval and the merchant fleets, both of whom urgently petitioned parliament for help. The help they had in mind was lighthouses. Parliament agreed, and decided to set up a committee that recommended the construction of at least four lighthouses at critical points around the Scottish coast. But it took until June 1786 for a bill to be passed 'for erecting certain Lighthouses in the Northern Parts of Great Britain . . . to conduce greatly to the security of navigation and the fisheries'.

A diary from 1782

In the east of the country, John Ramsay of Ochtertyre, Perthshire, was writing that in January 1782 there were hurricanes of wind accompanied by flooding of the River Teith three times in ten days. Severe frosts occurred during February and March and a heavy snowfall also took place in March. Snows and rain were characteristic of April and from mid April till May there were very cold winds, but it was dry. Mid May till mid June were characterised by heavy rain which chilled the young corn, the middle of July was characterised by ten days of hot weather followed by heavy rains and stormy winds culminating with a 'hurricane' on 24 August. In September, despite two weeks of fine weather, the oats were still green. In Perthshire it was snowing by 17 September. The ripening of the oats at the start of October was soon stopped by frosts on 4 and 13 October. The snows returned at the end of October, followed by north winds and frost. As a result, the corn was not cut till well into November, while further snowfalls prevented the potatoes from being lifted. These conditions led to widespread hunger. Parliament was told that in Inverness there were many good farmers with their wives and children begging in the streets, and that meal or any kind of victuals (provisions) could not be had for love or money.

1783 – a disaster across northern Europe

The year 1783 marked the end of the American War of Independence, but closer to home famine continued to rage, while emigration to Canada and America continued. Some reports from the northwest Highlands describe how people survived through the spring of 1783 by eating shellfish from the shore. Numerous landlords were so shaken by this famine that it led to the founding in February 1784 of the 'Highland Society of Edinburgh', dedicated to the economic improvement of the Highlands and the preservation of the Gaelic culture, this organisation developing into what is now known as the Royal Highland and Agricultural Society of Scotland.

Then things deteriorated even further. In June a major volcanic eruption started in the Laki area of Iceland. The eruptions became more extensive after late July 1783 and continued until January 1784. The effect on the weather of northern Europe was immediate. Across Scotland, clear summer skies were soon replaced by a haze of dust and a sulphurous fog which obscured the Sun for three weeks. In her diary from Kenmay, Aberdeenshire, Janet Burnett, unaware of the volcanic eruption, described how the leaves on the plants in her garden and the crops in the fields were withering yellow. In fact, the year then became known in Scotland as the *Bliadhne nan Sneachda Bhuidhe* (the Year of the Yellow Snow).

The weather diaries of Janet Burnett, 1758–80 and 1781–95

Janet Burnett of Kenmay, Aberdeenshire, kept a diary from 1758 until a few weeks before her husband died in 1780. When she moved to live with her sister at Disblair House in the parish of Fintray, she kept a second diary that started in 1781 and ended in 1795. Her two diaries show a great interest in the weather and its effect on farming, the garden and the countryside. The remarkable detail of her records makes her diaries an extremely valuable archive of past weather in Scotland for the second half of the eighteenth century. Although Janet had no idea that a large volcanic eruption had taken place in Iceland in 1783, her weather accounts for this time period are very instructive:

July 1783 . . . the 10th the same weather fogg most of the day – 11th Thunder at a distance in the morning, closs air and fogg all day – at eleven o'clock night, the thunder begun again and continued pretty loud with a vast deal of lightning till 2 o'clock in the morning of the 12th. This day vastly warm the fogs still continow. Some people says there has not been a day since the 3rd but that they have heard thunder – this and such a contnowance of thick fogg is uncommon in this country.

The leaves of the corn and bear [barley] is yellowed and the tops of the potatoes blackened – from what cause we know not as nobody will allow of any frost having been. The most of the broom bloom too is weathered. The mercury here keeps very high. We hear from London the weather is sultry hot and the barometer in the shade at midday has been above eighty degrees and one day near ninety which is hotter than under the Line [equator].

27th December 1783 – the wind hardly abated but snow most of the day. The snow very deep and hardly any travelling with wheel carriges – the Post from this to Old Meldrum 12 miles was 9 hours on the road – from the 27th to the 31st showers of snow and the kinest frost we have seen for many years no heat of the room makes any impression on the ice on the inside of the windows. The watter in a bason froze in half an hour at 10 o'clock fornoon with a good fire in the room. The 1st January 1784 the air milder, 2nd a good deal of wind and drift – at night a most violent storm of wind at South East. This hurricane of wind blowd all the snow in such wreaths as was never seen in this Country. Many of them 18 foot perpendicular. Many people was two days in their houses [due to snowdrifts] . . . at several other little harbours near this, great peaces of the rocks was rent off and thrown into there harbour, the sea came out 40 yards further then the oldest man ever remembers . . . The frost of the 31st (Jan) was most remarkable the thermometer fell five and a half degrees below the freezing point.

Janet's diary tells of snow and frost lasting until the start of May in 1783. For example, for February she tells us:

From the 7th to the 14th only one day without snow, constant frost and pretty calm the wind . . . 18th every day more snow . . . the storm much deeper than ever, and 'tis no better over all England and also in France – this storm is thought more sever then in the year 1740 as we have had a great deal more snow . . . the sholls of ice in the Don was so large as to choke up the usual bed of the river and turn it out of its cours in three different places . . . This storm has been almost universal. At Paris they never experienced anything like it. When it brok up the beginning of March the Seine rose 22 feet above its bed . . . in Ireland the poor was almost famished, their potatoes being so much spoiled by the intense frost. On March 13th a great fall of snow . . . 15th exceeding cold with loud wind . . . from the 22nd to the 26th snow every day and frost and as cold as when the storm was lying on the ground . . . little work can go on and everything as winter.   (Pearson, 1994)

The magnitude of the Laki eruption can be gauged by its catastrophic effects in Iceland. Approximately 53% of Iceland's cattle, 77% of the ponies and 82% of the sheep died, together with nearly 20% of the island's population.

Freezing conditions in 1783

The following account written in the *Scots Magazine,* 1784, brings a chill to the bones:

In the months of December and January there were greater falls of snow than has happened for a great many years past. It began at Edinburgh upon the 24th of December, and continued with very little intermission till the end of the month. The roads were rendered almost impassable, which in a great measure stopt all intercourse with the country. The diligences and slys which set out from Edinburgh on the 29th, after going but a short way from town, were obliged to return, it being impossible for them to proceed. They were subjected to the same inconvenience once or twice during the month of January, by fresh falls.

The showers of snow were frequently attended by high winds, which did a great deal of damage upon the coast, particularly at Aberdeen, where several vessels were driven ashore and wrecked. In the end of December the cold was excessive. On Sunday the 28th, at half past 11pm, the thermometer, exposed to the open air at the observatory at Glasgow, pointed at 4° above Zero; next night, about the same time, to 11°; and on the 30th, about 10 o'clock, to 4° below Zero. The post-boy with the mail from Dumfries to Thornhill, was frozen to death upon his horse. At Edinburgh, on Wednesday the 31st, at eight o'clock in the morning, Fahrenheit's thermometer, on the outside of a window, stood at 35° below the freezing point, being 3° lower than it was 14 January, 1780, and is perhaps the greatest degree of cold known in this country since thermometrical registers were kept. The instrument, laid on the surface of the snow in a garden just at sun-rise, fell to 48° below the freezing point.

The Icelanders seemed to be facing complete extinction. A committee was appointed in Copenhagen to devise means for relief. There was even a plan considered to evacuate the island and remove the entire population to Denmark.

In the years that followed the Laki eruption, Scotland's weather changed markedly. The most immediate consequence was a series of exceptionally cold winters. A report in the *Edinburgh Magazine* illustrates this vividly:

> from the 18th of October 1784 till the present time, which is a period of 143 days, there have been only 26 in which the thermometer has not been from 1 to 18 degrees and a half below the freezing point, which is a more constant succession of cold weather than has been known in this climate. Last year there were 89 days of frost, and in the year 1779 there were 84; in 1763 there were 94 days of frost, and in the celebrated winter of 1739 there were only 109, which are 12 fewer than in the present winter.

For people living in Scotland at this time, fear of starvation was the foremost worry. In the *Scots Magazine* of November 1784 we read that:

> the Lord Provost likewise received a letter from the Lord Advocate, setting forth that as the harvest has been so late, and the weather has continued so unremittingly bad, very serious apprehensions had arose in his Lordship's mind relative to the supply of provisions for the lower class of the inhabitants of Scotland for the ensuing year. His Lordship makes no doubt, but it has occurred to the Lord Provost, as a matter well worthy of the attention of the Magistrates, in what manner best to alleviate the distresses arising from so severe a calamity. The best method of giving charity, on such an occasion, his Lordship thinks, is, to contribute, according to the peoples' respective abilities, for keeping the markets from rising to any immoderate height.

In the far north at this time in Shetland there was a great famine, with the longest frosts and snow in living memory and food for neither man nor beast. A letter from Edinburgh, dated 6 May 1784, reads, 'I am much concerned at the melancholy accounts from your country. I hope, however, the distress of your people would be so far relieved by the supplies that would arrive shortly after the date of your letters, but I am much afraid the sad consequences of these last two seasons will be long felt in Zetland.' The newspapers reported that 'but for a great multitude of small fishes . . . many would have starved'. The cattle actually did starve. A petition on 27 February 1784 presented by the ministers of Shetland to the barons of the Exchequer declared that 'of the last eight crops, four have failed almost totally in so much that the four together would not have supplied bread and seed for one year'.

Opposite the title page in the *Scots Magazine* for several months in 1785 there appeared a description of the exceptional severity of the winter of 1784–85: 'The winter-season, from the first fall of snow on Oct 7th, 1784 . . . lasted 177 days, and, if about 12 days towards the end of January be excepted, the whole of this period was frosty or snowy, or both.'

There was some respite in 1787, when, for example in Shetland, between January and March, reports described how mild the winter had been, with little frost and snow. The harvest was much better than in previous years, and even better in 1788. In true Presbyterian style in Shetland, the minister of Dunrossness parish, an area badly affected by famines in the preceding years, publicly condemned the popular rejoicing of the best harvest for seven years. Another fine summer and harvest followed in 1789 but a series of warm years in the immediate future was almost beyond hope.

What followed, indeed, was more bad weather. In 1790 the spring and summer months were so wet in most parts of Skye and the Western Isles that it was impossible to cut or dry peats. Fuel was so scarce that year that people had to burn the heather roots that they had gathered for rope-making. The winter of 1790–91 was very stormy and wet. Sea ice was also very extensive in northern waters at this time, while much of Scotland continued to be surrounded by cold polar waters. With the cold water came the herring, and behind them the whale. In fact, reports from Shetland at this time refer to fantastic white fishing. They also describe many men lost at sea during the summer fishing (probably due to summer storms) and whales so numerous that, 'fisherman are afraid to venture off'.

Across the Highlands and Islands powerful social changes were afoot. The year 1792, known as the *Blianthne nan Ba* (the Year of the Sheep), was a key year in Scottish history, when many people were driven from their land to make way for sheep. The storms continued. December 1792 was one of the worst months, remarkable for the production of many deep depressions moving across the North Atlantic at unusually fast speeds and indicative of a very strong jetstream. A huge storm blew up on 9 December. Ferocious winds blew over the Shetland–Faroe Islands region, estimated at around Beaufort

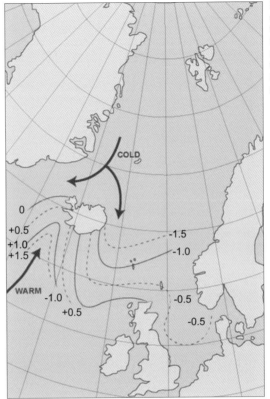

Reconstruction of ocean surface temperatures for the northern North Atlantic for 1792. The numbers represent ocean surface temperature changes (°C) relative to present (based on Lamb 1982).

force 11 and 12. Northern Scotland was badly affected and a report from inland of Aberdeen tells of winds all day on the 10th that were so strong that people could not remember anything like it.

Thunder and lightning in Alloa

Thunder and lightning due to the atmospheric disturbances were features of the summer and autumn of 1793 across Scotland. Prominent amongst these were thunderstorms on 2 July across almost the whole of Britain. The following account from the *Scots Magazine* for Alloa is typical of contemporary newspaper accounts:

> The lightning entered the chimney-top of a house. In one of the rooms on the ground-floor there was a woman, her daughter, of about nine years old, a young boy, and a dog. The

girl was scorched all over the body, as if dipped in a cauldron of boiling water. The mother was struck senseless on the ground, but recovered soon after. The boy suffered in the same way as the mother. The dog was instantly struck dead. In the middle of the floor of the other room in the ground-flat, two men and a woman were all struck, and laid flat upon the ground; one of the men only scorched a little in different parts of the body. In the room upstairs there was a women, a child in the cradle, a girl, and a boy. The woman was laid flat on the ground without any damage – the child unhurt. The girl had one of her arms much scorched and blistered; and the boy was drove under the bed from the middle of the floor, but not hurt. Some accounts mention, that there is a man killed at Menstrie, and two cows struck dead at Kersey.

The Goniel Blast

In 1794 a severe blizzard known as the 'Goniel Blast' took place in January. The blizzard was widely recorded in the Southern Uplands and led to the loss of life of many thousands of sheep and the death of several shepherds in Dumfriesshire. For several days the snow fell so heavily that in some areas the snow was 50ft deep. A total of 4,000 sheep perished in the parish of Eskdalemuir. An effect of the frost was that many of the sheep that died in Scottish glens at this time were fit to eat, the word 'goniel' referring to flesh fit to eat although not killed by a butcher. Meat prepared in this way was usually smoked and dried, and in fact the practice of eating goniel had been commonplace in the Borders for many years.

Descriptions of conditions in Edinburgh for the same time seem positively genteel, as described in Mossman's classic work on that city's weather, *The meteorology of Edinburgh* (1895–1903):

January 20–27, 1795 – A great frost. Continued snowstorm. Mail coaches delayed.

February 9. In the High Street a woman was dangerously wounded on the head owing to a huge mass of snow falling off the roof of one of the houses.

February 11. Very heavy snowfall; so deep was the snow that the
hackney coaches were frequently obliged to draw with four horses.
Mail coaches snowed up.

February 12. The snow lies excessively deep in the streets of Edinburgh
and in the neighbourhood. Three hundred soldiers and labourers
employed by the Magistrates to clear the roads to the coal-hills.

February 14. A gentle thaw commences, with the thermometer from
34 to 40 degrees; this, however, is soon again succeeded by frost.

Frost broke up on 3rd of March, having lasted 53 days.

The dearth that affected Scotland at the close of the eighteenth century also
occurred further afield. The following sentences from an account from Ireland
have a sinister echo of life in Scotland at this time:

> Continued rains, attended with an unusual degree of cold, occasioned
> an almost general deficiency in the crops, and a consequent failure of
> the usual supply of nourishment to the poor, already suffering under
> many privations . . . the state of the poor in the principal towns of
> Ireland, in the years 1799, 1800–2 were wretched in the extreme . . .
> the most melancholy accounts of the harvest arrive from all parts of the
> country; in many places the oats and other late corn remain on the
> ground not worth the reaping . . . the herring fishery very abundant;
> nevertheless, distress had commenced among the poor at the end of
> December . . . the poor of the country . . . are said to be perishing from
> the dearness, scarcity, and bad quality of all kinds of provisions, in
> consequence of the dreary harvest.
>
> (quoted in *Feast and Famine, Food and Nutrition
> in Ireland 1500–1920*, by Clarkson and Crawford.)

From Edinburgh we learn of a remarkably cold summer in 1799, 'the period
from the 20 March to 20 October was characterised by a great depression of
temperature, so much so that the harvest was not generally got in till the end
of November, and in high grounds till nearly the end of December' (Mossman
1895–1903). Testament to the many destructive storms that occurred at this
time comes from reports in December 1799 of a gale that lasted three days
and destroyed over 70 ships around the Scottish coast. The warship HMS *York*,
caught off guard by the storm, ran aground on the Bell Rock and sank with
the loss of all of the crew.

POSTSCRIPT

During the eighteenth century, any good patches of weather were few and far between. Moreover, those forced to emigrate had not only suffered as a result of the elements, but also from the injustices of the Highland Clearances. The two conditions conspired to deprive them of their livelihood and brought hunger to their children's bellies.

The rigours of our present climate are as nothing compared with the harsh, hostile weather experienced during the years described above. Occasionally, there was a hot summer or a fine autumn, but for most of the time, rain, damp, storms, snow, cold and even volcanic eruptions, were the order of the day. Only the herring, the silver darlings, appear to have flourished. It is a blessing that the oceanic and atmospheric changes that led to the southward expansion of cold polar water also led to the arrival of the shoals of herring, as they were also the processes that led to a southward displacement of the North Atlantic storm track, the very same processes that led to a marked increase in the frequencies of winter blizzards, storms and the 'Goniel Blast'.

CHAPTER 7
A CHANGE IN THE AIR (1800–60)

I had a dream, which was not all a dream.
The bright sun was extinguish'd, and the stars
Did wander darkling in the eternal space,
Rayless, and pathless, and the icy earth
Swung blind and blackening in the moonless air;
Morn came and went – and came, and brought no day,
And men forgot their passions in the dread.

Byron, from 'Darkness', 1816

INTRODUCTION

The nineteenth century began with wild winds, shipwrecks and the loss of souls in stormy waters. In the northern isles a fierce storm in January continued for two weeks, blowing a tempest with blizzards. Many ships were wrecked on rocks off Shetland. From Aberdeen alone as many as 80 seamen lost their lives in the southeasterly gales and blizzard conditions. The 'Goniel Blast' had returned, with many cattle and sheep perishing. By the autumn there were crop failures. The hope that came with the start of the new century quickly turned to despondency with the realisation that the dreadful weather that had marked the 1790s was continuing. Famine stalked the Southern Uplands and the price of food reached high levels. Added to that there were fears that a potato famine that had started in Ireland in 1801 would spread to Scotland.

With the storms and snow, landowners faced a dilemma. On the one hand there was a strong push to remove people from the land and replace them with sheep. On the other hand, loss of livestock was a near certainty due to the severity of the winters. Historian Tom Devine tells us that in 1802 on Tiree, Maxwell of Aros, the 5th Duke of Argyll's chamberlain, recommended in a report that 'the productive capacity of the estate could only support the population except under conditions of penury suggesting the need for emigration of about 1,000 of the population to North America'.

For reasons that are unclear the fisheries of 1802 and 1803 were poor. For the men, women and children making a living from the fish it was a disaster. Some maintained that the distress was much greater than the horrors of 1784. Many relied for their survival on charitable supplies of grain, meal and bread. The government, acutely aware of the loss of part of the labour market through emigration, brought in laws to restrict it, so for the poor there was no way out. To make matters worse, a strong El Niño developed in 1803, and with the El Niño came more North Atlantic storms. A taste of the severity of the storms comes from two accounts from Leith given in the *Scots Magazine* of January 1803:

> It blew very hard on Sunday night [9 January], accompanied with a heavy sea, and the gale continuing to increase, the high water on Sunday afternoon's tide exhibited a scene seldom witnessed. The prodigious roaring surf without, composed of contained breakers, and sometimes rising higher than the top of the lighthouse, being interrupted in its progress by the angle of the North Pier, rolled into the harbour with irresistible impetuosity, and occasioned such a violent commotion amongst the shipping, that many of them sustained damage by their ropes breaking, and from some of the mooring rings being torn from the pavement; and several to secure their ships, were obliged to bring on shore their anchors, and fix them in the streets, and in the doors of some of the houses. In the Sand Port there was a prodigious swell, two sloops were sunk, and others received considerable damage . . .
>
> In the violent gale on Tuesday [19 April], several of the ships at anchor in Leith Roads drove considerably, and some of the vessels lying in Leith, near the entrance of the harbour, suffered damage. A Danish vessel, the *Leon of Easterezen*, owing to the violence of the gale, and heavy sea, pitched away her foremast and boltsplit while at anchor in Leith Roads; and the *Dunrobin Castle*, from Virginia, laden with tobacco, and the *Princess Royal* parted from their cables and anchors and drove down the Firth.

The misery continued year after year. In 1804 the government granted £10,000 for the relief of the starving populace of Shetland. Then, after the extremely cold winter of 1805, a tremendous storm took place during Christmas 1807–08 across the north of Scotland. It was described as probably the most severe gale of the nineteenth century at Wick. Meanwhile, reports from Skye continued to describe famine caused by incessant rains that lasted throughout spring, summer and autumn.

The cold winters, and cold water, did bring the whales back to Shetland waters during the early 1800s. The available accounts describe huge numbers. For example, in 1805, 195 were driven ashore at Uyeasound in Unst then another 121 captured in the same area in April. In July 1807, 102 whales were driven ashore at Quendale Bay in the far south of the island. This was followed in September 1810 by three large schools of whales driven ashore, from which 1,000 barrels of oil were processed.

A ray of hope arrived in 1808 with a fine, warm summer across Scotland. But things turned for the worse in the autumn with more storms and high tides. In Edinburgh on 21 October, to the consternation of all, a heavy south-westerly gale blew down a building (which contained a model panorama of the Battle of Trafalgar) at the foot of the Mound. In November the tide levels at Leith were the highest in living memory. By January 1809 the cold had returned, along with easterly winds and blizzard conditions. Between Queensferry and Kinross the snow lay six to ten feet deep, while Sunday the 22nd was one of the coldest days that anyone could remember. The new harbour at Leith was so completely frozen over that sailors could pass from ship to ship upon the ice.

With the storms came many more shipwrecks. By this time the construction of lighthouses around Scotland's coastline had started – thanks to the genius of Robert Stevenson (grandfather of the author Robert Louis Stevenson). Work usually took place during summer but could not escape some of the violent storms that developed at this time of year. As many were to discover to their cost, sudden storms during the summer months were to be a feature of years when the North Atlantic storm track was displaced much further south than usual.

Shipwrecks and tides

The increasing frequency of storms took its toll on ships and sea. For example, in 1811 three naval battleships (the 98-gun *St George* and two 74-gun ships) were shipwrecked in a North Sea storm while returning from the Baltic. Two thousand lives were lost, double the British naval losses during the Battle of Trafalgar. November was particularly severe, with very bad gales and high tides. In Orkney there were nine wrecks in one day. The tides rose to exceptional heights, exceeding 20 feet in the Firth of Forth. By the middle of the month another gale blew up. The *Scots Magazine* reported, in 1811, that at Leith:

> two sloops broke loose above the lower bridge, and drove through the arch, by which their masts were carried away. One of them was driven out of the harbour, and went ashore to the eastward of the pier, but has since been got off. Leith harbour yesterday morning had a very confused appearance, the vessels lying in all directions.

The year 1812 saw renewed crop failures. Letters from Inverness describe how the gathering of harvested crops had been greatly delayed by unfavourable weather. From Shetland there were reports of a very severe spring, with intense frosts, heavy snows and northerly gales 'such as have not been seen in the memory of man. The whole year was bad. Corn rotted in the ground, and there were only three dry days during five weeks of September and October' (*Inverness Courier*, 1811). It was cold everywhere. In 1814, ice covered the lochs around Edinburgh for 52 days, from 3 January to 23 February. By the end of January the *Scots Magazine* was reporting that:

> in consequence of the intensity of the frost the navigation between Grangemouth and Leith is interrupted and the Great Canal is shut. The Carron is completely covered with ice. The Firth above Queensferry is impassable. The frost is far more severe than that of 1795 . . . [O]n February 6th . . . the greater part of the old timber bridge between fisherrow and Musselburgh was carried away by the great quantity of ice which floated down the River Esk, [on the] breaking up of that water by the thaw.

An enormous volcanic eruption

In 1815 a catastrophe took place that was to change the world. During April, an enormous volcanic eruption took place in Tambora, Indonesia. It was one of the biggest eruptions in human history, even bigger than that of Krakatoa, which was to follow in August 1883. Volcanic ash circled the globe, together with vast quantities of sulphate aerosols. The effects of the eruption were felt worldwide. For many months, sunlight was obscured by the huge quanties of ash in the atmosphere leading to, amongst other things, months of red sunsets. The effects of the eruption prompted Byron, living in Switzerland in 1816, to write his famous poem 'Darkness',

> *The rivers, lakes and ocean all stood still,*
> *And nothing stirr'd within their silent depths;*
> *Ships sailorless lay rotting on the sea,*
> *And their masts fell down piecemeal: as they dropp'd*
> *They slept on the abyss without a surge –*
> *The waves were dead; the tides were in their grave,*
> *The moon, their mistress, had expir'd before;*
> *The winds were wither'd in the stagnant air,*
> *And the clouds perish'd; Darkness had no need*
> *Of aid from them – She was the Universe.*

Several accounts describe the winter of 1815–16 as being long and severe, one from the *Scots Magazine* observing that with, '[O]ur winter has this year been of five months' duration. It began with frost and snow early in November; and on the afternoon of Thursday the 18th April, the snow fell thick and heavy, and the whole country around Edinburgh speedily assumed the aspect of mid-winter.' Hugh Miller refers to five successive winters of devastating storms between 1815 and 1820.

The climate change that followed the Tambora eruption happened gradually, as the huge quantities of ash in the stratosphere acted as a barrier to the penetration of the Sun's rays. The changes mostly started to take effect in 1816, the time of Byron's poem. The *Inverness Courier* reported that September 1816 was cold, with frequent showers of hail, sharp frosts at night, and snow on the higher hills, while many compared the weather with that of 1782 and expressed fear for their crops. By 1817 the coverage of sea ice across northern waters had increased considerably and storms were commonplace, with reports from Shetland describing the year as 'exceedingly tempestuous' and no fewer than 20 vessels being totally wrecked or stranded. The spectre of famine was again in the air. Between 12–16 January 1818 the country was struck by more storms. Buildings in Edinburgh were reported to have been severely damaged by westerly gales, while at Gordon Castle near the Moray Firth trees were blown down by winds estimated at between 100 and 120 knots.

Polito's menagerie on the mound

The storm of mid January 1818 caused chaos in Edinburgh. The *Scots Magazine* described how:

Last night we were visited by one of the most severe gales we have experienced for a long time. It began to blow at ten o'clock from the southwest, accompanied by heavy rain, and continued to increase during the night until it became a perfect hurricane. In the morning it had not abated in the least degree. From seven till nine it was particularly severe; so much so, that a considerable part of the lead on the Dome of George's Church was stripped off; at the same time the large wooden building erected on the Mound for showing Polito's menagerie of wild beasts, and since used for exhibitions of lesser note, was blown to pieces, and a great part of it carried into the North Loch; part of another temporary wooden erection, presently occupied as a wood-yard, was likewise blown down, and strewed in various directions; fortunately no person was hurt.

We would here call the attention of our Police to the impropriety of permitting such superficial erections to be placed in so exposed a situation as that of the Earthen Mound by which the lives of passengers are placed in the greatest jeopardy, in every gale of wind which blows. Several of these temporary buildings have been blown down before; very fortunately there were no wild beasts in them at the time, otherwise the consequences would have been dreadful. We are much afraid the gale will have been productive of the most disastrous and melancholy consequences among shipping on our coasts.

In the following years the gales and floods continued. Between 9 and 13 October 1819, a storm from the northeast caused about 150 vessels to be stranded or lost on the eastern coasts of Scotland and England. By November 1824 the *Inverness Courier* was reporting that across northern Scotland there had been, 'uninterrupted continuance of wind and rain for many weeks . . . [T]he River Ness . . . rising for some weeks . . . attained yesterday to such a height as has not been remembered by the oldest inhabitant in town, and now presents a magnificent but fearful spectacle ... In many districts a large part of the crop was not only unstacked, but uncut.'

There were occasional lighter moments, however. In 1819 Shetland, which had suffered such a battering from the elements, experienced an extremely mild spring and warm summer. In February, the Reverend John Bryden of Sandsting delighted in a second crop of artichokes in his garden ready for use.

The 'Long Storm' of 1823

Of all the winters that our ancestors had to face, one of the most severe was that of early 1823, known as the 'long storm', when the country was lashed by storms and blizzards. One of the most graphic and detailed accounts appears George Bruce's 1884 account, *Wrecks and Reminiscences of St Andrews Bay*:

> The storm commenced on the 12th January 1823 and continued almost without intermission until the 24th – slowly but surely enveloping the country beneath a white shroud of snow ... [A]fter a week's cessation it again set in with renewed and increased severity on Saturday night, 1st February, and continued with great violence until Tuesday forenoon, the 4th, accompanied by a most severe northeasterly gale. The roads were completely blocked up, the snow being drifted higher than the hedges and dykes – in some instances the wreaths being 15–20 feet deep ... [T]he stage coaches from Dundee, Cupar, St Andrews, and other towns, to Edinburgh were all stopped, and great numbers of people were employed on the different highways cutting through the snow ... [T]he houses were covered with snow – most of the windows partially obscured by the drift sticking on the outside – in many cases totally blinded ... On Saturday the 8th, the thermometer fell 20 degrees below the freezing point ... it continued blowing and snowing for, more or less, nearly 6 weeks, embracing both land and sea in its bitter, cold, icy grasp. It was not only the longest snowstorm, but one of the most prolonged and severe sea storms of the present [nineteenth] century ... [A]lthough 1827,

> 1838, 1881 and . . . 1882 . . . seemed to vie with it. It was fully 3
> months before the snow fully melted away . . . So deep was the
> snow drifted in several parts of the City that some tunnels had
> to be dug, or scraped out . . . to reach the elevated snow-paved
> streets, and also let in the light of the Sun . . . two old people
> were dug out of their house in a tunnel about 6 feet deep which
> could allow men to pass underneath the snow.

The year 1826 came as a big surprise to most. The reason was that it was hot
– very hot. In fact, the year came to be known in the Gaelic as *Bliadhna an
Teas Mhóir* ('the Year of the Great Heat'). No rain fell from May until August,
with main rivers, lochs and springs running dry. As a result the corn crop was
so short that it could not be cut, and had to be pulled out by the roots. There
was a heatwave in Edinburgh that culminated on 24–30 June, and an early
harvest across most areas of Scotland. Across the east of the country cutting
began about 10 July and by the 29th many fields were cleared. In fact there
was a double crop, the second harvested in October.

The winter was cold, however. On 22–24 November there was a severe
storm that hit the western Highlands with terrible gusts of wind, and snow in
huge flakes. The storm increased in ferocity as it travelled eastwards across the
Highlands and there was great damage at Inverness, where 11 people died
from the cold as they tried to get back home to their own districts after the
Martinmas fair at Inverness. The storms continued through the cold winter.
The *Inverness Courier* describes how severe weather set in on the first day of
the New Year and continued unabated: 'Frost, snow, thaw, and gales of wind
alternated in rapid succession . . . the rivers flooded to an unprecedented
extent.' Snow still lay in the fields at the start of March – in fact in the centre
of Edinburgh at this time piles of snow (particularly around Waterloo Place),
were six feet high. Storms again continued throughout the summer months
and from distant St Kilda on 8 July 1827, hurricane-force winds struck the
island with devastating effect. The repeated occurrence of storms during
summer came to be a feature of Scotland's weather during the nineteenth
century, as well as of the previous century. Never was this more true than on
3 and 4 August 1829, when a violent storm hit the northern Highlands
causing the Moray floods.

After The Moray floods

The *Scots Magazine* provides this graphic account of flooding and casualties of the storms that raged across eastern Scotland after the Moray floods of 1829:

> Tuesday, August 4th 1829. At the time our last papers went to press we noticed that heavy rain was falling, accompanied by high wind; as the night advanced the wind increased to a hurricane, blowing from the north-west, and the rain fell in torrents. The storm was severely felt in the Firth, at Newhaven, and also all along the northern shore, at Burntisland, Kinghorn, Kirkcaldy etc., where it was also accompanied with peals of thunder, and the most vivid flashes of lightning.
>
> We regret extremely to mention, that the Newhaven fishermen have sustained a greater loss in boats by this storm than in any season for upwards of twenty years past. Out of twenty-five that were moored off the stone piers, three only rode out the storm and on Tuesday morning the coast in that vicinity was covered with fragments of wreck, masts, oars etc. and presenting a distressing scene.

This storm will always be remembered for the incredible amounts of rain that fell across the Grampians. A furious northeasterly wind created high seas which wrecked many ships and broke open the harbour at Garmouth, near Elgin, washing away part of the village in the early hours of 4 August. Exceptional rainfall caused flooding in lochs and rivers to levels never previously reported, and, it is believed, unequalled since. Torrents of water came down Speyside from the northern flank of the Cairngorms. The oldest people in the areas worst affected observed that the flood levels exceeded those of the greatest remembered previous floods, which took place in 1768. At least nine bridges, some of them recently constructed main-road bridges, and many houses and other buildings, were destroyed by the flood at various places in the eastern Highlands of Scotland. Many lives were lost.

After the wet summer of 1829, the remaining months of the year were all colder than usual and the winter that followed was severe – in fact one of the severest across all of northern Europe, with cold easterly winds blowing off the continent. An indication of cold water again surrounding Scotland may be provided by historians who point out that the 1830s was a time when the herring fishery in Scotland again approached the boom times of the 1790s. For those in the western Highlands and Islands, this was also a time when the boom in kelp production that had started in the 1790s came to an end, and the incomes of many poor people all but disappeared. Against this background of bad weather, crop failures and the collapse of the kelp industry, the cruel process of evictions continued energetically – for example on Islay in 1831. Devine's account, *The Great Highland Famine*, published 1988, highlights the decade of the 1830s, when an estimated 130 souls left Islay, to be followed during the 1840s by a further 1,200.

A tragic storm occurred in Shetland during the summer of 1832 that led to the loss of 31 boats, in which 105 people lost their lives. More gales followed in 1833. For example, on 20 February a severe northeasterly gale struck eastern Scotland, with many vessels lost, including four or five fishing boats and several men lost in the Firth of Forth. The familiar summer storms occurred again – this time the worst being a hurricane that took place in Shetland on 27 August. By November we read of another off mainland Scotland that increased to a 'perfect hurricane' so violent that it prevented passage between Newhaven and Kirkcaldy and the steam boats to Stirling were forced to return to the chain pier (*Scots Magazine*). A bitterly cold and snowy winter followed during 1834–35. By early March 1835, the snow south of Edinburgh was eight to nine feet deep. By the middle of the month the *Caledonian Mercury* was reporting that 'we still have very stormy and variable weather. In some districts the snow is deeper than has been witnessed for 20 years, and the sheep are suffering.' By 1835 the herring yields in Shetland reached a record 32,000 barrels.

Across the Highlands and Islands, many suffered from a cold, wet spring that led to late sowing of the crops, and by harvest time the unripe corn was being battered by rain. During the first few months of 1836 cold and rain caused the ground to be tilled with great difficulty. There was very little cattle feed and many animals died. Nearly 700 head of cattle died in Lewis, as well as several thousand sheep. The snows that started to fall during early December 1835 continued unabated until March 1836. The north of Scotland was badly hit, with some commenting that 'the snow was at a greater depth than has been seen for 15 years past'. The summer and autumn of 1836 were also wet and, as a result, the winter of 1836–37 was associated with dearth and famine. To make matters worse, the potato crop failed across the Highlands and Islands that autumn. Not only was food scarce, but the peats needed for winter fuel had not been cut in the summer because of the heavy rain. In some cases people had to burn their turf huts and cottages for fire. There are accounts describing how some even had to draw lots to select whose house was to be dismantled for fuel.

The snowstorms were at their worst during February and March 1837. A writer in the *Edinburgh Advertiser* stated that 'the severity of the weather and its long continuance at this season of the year are altogether unprecedented in our latitudes', while in the *Glasgow Chronicle* on 12 April we read that the Campsie and Kilpatrick hills were then white with snow and everything bore the appearance of the depth of winter. The wheat had been so badly damaged by frost that the farmers had harrowed it down and were sowing oats instead. Widespread snow again fell across the country on 8 May.

In Shetland the herring yields continued to hit high levels. Devine describes how a better summer occurred in 1837 but on Tiree the grain and potato crops failed during the spring and as a result a quarter of the island's population was dependent on the charity of others for food. That winter, further storms led to an unusual occurrence in Orkney, at Otterswick on Sanday, when a severe northeasterly gale caused the sea to scour the beach, laying bare an ancient forest floor with black moss and big fallen trees (trunks up to 60cm thick and bigger than any trees that now grow in Orkney), which had evidently been submerged by the sea and buried by sand for some thousands of years. Snow and blizzards returned again during the winter of 1837–38, especially during the spring of 1838, with snow on the ground from January until early May. One report from near Huntly describes people walking over the tops of two farmhouses due to the depth of the snowdrifts.

Lighthouses, storms and shipwrecks

With considerable numbers being lost at sea in storms and the wrecking of ships on Scotland's coastline nearly every winter (and summer too), the push was on to build more lighthouses and make life safer for those at sea. The years 1838 and 1839 were highlighted by three particularly severe storms. First, it was the year when a big North Sea storm on 7 September caused the wrecking of the Dundee-bound passenger steamship the SS *Forfarshire* off the Farne Islands on the Northumberland coast, and the rescue of nine of the passengers by the Farnes lighthouse keeper together with his 22-year-old daughter, Grace Darling, this event ultimately leading to the founding of the Royal National Lifeboat Institution.

During January 1839 an incredible storm struck Wick. The *John O'Groats Journal* of 9 January describes how:

> [O]n Monday evening and Tuesday morning last . . . one of the most tremendous gales of wind ever experienced . . . with the exception of the memorable 'windy Christmas' about 32 years ago nothing approaching it in violence had been felt in this country. The wind was from the NW . . . the mercury was unprecedently low [an astonishing 925.2 mb at Sumburgh in Shetland] . . . and everything denoted a northern hurricane.

Tragedy in Shetland

On Tuesday, 9 September 1840, an autumn storm struck Shetland with severe consequences. The *Shetland Folk Book* contains an account describing how five boats went down with all hands that night, and over 30 men lost their lives. In Lerwick there was other chaos with boats dragging and driving everywhere, many being smashed to pieces on the shore. There were similar scenes at Scalloway and elsewhere. Thirty boats were totally lost and scores of others were damaged. The destruction of many boats, together with nets and other materials, had near fatal consequences for the Shetland fishing fleet. The financial consequences of the storm contributed significantly to the closure of the Shetland Bank, which was later declared bankrupt owing approximately £60,000. As the years passed, the Shetland fishing industry rose again, although for 15 years after the tragedy of 1840 folk still spoke of the '. . . hungry '40s'. It took another 40 years for the herring industry to get back on its feet. Boats which had been hauled ashore in 1840 were never launched again and left to rot on the shore.

Suffering in St Kilda

With conditions as described across the Scottish mainland, one shudders to think what life must have been like on St Kilda. A letter from a visitor to the island in 1841 described the struggle for survival of the islanders in the face of the harsh climate:

> [T]heir slight supply of oats and barley . . . would scarcely suffice for the sustenance of life; and such is the injurious effect of the spray in

winter, even on their hardiest vegetation, that savoys and german greens, which with us are improved by the winter's cold, almost invariably perish. The people are suffering very much from want of food . . . They literally cleared the shore not only of shell-fish, but even of a species of sea weed that grows abundantly on the rocks within the sea-mark . . . Now the weather is coarse, birds cannot be found, at least in such abundance as their needs require.

Despair of the 1840s

As the 1840s progressed, the country continued to be battered from all sides. Not only did winter gales take their toll on those at sea, but violent gales continued to occur during summer and autumn. In 1844, for example, hurricane force-10 winds from the west and southwest struck the west and south of Scotland on 12 and 13 June. In August 1845 the weather was described as 'very wet . . . the general complexion of the season disastrous in the extreme. Previous Wednesday a terrible storm at sea' (*Inverness Courier*). The effects of such poor weather were added to by the great potato famine of Ireland, which had started in 1845 and had begun to spread into the Hebrides the same year, with the most serious failures in Islay and mid Argyll.

By 1846, famine had spread across the Highlands and Islands. Although the spring was mild and pleasant and the early summer warm and dry, with a heatwave in June, in July it began to rain, and with the wet weather came more potato blight. The winter of that year set in early and proved cold and stormy with frequent gales and snowstorms. In his history of the Highlands and Islands of Scotland, James Hunter explains that 'to the incessant cold and hunger – intolerable enough in themselves – were added sickness and disease. Typhus and cholera broke out in several places. The shellfish scavenged from the beaches produced dysentery when eaten.' Devine adds that on Tiree, the potato blight first became obvious during October. At that time the Marquis of Lorne concluded that only 400 of the island's inhabitants (which numbered slightly over 1,400 in the 1841 census) could be deemed independent of the need for aid.

The famine continued in many areas of the Highlands and Islands in 1847. Hunter describes how, on Barra, there were 'few families with any food at all . . . [T]he situation was equally ghastly. Everything that could be eaten – including seed corn needed for the spring sowing – had been eaten; and the island's population was subsisting on a debilitating diet of shellfish.' Devine points out that, in January that year, the people of Barra were reported as being in a state of absolute starvation. The storms continued and, when the *Exmouth* set sail from Londonderry on Sunday, 25 April 1847, it became caught in mountainous seas and hurricane force-11 winds. The ship was wrecked on the rocks of the Rhinns of Islay, with the loss of 251 lives. Then, following a summer with an unusually good harvest, the weather broke once again, in the early autumn, and for several weeks the whole of the northwest Highlands and Islands were swept by almost incessant rain and gales. Crofters' corn was flattened and practically destroyed, while a new outbreak of blight devastated the already scanty crop of potatoes. On Tiree that year, a further 340 emigrated from the island while on Rum, no dry peat was available as fuel for the winter.

By the autumn of 1848 the potatoes had failed more or less completely and the grain crop was so late that in many areas it remained unharvested. In

Black Saturday at Wick

The worst catastrophe ever recorded along the coastline of Caithness took place on 19 August 1848. Although August is not normally noted for storms, a number of years are known for exceptional storms that took place during summer as well as winter. This catastrophe developed when the barometer showed a sharp fall in air pressure while the wind shifted to an easterly gale. By dawn the following morning the sea was 'studded with boats all running before the wind, the crews evidently careless of where they landed'.

Wrecked boats were floating in every direction while crowds of boats were flying for shelter wherever the crews thought'. Foden describes how 37 souls were drowned. Of these, two were from Wick, six from Poultneytown, one was from Staxigoe and one from Thurso. Six came from Orkney. The largest number from any one place was 13 from Lewis. The others, mostly crewmen, were from various places in Caithness and Sutherland, including Bower, Tongue, Assynt and Lybster. Some boats were lost or severely damaged, and dozens more injured but reparable. The effects of the storm were also felt more widely, with eleven lives lost at Peterhead, seven at Stonehaven and five at Johnshaven.

Wester Ross, for example, crofters' corn was still green when the first snow fell in October. Matters were made worse by a very poor herring fishing season. In the north of Scotland, at Wick, a terrific storm blew up on 19 August. As described in the *John O'Groats Journal* of 25 August 1848, the state of the weather was fearful, 'the [Poultneytown] bay was almost one entire sheet of wave . . . [A]ltogether 37 fishers were drowned . . . [S]ome boats were lost or severely damaged, and dozens more injured but reparable.'

The start of 1849 was no better. On 10 January a great easterly gale and heavy seas washed away heavy harbour defences at Peterhead. '[T]he weather throughout the week has been exceedingly bad. One storm of wind and rain has succeeded another, and lightning has been frequent in the evenings. Rivers in flood' (*Inverness Courier*). There is reason to believe that the cold polar waters may have pushed even further south by this time, with huge catches of herring all along the west coast from Lewis to Argyll. The *Inverness Courier* describes how, on Lewis on 1 June, fishing was 'uncommonly productive', at Lochcarron, 'never in the memory of man was there such an appearance of herrings on the coast' and, in Argyllshire (10 August), the fishery was 'productive . . . almost beyond remembrance' while, on Skye (17 July), 'herring fishing exceeds anything that has taken place for the last 40 years'.

By the start of the 1850s many in the Highlands were in severe distress. Devine has described how during 1851 there was another petition from poor persons in Tiree for aid to emigrate – since they were cast into penury on the termination of the Central Board that had previously provided wages through drainage and other works projects. On Tiree that year there were 465 people who emigrated. Devine states that, on Iona, 'conditions of the "crofter class" had deteriorated greatly since 1846, [and] many were forced to sell part of their [cattle] stock . . . [M]any small crofters (£3–£8 rent per year) were forced to sell off stock to buy food.' On Sleat, Skye, 'the circumstances of the people have progressively deteriorated, from year to year, since 1846' and, on Barra, 'of 230 persons paying rent to the proprietor, there are about 80 who have no stock of any kind'. By January 1852 the Highlands were 'in the grip of a severe snowstorm, the heaviest, it was believed, since 1826' (*Inverness Courier*).

Even the emigrant ships were sometimes caught up in the storms. Nearly all such ships would cross the ocean during summer despite the danger of an occasional violent summer gale. Such a disaster happened in June 1850, when the steamer *Chevalier* took 129 Raasay people bound for Australia, but news came through on 29 November that the ship had been wrecked off Jura in a storm.

Raasay House weather records

A detailed record of Scotland's weather for the second half of the nineteenth century comes surprisingly from weather diaries kept at Raasay House opposite Skye. The landowner (appropriately called Dr Rainy) maintained a frosty relationship with the local people, culminating eventually in his clearance of people from the land – actions so movingly described by Sorley MacLean in his poem 'Hallaig'. The weather diaries also contain vivid of accounts of life in the mid nineteenth century. For example, on 29 November 1854 he describes the gales that caused the wrecking a few years earlier of the *Chevalier* steamer and the drowning of the Raasay men, women and children on their way to a new future in Australia. They also describe the snowstorm and frosts of January 1854, when air temperatures plunged to -12°C. At this time, the whole of northern Europe experienced freezing winter temperatures and snowstorms that blocked roads and railways and inflicted considerable loss of life and shipping.

The cold winters of 1851–52 and 1852–53

The snows returned with a vengeance on 13 January 1852. Most of the snow fell in the north and east of the country. Movement north of Perth was only possible with great difficulty. The *Caledonian Mercury* reported on 15 January:

> Loss of life in Strath Tay by the snowstorm last week which the people in that district declare to be the severest . . . known for 30 years. North of Inverness . . . two persons perished in Lochaber; 3 persons died in the borders of Banff and Aberdeenshire; large numbers of sheep wintering on low grounds as well as on the hills, have perished in the drifts; in the Moray Firth from the severity of the wind . . . there has been a loss of shipping unparalleled on our coasts for many years past. Some of the snow drifts near Huntly were 40 to 50 feet deep.

More was to come the following winter. Reports from the Borders mentioned that old shepherds there had not experienced such snowstorms for 30 years. The *Caledonian Mercury* of 5 March stated that, in Banff, 'the snowstorm which began on 10th February has continued with more or less violence ever since'. Many equated this winter with the dreadful blizzards of 1838.

The winter of 1860–61 was also cold and snowy. The first hints of this come in a short note in Dr Rainy's Raasay diary for 4 October: 'wet and stormy day. Very squally with heavy showers of rain but the Cuillin Hills capped in snow last night.' The snowstorms had set in on a grand scale across the country and, by mid December, 'a great snowstorm took place across central and southern Scotland on 19 December 1860, it had a severity . . . that exceeds anything experienced for probably 20 years'. Even across Edinburgh the snow was at least 2 foot deep. This was accompanied by very low temperatures on 26 December that plunged to -17°C at the Botanic Gardens in Edinburgh. People struggled to remember temperatures as low – some said that the last time it had been as cold was between the years 1812 and 1814. Boxing Day 1860 was also famous as the day of the 'bitter black frost', when freezing fog accompanied a fall in temperature to between -10 and -12°F. The worst areas affected included Kirkcaldy, Crieff, Greenock, Perth, Alloa, Cupar, Falkirk, Kelso and Galashiels. When the thaw came in mid January 1861, huge blocks of ice were to be seen drifting in the floodwaters.

CHAPTER 8

A CATALOGUE OF DISASTERS (1861–99)

The first hint we got of any disaster
was a number of oars floating in the water,
for we had seen no other boat during the night.

John Fraser, from 'Tragedy at Gloup', 1881

INTRODUCTION

As far as we can tell, the horrendous weather that had prevailed for the most part from the 1750s until the 1860s continued in the years that followed. The comparison is, however, a difficult one to make since the way weather conditions were reported changed. With some important exceptions, most reports of the weather during the early 1800s amount to descriptions by observers. By contrast, from the 1860s onwards, meteorological conditions were carefully recorded, in most instances as several readings each day, at dozens of locations around Scotland.

The majority of the weather readings were made by the keepers of the many lighthouses now scattered around Scotland's coastline. Weather recording was also set on a more formal basis as a result of the establishment of the Scottish Royal Meteorological Society in 1867. From that year onwards, the duties of each lighthouse keeper included the recording of all aspects of daily weather, including the measurement of air temperature, pressure, wind direction and strength, cloud cover, snowfall, fog and even the state of the sea, whether rough or calm. The keepers were also required to record any other meteorological phenomena worthy of note. These included thunder, lightning and the northern lights – the notes of the keepers at Muckle Flugga lighthouse in northern Shetland even include descriptions of distant earthquakes rumbling beneath the ocean waters. The keepers also made notes of times of the most devastating storms. One description of a storm in 1862 by the

170

keepers on the Monach Isles lighthouse out in the Atlantic Ocean west of North Uist describes how the lighthouse tower had started to shake and the crew were in fear for their lives.

The start of the giant storms

When a ferocious storm ripped through the Outer Hebrides on 11– 12 January 2005, there was much speculation as to whether or not any similar giant storms had struck the islands in the past. It is worthwhile contemplating what happened during the latter part of the nineteenth century. The late 1860s represented the start of a 30-year period when Scotland was to be struck by successions of severe winter storms (as well as some frightening events during summer). The first signs of the winds of change came in December 1862, when a damaging storm swept across the Outer Hebrides. The gale was recorded by John MacDonald of Bernera on the Isle of Lewis and quoted in the *Inverness Courier* of 8 January 1863:

> [T]he gale commenced about noon on the 18th and did not abate till 7 a.m. on the 20th, and exceeded in severity, force and duration anything I have witnessed for at least 20 years . . . [T]he boisterous raging of the Atlantic was fearful to behold. An island, named the Old Hill, which is several hundred feet high and about 3 miles distant from Bernera, was frequently covered entirely with the spray. Fish of various kinds were choked and driven onshore . . . lobster creels and fishing materials of every description were lost in all directions. The tide, which was the highest ever witnessed, the rise having been about 5 feet above the ordinary mark – swept away and damaged a number of our fishing boats; and rocks hundreds of tons in weight, along the shore, were torn asunder. In fact, the scene surpassed everything seen or heard of before amongst us.

Another disastrous storm occurred in 1867 in the Shetlands, when the islands were struck by hurricane-force winds. Yet another huge storm blew in on 24 January 1868 this time recorded as hurricane force 12 across Lewis. Even Edinburgh felt the effects. There, 24 January came to be known as 'Windy Friday', when winds reaching the force of a tropical hurricane swept across the city. A gable in Duke Street was blown down, cabs were overturned and many buildings were damaged.

A consequence of the detailed recording of weather in meteorological logs is that it becomes difficult to compare this type of weather information with the more descriptive accounts that had gone before. We may never know how severe the weather conditions were felt to be in the latter decades of the nineteenth century, compared with earlier decades. We do know, however, that some of the weather extremes, particularly the storms, are now established as notable events in Scottish history.

By the start of the 1870s people were beginning to wonder if Scotland's weather was ever going to change. After all, an entire generation of Scots had lived through a period of calamitous weather that appeared not to have changed much over 50–60 years. From the 1870s onwards, winters were either extremely cold, with snow lying for weeks on the ground, or they were incredibly stormy. By and large summers and autumns were wet, with only a few warm, dry summers interrupting the miserable dampness.

The year 1870 was only a few weeks old when a catastrophic storm battered Scotland. The effects of the February storm were most severely felt at Wick, when a severe storm broke out and continued without a break for three days, with the result that part of the peir, measuring 380 feet, was destroyed. At the end of February another storm struck. This time it was a snowstorm which, according to the *Scots Magazine*, 'commenced on Wednesday morning last, and only gave way yesterday evening [and] has proved the most severe and long-continued that has visited this district for many years. During the whole of Friday night, snow fell without intermission, and on Saturday morning the streets were found to be covered to a depth of nearly twelve inches.'

Below follows a list of days in 1871 at Lews Castle, Stornoway, when winds blew at force 10 or, at the highest level, hurricane force – equivalent to force 12:

Lews Castle, Stornoway, 1871
Jan 1 (hurricane force 12), 4, 6, 15 (all force 10) and 16
    (hurricane force 12)
February 22 (hurricane force 12) and 23 (force 10)

March 1, 6, 7 (force 10), 12 (hurricane force – described locally
   as 'a terrific gale') and 20 (force 10)

April 18 and 19 (force 10)

May 3 (force 10)

August 1, 22 (hurricane force 12) and 23 (force 10)

September 5 and 20 (force 10)

October 14, 21 (force 10), 22 (hurricane force 12) and 27
   (force 10)

November 13, 19 (force 10) and 20 (hurricane force 12)

December 16, 17, 18, 23, 24 (all force 10) and 31
   (hurricane force 12)

Figures like these are astonishing. They demonstrate the occurrence of
hurricane-force winds on several occasions throughout the year, including
two during August. Although 1871 marked the start of a very strong El Niño,
it would be naive to attribute weather like this solely to climate perturbations
across the Pacific.

One thing is for sure – calm conditions did not return in 1872. On New
Year's Day, a severe gale roared across northern Scotland, with much property
damaged, many people injured and structures such as Wick pier destroyed by
the sea. Tom Stevenson (another of the lighthouse Stevensons) later attempted
to repair the harbour wall, including the addition of a 2,600-ton foundation
block, only to have it washed away in a later storm in 1877.

A bad day for Helen Whigham and John Gilchrist

The storms that raged across Scotland at this time also affected life in
the cities. For example, the *Scots Magazine* faithfully reports from
Edinburgh that:

[O]n Saturday, January 18th 1873, the unsettled and disagreeable
weather to which we have been so long accustomed reached a
sort of climax in a furious storm of wind and rain. Throughout
the whole day a southwesterly gale swept over the city, accompanied by drenching showers, which cleared the streets of all
but those whom business compelled to venture abroad. A good
many slates and chimney cans were blown down and one or

two accidents are reported. About noon, Helen Whigham, 45 lamp post in North Bridge by the violence of the wind. She was conveyed to the Royal Infirmary, where it was found she was suffering from a severe wound on the right temple, and after the wound had been dressed she was taken home. A man named John Gilchrist, residing at Elizabeth Field, Bonnington was walking along the pavement in Greenside Place, when he was struck on the back of the neck and head with a heavy chimney can, severely cutting his head and stunning him.

Peril at sea

During 1875, an extremely severe storm off northeast Scotland between 15 and 28 October led to the loss of 15 vessels, mostly between Aberdeen and Peterhead. In his history of shipwrecks in northeast Scotland, D.M. Ferguson relates how, 'a south-easterly sprang up on the morning of 14 October and continued with increasing violence till the end of the following week . . . [T]he huge seas which hammered the coast caused considerable damage to the harbours at Stonehaven and Aberdeen . . . [I]n the latter a 60-ton block of masonry was torn from the North Pier and later discovered 100 yards away in the bed of the navigation channel.'

Ferguson also describes how in late December 1876, 30 vessels were lost in another storm in the north of Scotland: '[I]n terms of ships wrecked and lives lost in December 1876 precise totals will never be known as several of the casualties remain unidentified and even such an authoritative source as the Lloyds List was unable to give a complete record of events, so overwhelming was the magnitude of the disaster . . . [but] at least 150 lives [were] lost.' The locations of the vessels lost gives some idea of the storm centre. These include Golspie, Stonehaven, Rattray Head, Donmouth, Keiss Castle (Caithness), Dornoch, Tain, Peterhead, Cruden Bay and Lossiemouth. According to Ferguson, 'without doubt the storm of 22–23 December 1876 was the most terrible in terms of losses at sea that the North East of Scotland has ever experienced. At its height it blew force 12 from the east and was accompanied by snow and latterly thunder and lightning. The surge in Aberdeen harbour was so severe that at one point, one of the retaining chains on the gates parted and they had to be opened to prevent further damage.'

The Uig flood

A strange thing happened on Skye on 14 October 1877. It happened on the land of the laird of the Kilmuir Estate in Uig, Captain Fraser. Fraser was, by general agreement, a very unpopular landlord and caught up in many of the bad deeds and injustices prevalent at that time in the history of the Highlands and Islands. The rain had fallen continuously for over 24 hours. Northern Skye had borne the brunt of the rainfall. In Portree, much of the town centre was flooded. Several of the bridges in northern Skye were washed away by the floodwaters.

But the vast majority of the flood damage was on the Kilmuir Estate. The floodwaters came down into Uig Bay, washed away crops and drowned sheep, many of which were swept out into the bay. Even part of the graveyard was washed away with some of the skeletons piled against the lodge walls and others floating in the sea. Many said at the time that it was God's wrath that was being acted out on Captain Fraser, with some lamenting that it was pure bad luck that the laird was absent when the floods took place and others reflecting on the prophecies of the Brahan Seer (see Chapter 1).

Disaster on the Tay Bridge

Shortly after Christmas, on Saturday, 27 December 1879, a bad storm swept across Lewis. It was recorded there as force 12, with winds from the southwest. By the next day, the winds had moved round to the northwest but were still measuring force 10. As the storm swept eastwards across the mainland it did not abate. Reports from Edinburgh also describe a severe storm from the southwest that Saturday, which did not subside until the Sunday morning. All day the sky continued to have a very dark and threatening appearance, and in the evening, the wind again blew to the force of a gale in the southwest.

The *Scots Magazine* reported how 'just a few miles to the north on Sunday December 28th, the most terrible railway accident which has ever happened in Scotland occurred when a large portion of the Tay Bridge having been blown down causing the total destruction of the North British train from Edinburgh due in Dundee at 7.20, and the loss of nearly 200 passengers'. The storm was estimated at force 10–11 and was blowing down the Tay, striking the bridge along its side. The collapse of the rail bridge, the pride of Victorian engineering, stunned the general public. A subsequent Court of Inquiry concluded that the disaster was caused by the use of design structures that were insufficient to allow the bridge to withstand the force of the storm at the time. Sir Thomas Bouch, the bridge designer, was held responsible for not making sufficient allowance in the bridge design for the effects of hurricane-force winds.

1881 – another catastrophic year

After another terrible storm on 29 October 1880, reported by the *Caledonian Mercury* as having caused widespread loss of life, 1881 did not begin promisingly. This was the year when the cover of sea ice across the northern North Atlantic was at its most extensive since 1800. As early as January the whole northwest, north and east coasts of Iceland were blocked by ice that lasted till the beginning of May. In April the ice began to spread to the south coast, and in May, a very broad belt of ice extended along the east coast, and almost completely surrounded the country. From Fraserburgh, Captain Gray, captain of a merchant vessel that regularly plied northern waters, wrote a letter to the *Royal Geographical Society Journal* describing the enormous cover of sea ice at this time and expressing fears that a new ice age was about to begin.

With the southern extension of sea ice came the southward movement of cold polar waters and, with this, a steeper thermal gradient across the North Atlantic and many more storms. It is no surprise that the harvest of this year was very poor in the Highlands and Islands. The dreadful weather may also have contributed to social unrest across the area, leading in the summer and autumn of that year to the first rent strike there, by the Braes crofters, marking the start of the Highland Land War. By late August 1881 the weather had proved disastrous to grain crops: '[M]any fields have been so much "laid" that much difficulty will be experienced in cutting them with machine' (*Scots Magazine*). Most of the rains came from a very large number of Atlantic storms, some of which have lived long in the memory and several of which are still well known. One of the worst disasters happened in mid July, but other dreadful events took place in October and November.

A silent winter

The year 1881 began in silence, however. The winter of 1880–81 was one of the most memorable snowy winters of the century, starting in mid October and continuing until March. Reports in the *West Country & Galloway Journal* for March describe how:

[t]he snowfall was very heavy, and the drifting was of such a character that it was impossible to keep the railway lines clear. The North British Railway was blocked south of Hawick. The main line of the Midland Railway was also closed. In the north, the Highland Railway was completely blocked between Dalnaspidal and Dalwhinnie. The passengers of one train had to remain overnight in the carriages, and were relieved on Friday with difficulty by a squad of men, and the majority took refuge at the Dalwhinnie Inn. The Caithness section of the Highland line was also blocked.

The efforts made on Friday night to clear the railway lines and to recover the trains buried in snow on many of the systems were frustrated. The whole work, in fact had to be gone over again, and it was not until Sunday that any real progress could be made in relieving the block. On the Caledonian Railway the line between Glasgow and Perth was cleared; but a huge snow-wreath on a level with the telegraph wires stopped the way to Aberdeen. The Granite City, indeed, was up to Sunday night completely isolated, the telegraph lines being interrupted as well as the railway. The Callander and Oban Railway was also blocked on Saturday, as well as the Wemyss Bay line, but the other portions of the Caledonian system, including the lines to the south, were clear. In Fifeshire, the traffic was on Saturday and Sunday considerably impeded.

Ferguson describes conditions at sea:

The casualties suffered in the storm of March 1881 were appalling by present-day standards: at least sixteen vessels were wrecked with the loss of over seventy lives . . . and this takes no account of the huge amount of unidentified wreckage that also came ashore . . . The wind blew from the southeast and was accompanied by heavy falls of snow which blocked roads and railways with huge drifts up to twenty feet deep, bringing life to a complete halt.

The coastal areas principally affected were Peterhead, Aberdeen, Stonehaven, the Ythan estuary and Cruden Sands.

The Gloup disaster

In July catastrophe struck – this time in Shetland. The *Shetland Times* reported: 'It was on 20th July . . . that a sudden gale sprang up, bringing in its track death, sorrow and suffering. And not since that date have we had such a gale at the season of the year in Shetland.' In a *Shetland News* interview with a survivor 50 years after the event, John Fraser of Lerwick describes how:

[a] fleet of about 30 boats was at sea the night of the disaster, 26 from the north half of Yell, most of them from Gloup, with others from places such as Gutcher and as far south as Whalfirth [near Mid Yell]. There were a few among the number out from Unst and Feideland. The night was very fine, and we went off from the land about twenty miles, though it is difficult to recollect the distance after so long an interval of time.

The storm struck us suddenly, and as soon as it struck we were in a fearful sea, and in darkness, in spite of it being the month of July. In our boat we held to our lines and did not leave our position till we had got all our lines on board. We then set sail and turned for home, sailing before the wind. In such a sea it was necessary to steer for each wave, veering away from side to side according to the precise direction from which the wave pursued us. Two men stood by the sail (a square sail) in order to handle it, both for the veering, and because, if a sea threatened to break over us, the skipper would make them lower the sail, thus easing the boat and allowing the wave to go past us before breaking.

At last as the day broke (about 4 a.m.) we saw that we were nearing the land – it was then pouring with rain as well as exceedingly tempestuous, with a dark overladen sky. The first hint we got of any disaster was a number of oars floating in the water, for we had seen no other boat during the night. As we approached the haven at Gloup Voe we saw an empty boat driving ashore, overturned on its side, mast and sail keeping it in that position. Then as we entered the Voe itself, we saw a great concourse of people – wives, sisters, parents, and some children – gathered on the shore with a great lamentation, and a boat manned by twelve men rowing towards us to get hold of the upturned boat. The people had come from miles around to view what they dreaded and expected, for the storm had broken suddenly in the midst of a fine night, and they knew their men were at sea. When we landed they asked if we had seen any other boats, but of course we said we had not.

According to the *Shetland News*, Mr Fraser stated that there were six boats carrying a total of thirty-six men (six men to each six-oared boat) lost from Gloup alone or thereabout. His father and brother were also out that night; they were all in different boats, but were all saved, so that their house was not visited by any of those who came to succour the distressed. But he recollected how the hearts of all, rich and poor, were opened; how food and clothing poured into the district; and how certain people from the south were exceedingly kind. He stated that the money raised formed the nucleus of what is called the Fishermen's Widows' Relief Fund, and that the widows got 17 shillings every quarter in perpetuity after the disaster, an insufficient sum, he said, though he agreed that only by investing the money and using nothing but interest could they have been given anything at all in perpetuity.

'Black Friday' in Eyemouth

In mid October tragedy was to strike again. A huge storm formed over the North Sea and, as the *Scots Magazine* reports:

> The rough weather of the last two or three days culminated yesterday in a severe gale, which seems to have extended over a wide area, and occasioned considerable destruction of property as well as lamentable loss of life. In Edinburgh the storm, which was accompanied by a fall of the barometer to the extent of over an inch, commenced at a late hour on Thursday night. The wind having veered from northwest to northeast swept over the city in tempestuous gusts, which became more violent hour by hour.

In the fishing village of Eyemouth, 14 October 1881 is known as 'Black Friday'. The fishermen who put to sea that morning in calm weather were struck by the sudden storm. The boats made for land but many did not reach it, with some vessels capsized or wrecked on the reefs near the entrance to Eyemouth harbour. A total of 189 men lost their lives on that day, leaving 93 widows and 267 fatherless children. By most people's reckoning, the Eyemouth tragedy was the worst fishing disaster in Scotland's history. Today a memorial stands at the sea front and a beautiful tapestry hangs in the Memorial Room in Eyemouth Museum, together with a list of the names of all the boats and the crews who drowned.

The west coast suffered devastating storms too. On the night of 23 November 1881 one resulted in the destruction of the slate quarries of both Easdale and Eilean A'Beithich in Argyll. Huge waves swept over the entire coast and by morning the quarry workings lay flooded and useless. Later attempts were made to salvage the industry, but it was never again to flourish as in the past.

The year 1882 brought a very similar pattern of weather. Sea ice continued to cover huge areas of the northern oceans. Storm tracks over the North Atlantic continued to be displaced southwards. Some of the storms approached the Scottish mainland with a vengeance. The first battering came on 5 January. The *Scots Magazine* described a 'furious gale, occasioning great destruction to property, though, fortunately, so far as yet ascertained, comparing favourably in other respects with the direful hurricane of November [1881], has raged for the last 24 hours over, apparently, the whole of Scotland and the north of England'.

Life was bleak. The autumn of 1882 gave way to by far the worst and most difficult winter experienced by the crofting population across the Highlands and Islands for many years. According to Hunter:

> Crofters' corn, most of which had remained unharvested because of prolonged rain in August and September, was largely flattened and destroyed by an exceptionally severe southerly gale. All the islands and the entire north-west coast of the mainland were affected by the storm which, as well as adding to the agricultural havoc already wrought by the blight, caused no less than 1,200 boats to be damaged or destroyed, and brought about the loss of an immense quantity of nets and other fishing gear.

As a consequence, during the winter of 1882–83 the crofting population found itself suffering under conditions very similar to those of the starved 1840s.

Oh – to live in the capital city!

Amid the fearful winds and rain, the reports from Edinburgh have an almost surreal quality about them. For example, following a storm on 10 January 1882, the *Scots Magazine* describes how:

> a violent gale from the southwest was experienced again yesterday in Edinburgh, though, happily, unaccompanied by such

accidents to life and limb and destruction to property as characterised the storm of Friday last. In the early forenoon, especially, the wind was very high; and in such exposed thoroughfares as Princes Street and the Bridges walking was rendered rather difficult.

No accidents were reported at the Infirmary last night; and the most of the rickety chimney cans in the city having apparently been blown [away] on Friday, few were left for the wind to operate on yesterday. Upon an old tenement on the west corner of Chambers Street the chimney cans were discovered in a dangerous condition in the morning, and in course of the forenoon were cleared away by a chimney sweep who went upon the roof for that purpose. The storm was singularly enough not attended in the Edinburgh district by any marked fall in the barometer.

Between Thursday night and yesterday morning about 120 fishing boats sought refuge in Leith Harbour from the fury of the gale. The fleet are decked vessels of the largest size, and most of them got to the deep-sea fishing ground, about 100 miles beyond May Island on Tuesday for the usual week's fishing, with few exceptions, they were all engaged in the line fishing when the gale came upon them on Wednesday morning, and yesterday morning as the fleet came up the Firth scudding before the gale, sometimes four and five abreast and rounded the river heads, a very fine and unusual spectacle was presented. The southeasterly gale favouring Leith as a harbour of refuge, most of them were making for this port. Large crowds gathered to see the unshipping of the fish, which seemed rather too plentiful.

More big storms followed in 1883 but something worse was to happen later in the year. The start of the year was snowy. In early March a storm with winds typically around 80–90 knots affected the whole of the North Sea, especially the northern and western parts, the Hebrides and the northern part of the Irish Sea. There were also the now characteristic summer storms. For example, on 9 August 1883 the *Scots Magazine* notes in characteristic Edinburgh style:

[Y]esterday was one of the coldest, stormiest, and most disagreeable days which have been experienced in Edinburgh this season. A boisterous wind from the southwest brought with it blinding rains, which lasted during the greater parts of the day. Numerous rickety chimney cans succumbed to the violence of the gale, which also played sad havoc amongst trees and shrubs in different parts of the town. The only damage reported to the Burgh Engineer as resulting from the gale in Edinburgh was the blowing down of a number of hoardings. The weather in the Firth was very boisterous, much damage being done to shipping.

Krakatoa and the aftermath

The year 1883 was disrupted by one of the biggest catastrophes the world has ever known. Far away, in Indonesia, the volcano of Krakatoa erupted, filling the atmosphere with ash and causing a huge tsunami in the Indian Ocean, similar in magnitude to that of Boxing Day 2004. The world's weather was about to change again. Scotland – already being pounded by stormy weather – was, as elsewhere, about to experience the effects of this huge, though distant, eruption on top of its own weather and climate. The main change was that the enormous volumes of ash in the stratosphere inexorably led to a further cooling of climate. By the end of the year, reports had turned from falling temperatures to storms. In December 1883 the *Royal Sea Express*

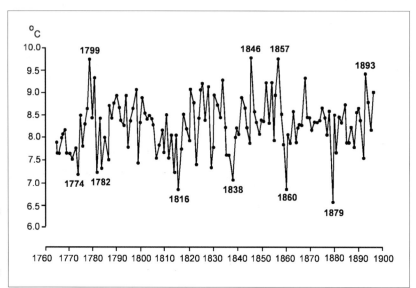

Graph of mean annual temperature for Edinburgh between 1760 and 1900. Note that among the coldest years, the year 1816 followed the volcanic eruption of Mt Tambora in Indonesia. By contrast, the cold year of 1782 preceded the Laki eruption of 1783 in Iceland.

newspaper reported that the total number of shipwrecks for the year was an enormous 1,914, compared with 1,747 in 1882.

In the years that followed, the changes to the weather and climate were made even more extreme by the onset of a severe El Niño that was affecting weather worldwide and which for Scotland may have increased the frequency of gales or kept them at a high level. January and early February were particularly bad months. On 27 January 1884, off Shetland, a succession of cyclones reached a near record low pressure of 930–932 mb. On 16 September 1885 a letter in a bottle was washed ashore on Lewis. It was addressed to Dr Rainy from Raasay, one of the leaders of the Free Church of Scotland, and was written by the minister of St Kilda, the Reverend John Mackay. 'I beg leave to intimate to you,' he wrote, 'that I'm directed by the people of this island to tell you that their corn, barley and potatoes are destroyed by a great storm which passed over the island on Saturday and Sabbath last. You will be kind enough to apply to the government in order to send a supply of corn seed, barley and potatoes. They never saw such a storm at this time of year.'

The Ben Nevis observatory and Clement Wragge

With such chaos at sea and on land, a proposal had been circulating to construct a weather observatory on the top of Ben Nevis. If scientists could understand the links between weather at low and high altitudes then there was a possibility that improvements in weather forecasting could be made – to the benefit of all. Accordingly, plans were drawn up in the late 1870s by Thomas Stevenson, the lighthouse engineer and father of the writer Robert Louis Stevenson, for a new weather observatory on the top of Scotland's highest mountain. The initial idea was that the costs could be borne through public subscription, but by 1880 it had become clear that insufficient funds were available.

To the rescue came Clement Wragge, who offered his services to the Scottish Meteorological Society to climb the mountain every day during the summer of 1881 to make observations at the summit simultaneously with observations made in Fort William by his wife. The process was repeated the following summer from June to November. Were it not for the drive and stamina of Clement Wragge and the widespread interest generated by his detailed weather observations, a subsequent appeal to the public for construction funds might not have succeeded. As it turned out, sufficient money was raised and the observatory was officially opened in 1883.

The observatory was continuously manned, weather readings were taken every hour, sometimes in horrendous weather. A road was constructed up to the summit and people using it were charged one shilling. There was even a restaurant erected on the summit by one of the Fort William hotel-keepers, and people could shelter there overnight during the summer months. In 1893, the famous Scots explorer, Speirs Bruce, as part of his preparations for his 1902 voyage to Antarctica in the *Scotia,* was asked to be a member of the staff of the Ben Nevis observatory. Like many others, he was extremely concerned at the closure due to lack of funds of the observatory in 1904.

Soon after Clement Wragge learned that he was not to have employment linked to an observatory, he emigrated to Australia. He eventually became head of the Australian weather bureau. He later became famous because of his idea to give names to the biggest tropical hurricanes (Hurricane Katrina etc), but in Clement's case he elected to use names of people he did not like!

The storms continued to rage. On 2 March 1886 the *Scots Magazine* reported:

No such sudden and severe snowstorm as that which raged yesterday in the Edinburgh district has been experienced for many years. The winter has been a long and hard one, but the storm of the 1st and 2nd March has not had its parallel this season, and it will take its place among other memorable storms. Up to 8 o'clock it had been blowing hard and snowing and drifting for something like 30 hours almost without intermission, and the temperature being low the whole face of the country lies under a white, snowy fall . . . [with] snowed-up trains, blocked roads, dislocation of traffic, and general inconvenience and discomfort to all concerned . . . The storm, which began about 3 o'clock on Monday afternoon, and had continued to rage all through the evening, showed no signs of abatement yesterday morning. On the contrary, the wind, which was blowing from the northeast, seemed to have gained in force and the storm altogether in intensity.

In the face of the cold, rain, snow and high winds, hunger was never far away. In 1892, for example, the Minutes of the Shetland 'Yorkshire Friends' Quarterly Meeting recorded that:

> during the late and disastrous harvest . . . the crofters were almost in a state of starvation and few of them had any seed corn with which to sow their fields. Committees were formed in various villages in the Northern Islands who undertook the careful distribution of seed corn . . . providing a maintenance for many starving families, amounting to a population of nearly 3,000 people.

The obvious effects of Krakatoa on the world's weather and climate lasted no more than ten years. By the close of the century, change was on the way – and it was for the better. Most of the weather records for Scotland show that the end of the century was marked by a significant decline in winter storminess. It was not an instant change, but one which started during the early 1890s and was well-established by 1905. With this change came a decline in rainfall and a reduction in winter flooding. The cause of the change is not known. Certainly, in the summer of 1895 Scotland experienced a heatwave. Edinburgh was no exception. The weather descriptions in the *Scots Magazine* are revealing (note that temperatures are given in degrees Fahrenheit):

> September 3–17. The mean temperature of these fifteen days was 63.6° or 8.5° in excess of the normal. From the 4th to the 6th the maximum temperatures were over 80°, being 82°, 82°, and 80°, while the minima were 59°, 57.6° and 62.6°. The mean temperature was 70.5° on the 4th, 70° on the 5th and 71° on the 6th, this being the only occasion in eighty years on which each of three consecutive days had a mean temperature in excess of 70°. The nocturnal warmth from the 3rd to the 8th was very unusual, the mean of all the minima being 60°; the air was unusually damp, which made the heat very oppressive.

Another dry summer followed in 1899, with no rain during late May, most of June and August. As the nineteenth century drew to a close, the experience of most Scots was of the tremendously warm summers of 1898 and 1899. Few were expecting a return to the horrors of the 1880s. Life was at long last good, and in the cities people were able to escape the factories in the middle of the day and sit in the sun with their lunch.

Captain Gray's map of the Norwegian and Greenland Seas for the early 1880s showing the enormous extent of sea ice cover. Captain Gray believed that the huge cover of sea ice was a forewarning of an impending ice age.

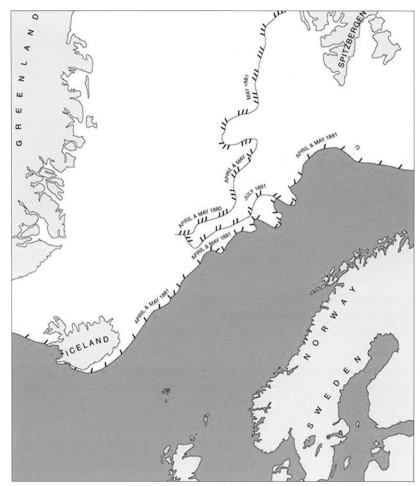

POSTSCRIPT

We ought never to forget how dreadful the weather was during the later part of the nineteenth century. The trend of exceptionally stormy winters reached a peak during 1880–82 and was then followed within months by the eruption of Krakatoa and its devastating impact. By the early 1890s, however, a shift to more genial weather had become established so that by 1897 one might be forgiven for thinking that there had been a general climate change, with some global warming thrown in for good measure.

CHAPTER 9
THE TWENTIETH CENTURY –
A NEW DAWN

Amateur gardeners were to be seen until darkness last night repairing
the ravages of winter in their gardens and optimistically planning for
flower beds and vegetable crops for the summer.

Edinburgh Evening Despatch, April 1947

INTRODUCTION

So did the start of the twentieth century bring with it a long-lasting improvement in weather and climate? Well – not exactly. In fact, the new century
started with a fearsome storm that raged across northern Scotland. Shetland
was badly affected, with the *Shetland Times* reporting a 'hurricane' with terrible
effects, great damage to property, shipwrecks on the coast and serious loss of
life at Delting, where four boats and 22 men were lost leaving 15 widows and
61 other dependents. Another severe storm struck at the end of the year on
20–21 December, with the wind recorders at Blackford Hill, Edinburgh,
measuring wind speeds that reached up to 93 mph.

But the climate was clearly changing. The 1901 storms were the exception
rather than the rule. A warm summer was to follow during 1901. Yet a curious
aspect of the climate remained – icebergs. The turn of the century was a time
when there was an increased frequency in the reporting of icebergs that had
broken off from polar glaciers and strayed southwards into the North Atlantic.
One such example was in 1902, when an iceberg was observed off the coast
of northern Skye. The tragedy of the *Titanic* followed during April 1912. Then,
as late as September 1921, a warning was posted in the Kirkwall harbour office
in Orkney, of two icebergs located 200 miles to the west of the archipelago.

Another major change was in respect of the annual extent of sea ice across
the northern ocean. By the start of the century there was a marked reduction
in the extent of sea ice, such that the coastline of Iceland became entirely free

of sea ice between 1905 and 1910. Sea-ice extent has never since covered such vast ocean areas as it did during the 1880s and 1890s. Although never studied in detail, this change in sea-ice coverage may have had a profound effect on the circulation of the northern North Atlantic and its impact on the atmosphere.

Hot summers were to follow – especially that of 1911. During this year, in Orkney, Kirkwall enjoyed just over 78 hours of sunshine over five successive days between 9 and 13 July, with temperatures the highest recorded since 1890. By the time of the outbreak of the First World War in August 1914, people were becoming used to warmer, drier summers and less stormy winters. The change to more benign weather became even more settled between 1920 and 1929, with the major shift taking place soon after 1926–30, with a reduction in climate extremes that was to last until the late 1960s. The trend was towards a preponderance of anticyclonic circulation, with clear skies and warm conditions during summer but winters that were cold and dry. If snow fell, there was a good chance that it would stay on the ground for longer periods of time.

The pre-war years

In the years leading up to World War II the fickleness of Scottish weather continued. Blizzards affected the country in January 1934, followed by intense cold and further snow in February. The weather was so severe that in Argyllshire deer were coming down off the snow-clad mountains and raiding stackyards in Glenorchy and Glen Etive. The snows lasted in the north of Scotland till April, when the thaw led to floods triggering several landslides. Near Stornoway, the sea, driven by a northeasterly gale, broke through a beach, leaving shellfish scattered across fields. High pressure returned during the summer of 1934, leading to a heatwave. Temperatures in Edinburgh reached between 26°C and 35°C in the shade during early July, while Tobermory, on Mull, was the warmest place in Scotland! In Buckie, a sparrow arrived in a chemist's shop, unable to stand due to melted tar on its feet. By the autumn the ground was rock hard in many areas, so when the rains came, water was forced across the ground surface. The result was more floods throughout November and December.

By January 1935 the snows and floods had returned again. There were many shipping accidents while in February the Clyde burst its banks near Hamilton. Many roads were blocked by drifting snow that continued to affect the north of Scotland even as late as May. Unlike the previous year, the summer of 1935 was very wet. The following report from Shetland appeared in *The Scotsman* in late July:

The case of the Orkney flying pig

Between January and April 1934 the Orkney Isles suffered a succession of gale- and hurricane-force winds. On 18 January parts of the road at Scapa and Carness were washed away and houses in Stromness flooded. Three weeks later, strong winds continued at 73 mph or more for five days, reaching hurricane-force speeds of 88 mph. Such high velocities were not recorded at any time earlier during the twentieth century, although winds at Kirkwall reached in excess of 100 mph on 23 January 1938. In April 1934 gale-force winds and heavy rainfall allowed water to enter St Magnus' Cathedral in Orkney through cracks in the copper spire and flooded the pulpit area. There was also the case of a pig belonging to Mr Peter Johnston of Gaitnip Farm, East Mainland, which was blown through the air over a distance of 50 yards – when the hut in which it was resting blew over – and lived to tell the tale. Never again believe that pigs can't fly . . .   (Hazell, 2000)

Shetland was visited during the weekend by the most severe and pro-longed rainstorm experienced for many years . . . in the north part of the mainland the loch of Brei Wick has disappeared. The sand and rocky strand, 70 yards wide, which separated it from the sea became undermined, and was swept away, and the loch emptied itself into the Atlantic.

Coastal damage was not limited to the islands. Storm waves, together with exceptionally high tides, swept away large sections of sea wall between Buck-haven and East Wemyss in Fife – this provides a good example, if any were needed, that severe coastal erosion was very common in the age before so-called global warming.

As the Second World War approached, the whole of Britain was again experiencing wonderful weather. Winters were rarely characterised by stormy interludes, while many of the summers of the 1930s corresponded with the popular image of endless days spent whiling the hours away in warm sunshine. When war broke out in 1939, Scotland had experienced a dry spring and summer with a brilliant month of June and a wet and cool July. Winter storms were above average, with some violent episodes particularly in October followed by a cold, dry winter. In fact January 1940 was the coldest month for 45 years but was then succeeded by a heatwave and drought that June which broke all records.

The following year, 1941, was very unusual in that there was a shortage of rain across the country, accompanied by a general lack of sunshine and severe snowstorms between January and March. Prolonged snowstorms were also a feature of the start of 1942. They were followed by a dry spring and a horrendously wet summer. In fact, Fort Augustus was not a great place for a summer break in 1942 since nine inches of rain fell there during August alone. The worst day was on 11 August when, further west, more than three inches of rain fell in Glenmoidart and Kinlochhourn. Another wet summer followed in 1943, while 1944 was much the same, with commentators describing the year as having been characterised by a lack of sunshine throughout spring and summer and excessive rains between September and November. The cold winters continued to be a feature of the war years. For example, January 1945 was thought to be the third coldest of the previous 50 years, with snowstorms locally the most severe in living memory. One of the worst gales occurred during this year also, on 18 January, when wind gusts at the Bell Rock lighthouse reached up to 95 mph and up to 75 mph over the Forth Rail Bridge. But by far the snowiest winter came during 1946–47, after the guns of war had gone silent.

Chaos in the blizzards

Across the western Highlands February 1947 was the driest and coldest month since 1914, with an average temperature at midday barely above freezing. Lochs, rivers, wells and even the sea in shallow bays were frozen.

In northern Skye, the end of March marked the end of a 67-day period of partial drought, with just over an inch of rain having fallen since early January and the average temperature 6.5 degrees below normal. On 28 January 1947, *The Scotsman* reported with a hint of irony that 'Edinburgh saw only a glimpse of the sun yesterday when it came out for half a minute at 2.20 p.m. The weather remained cold and snow lay in the higher parts of the city . . .'

For most, the winter of 1947 was bitterly cold. By the end of January temperatures across the east of Scotland had dropped to well below freezing. Snow carpeted the country and by early February snowploughs were out trying to open roads blocked by blizzards. Near West Linton, for example, 70 vehicles were caught in the snow and near Roxburgh a railway snowplough was engulfed by the blizzards and had to be dug out. By mid February large numbers of people were out skating on the ponds and lochs around Edinburgh. Near Fort Augustus, an astonishing 27 degrees of ground frost was recorded.

Localised ice floes were reported drifting in the Solway Firth. There were even reports of RAF aircraft shadowing ice floes and icebergs in the North Sea, with plans in place to bomb some of them if their continued drift looked likely to pose a danger in the busy shipping lanes. Aircraft were even dropping food supplies to isolated communities cut off by the snow. By the start of March, the newspapers were reporting that, in Fife, the villages of Largoward and Peat Inn had been isolated for many days, with drifts of snow in some places up to the eaves of the houses. Loch Lomond was frozen over between Balloch and Inch Murrin, with skaters out on the ice at Luss, Balmaha and Balloch. In the Borders, shepherds were concerned that the blizzard conditions were lasting into the lambing season. Some farmers were working 36-hour shifts in order to keep their sheep safe. Feed was running low and there was a fear that the following winter the sheep would suffer due to a lack of feed.

Then, just as reports of a thaw were in the air, Scotland was hit by another bad blizzard in mid March 1947. Even Prestwick airport, normally snow free during winter, was closed due to snowdrifts across the runway. Road and rail transport were disrupted nearly everywhere. A train from Edinburgh Waverley containing the Scottish rugby team heading for Twickenham was blocked by snowdrifts near Carlisle, the train remaining stuck for many hours.

Then, as always happens, with the thaw came the floods. In the southwest of the country the flooding was particularly bad. The only way of reaching Wigtown and Whithorn, for example, was by tractor, with local farmers reporting losses to livestock as high as 75%. Also because of the floods and snow, a train to Stranraer was stranded at Dumfries for five days before finally reaching its destination.

By spring, the thoughts of many turned to holidays. The following report from the *Evening Despatch* for April 1947, summarised things well:

[T]he Edinburgh Spring Holiday began promisingly on Saturday, with blue skies and sunshine, but conditions deteriorated yesterday, and high winds and heavy rain this forenoon shattered prospects for holiday-makers . . . Umbrellas, capes and raincoats were prominent today as a steady stream of people boarded trains for the North, South and West at Waverley Station.

Yet the summer was fine. Dry but cool, with almost no rain between July and September. In Glasgow, 31 July was recorded as the hottest day for four years at 30°C in the shade. In fact, August 1947 was generally considered to have been the driest across Scotland since 1825.

Whenever heatwaves occur in Scotland, fogs tend to develop over sea areas and the coast as the warm air is cooled from beneath by seawater. With the fogs came accidents at sea. The summer of 1947 was not particularly bad. It started near Dunoon during mid August when passengers on the LMS steamer the *Duchess of Hamilton* were startled to find the MacBrayne turbine, the *St Columba,* heading straight for its stern. Reports describe how 'superb seamanship' averted what could have been a major disaster. Fogs interrupted steamer services in Orkney and Shetland, while dense fog in the Forth estuary caused two ships to run aground. A fishing boat, the *Springfield* from Buckie, sank after a collision in fog with a trawler off Fraserburgh. Even in the far west in Lewis, the island was without mail for the first time on record because of fog across the Minch.

The summer floods of 1948

During the summer of 2007 many despaired of the weather, having been kept indoors due to torrential rainstorms. But to find a similar time in the past we need look no further than the summer of 1948, when the heaviest rain for many years caused widespread damage. The grain harvest was put in jeopardy as corn 'stooks' stood in pools of water in the fields. Farmers were also fearful of the appearance of potato blight, caused by the damp conditions. During the summer storms, five bridges between Edinburgh and Newcastle were washed away and six landslides blocked the Main East Coast railway express.

Berwick was more or less isolated by floodwaters as the River Tweed broke its banks while farmers desperately tried to rescue livestock in danger from the floodwaters. People in the village of Eyemouth, devastated by the fishing disaster of 1881, this time found their houses located on the other side of an embankment against which floodwaters had risen to a height of 30 feet, creating an area of water 300 yards wide and 5 miles long. Fortunately the embankment held. A man in the nearby village of Cumledge was less lucky; he watched in horror as a trunk containing his life savings of £120 was washed away in the floodwaters.

You've never had it so good?

By the start of the 1950s the war was starting to become a memory, ration books were soon to disappear and by the middle of the decade the Macmillan government was telling people that they had never had it so good. But at the start of the decade the weather was distinctly unpleasant. The first half of 1951, for example, was exceptionally cold, with patches of snow still visible on many hills by late August. The following winter of 1952 repeated the pattern of severe cold and blizzards. On 14 December there was a 12-inch snowfall accompanied by a very strong northerly wind causing 15-foot drifts in parts of Skye which was given much prominence in BBC news bulletins at the time.

The North Sea storm surge tragedy of 31 January 1953

On the last day of January 1953 a devastating storm developed in the North Sea. The north winds, driving southwards, led to tremendous sea floods in the southern North Sea, especially in the Netherlands and southeast England, where many perished as the sea broke through coastal defences. Eastern and northern Scotland were also badly affected, mainly as a result of the surge of seawater that flooded across coastal lowlands and damaged harbours and ports. In Orkney, Kirkwall was subjected to sustained wind speeds of near 125mph, with destructive waves washing away large areas of sea wall while at sea 14 Humberside fishermen on the Grimsby trawler *Sheldon* lost their lives. Most of the damage along the Orkney coastline was due to the coincidence of the peak of the storm with exceptionally high tides.

The storm is also associated with the heroism of Hamish Flett, captain of the passenger steamer *Earl Thorfinn*. The little ship was feared lost in the storm somewhere between Westray and Stronsay in a 100-mph hurricane and nil visibility but the captain took the ship southwards before the wind. During the crisis the ship's steam steering gear was lost. The crew somehow managed to steer the ship by hand before finally berthing in Aberdeen 30 hours later and delivering the ten passengers, aged between 18 and 73, from their ordeal. The hurricane also led to major changes in the landscape, with the island of Sanday almost divided in two.

Two days later there was probably one of the worst storms of wind and snow ever experienced in the Highlands. On the night of the 17th there was a storm which caused extensive structural damage with 100mph gusts crossing the Hebrides. Then, after a mild spring and cool summer, there was a very cold spell from September to December, as cold a winter as had occurred for over 70 years. After a mild 1953 the weather changed again, with November and December of that year being the warmest for almost a century and 1954 being renowned as the wettest year since 1903. On Skye, for example, it was the worst harvesting weather for 50 years. From 23 August to 31 October there were only three completely dry days.

By the mid 1950s much of northern Scotland was again paralysed by blizzards. During January and February 1955 conditions were dire on the mainland of Scotland, with the stranding of thousands of sheep and cattle, especially in Caithness and Sutherland. The threat to livestock led to missions of mercy, still remembered as 'Operation Snowdrop'. Thursday 24 February may have been the coldest day of the twentieth century, recorded as -10°C on Skye – equal to 18 degrees of air frost. A total of 170 degrees of frost was recorded during February at Struan, where snow lay for two and a half weeks till the thaw came. It is ironic, then, that a fantastic summer followed – especially during July and August. The harvest came early and thousands flocked to the beaches – it was to be one of the finest Glasgow Fair Fortnights on record.

Policeman guards the Highland Park

Severe gales struck Orkney on 12 January 1955 with temperatures as low as -4°C and 70mph winds. Children were trapped in schools and all transport came to a stop. By 14 January drifts up to ten feet deep were recorded, while on 16 January another 14 inches of snow fell. Conditions remained desperate until 24 January, with transport restricted to boats and ferries. After a brief respite, a second blizzard struck on 16 February, bringing down power lines, and closing all roads as well as the airport. The roof of a warehouse at the Highland Park whisky distillery caved in under the weight of 3 feet of snow, crashing down on the stock of 3,000 casks containing 23,000 gallons of whisky. A police constable was sent to mount guard on the precious stock.

(Hazell, 2000)

It was not to last, however. The following year, 1956, started with yet another cold snowy winter and a dry spring but then the coldest August for 100 years. Winter storms were never far away and on 12 December a reminder was served of their power, with gusts of 110mph at Benbecula, 104mph at Lerwick and 101mph across Tiree. There was a hint that change was on the way in 1957, when there were few severe snowstorms – was the climate becoming milder? Heavy snowfalls at the start of 1958 put paid to that idea. So also did a summer that was universally wet. But the weather has a knack of providing us with conflicting signals, since the following year, 1959, was said to be the best summer in living memory, breaking all sunshine records. Storms came late in the year with a vengeance. On 2 December the sea flooded across Stornoway airport. Then between 6 and 11 December, a series of strong southeasterly gales caused loss of life at sea including the entire crew of the Broughty Ferry lifeboat when answering a distress call from the *North Carr* lightship. Then the start of 1960 followed with blizzards, a severe frost and a miserable damp and dull summer that contrasted starkly with the summer before.

The year 1961 was unusually mild. Again July and August were wet and there were plenty of storms – in fact no fewer than four months during the year experienced wind gusts in excess of 100mph. Bad snowstorms came in December 1962 and more were to follow at the end of a miserable 1962, the coldest year in Scotland since 1922. The blizzards arrived in November 1962 and were to continue throughout the winter. Rail and road traffic were badly affected, with road vehicles and trains alike trapped in deep snowdrifts. The storms of November and December 1962 drew comparisons with those of March 1947 and February 1955.

Big changes in the North Atlantic

During the 1960s a big change took place that started to affect the climate of the North Atlantic region. The curious thing about the change was that it was almost invisible. At the time nobody noticed except a group of scientists who were monitoring changes in the temperature and saltiness of the North Atlantic Ocean. What they noticed was something that was to dominate our thinking on climate change from then until now – parts of the North Atlantic were accumulating large amounts of fresh water across the ocean surface.

The first big area of predominantly fresh water was observed across the ocean surface east of Greenland in 1967. During later years it moved across the northern North Atlantic by ocean currents taking it off Newfoundland in 1971–72 and gradually back again towards northern Europe, before finally returning to the Greenland Sea by the early 1980s. This giant pool of fresh water became known as the Great Salinity Anomaly and is thought to have resulted from an enormous discharge of ice from the Arctic Ocean in 1967. Scientists have no idea how this huge amount of relatively fresh water moving slowly around the northern North Atlantic may have affected climate. One view was that cooler surface waters resulted in less evaporation from the ocean and this might have caused decreased rainfall over Scotland. Another opinion was that it may have altered the position of the North Atlantic storm track, thus influencing patterns of winter storminess across Scotland.

The most important consequence, however, was that such enormous areas of fresh water sitting on top of saltwater made it difficult for the surface waters of the North Atlantic to descend to the floor of the ocean, thus disrupting ocean circulation. Since this circulation is the means by which heat is released from the ocean into the atmosphere, the disruption implies not only that ocean circulation was slowed down, but that the amount of heat released from ocean to atmosphere was also reduced.

The accumulation of large volumes of fresh water over the ocean surface of parts of the North Atlantic has continued off and on from the late 1960s until the present. Today, scientists are also concerned about even larger volumes of fresh water that have accumulated over the Labrador Sea in the western North Atlantic. So great has been the influx of fresh water that in some areas the depth of relatively fresh water exceeds 1km. Where has it all come from? Popular wisdom is that it has come from melting glacier ice from the ice caps of the eastern Canadian Arctic and also from the Greenland ice sheet. So we are left with an unsolved puzzle. Undoubtedly such huge volumes of fresh water have influenced and are influencing regional climate, but it is almost impossible to tell what changes in climate are the *direct* result of these processes.

Underlying this thinking is the idea that such changes have been detected only because of detailed monitoring of ocean conditions during the latter half of the twentieth century. Does this mean that similar changes may have taken place earlier in history and that we simply have no means of demonstrating that they ever took place? For the purpose of understanding changes in Scotland's climate and weather we just have to remember that the ocean changes that have taken place since the start of what is now called the Great Salinity Anomaly in the late 1960s may have played a big part in shaping the patterns of weather and climate change that have occurred during our lifetimes.

The cause of the bad weather lay in easterly winds blowing off continental Europe and collecting moisture on their passage across the North Sea. It was one of the worst winters in living memory. Spring was late, the summer was wet and damp, and the harvest was damaged. In some badly affected areas helicopters dropped supplies of food to snow-bound farms and villages. Then after the thaw that started in early March flooding was again severe. By contrast 1964 was mild and dry, with a reasonably dry summer. The winds were to shift to north by 1966, leading to more cold and wintry conditions, followed by disastrous flooding during August and December. The dull conditions continued through 1967, with the exception of a wonderful June. The great snows seemed to be disappearing and 1968 was to be remembered for the remarkably low number of gales as well as another 'flaming' June. The weather for Skye typified most areas. June was brilliant, with over 240 hours of sunshine. As rain soaked Ascot, stopped play at Lords and opened the umbrellas at Wimbledon, there was heat shimmering over the slopes of the Cuillins. By July, the drought was largely compensated for by the abnormal dews that were sometimes so heavy they could be heard running off the roof into the gutters. August was wonderful too, leaving most to forget the horrendous rains at the start of the year.

In the year that followed, the extremes between winter gales and summer heatwaves continued. On 7 February 1969, a gust of 118 knots, the second-highest wind speed ever recorded in the British Isles, was measured at Kirkwall Airport in the Orkney Islands. In the blizzard, staff at the airport dived for safety as they expected the building to collapse. A warm summer followed. By November, the astronauts on Apollo 12 were looking down over a cloud-covered northwest Europe as the winter gales gathered in the Atlantic.

Scottish football suffers in the snow and frost

The start of the 1970s in Scotland was gripped in a severe snowy winter; even Jock Stein, the manager of Celtic, sent his players home on 10 January and told them not to report to Celtic Park until the following week. Northerly winds meant widespread snow and frost but plenty of sunshine. By the end of the month tragedy had struck, with the Fraserburgh lifeboat capsizing in heavy seas and six crewmen losing their lives.

The summer was again to bring fine weather. June was one of the warmest and sunniest for over 30 years, especially in the west. Then came the autumn and winter rains. Drought followed across much of Scotland in 1971; in Orkney, for example, people on the isle of Shapinsay described how the well in the castle had dried up that summer, something that had not occurred for 130 years. In fact, during April hardly any rain was recorded anywhere in Britain. But the dry winds were coming from the north, giving a cold nip to the air. The storms returned with force at the end of the year. It was the stormiest December for 30 years and it coincided with a very strong El Niño. The cold and the snow returned in January 1972 as temperatures plunged. By summer it was dry but still cold; in Skye it was the coldest it had been for 30 years, yet it remained mostly dry till mid October.

By the start of 1973 many were remarking how mild it was, and how few frosts there were. Perhaps Scotland was feeling the effects of the Great Salinity Anomaly as it moved around the northern North Atlantic? Perhaps global warming had already set in or maybe the continuing El Niño was affecting world weather patterns? By late March a large anticyclone became centred over Scotland. Temperatures were significantly lowered and the winds returned to the north only to be succeeded by one of Scotland's wettest winters. Things were soon to improve. The summer of 1976 was one of the driest on record. Weeks of prolonged sunshine brought out the deckchairs and the bikinis. Golfers everywhere had a summer of hitting long drives on fairways that were baked rock hard. Another roasting summer followed in 1977. It brought back memories of the summer of 1968 and the Beatles. There were even reports of people in the west of Scotland collapsing from sunstroke.

But change was on the way. During 23–25 November 1981 a huge storm struck Scotland. It affected most areas, from the Faroes in the north to the

Netherlands in the south. In the central North Sea 100-knot wind gusts caused the oilrig *Transworld 58* and the Sedco/Phillips service platform to drag and break loose from their anchors. During the winters of 1982–83 and 1983–84, storms battered Scotland. At the time, many were of the opinion that it was a period of storminess unequalled in living memory, although beyond living memory we know that storminess was much more severe during the latter decades of the nineteenth century. In looking back on these ferociously stormy winters of the early 1980s, we ought not to forget that this period also coincided with another very severe period of El Niño circulation that scientists know to have disrupted weather systems around the globe.

PART 4
PRESENT AND FUTURE

CHAPTER 10
GATHERING OUR THOUGHTS

The Wintry West extends his blast,
And hail and rain does blaw;
Or the stormy North sends driving forth
The blinding sleet and snaw

Robert Burns, from 'Winter, a Dirge', 1786

INTRODUCTION

The last decades of the twentieth century formed the age of numbers. Technological advances were so great that the Earth's weather and climate were starting to be monitored closely by thousands of instruments measuring everything from minute changes in sea level on remote Pacific islands to temperature changes on the floors of the oceans. Add to that an array of satellites providing a continuous stream of data on the Earth's weather systems and it would seem that nearly everything that could be measured was being measured.

The last two decades are especially important for another very important reason. This has been the time when the issue of global warming has reached our TV screens and newspapers and has come to dominate our thinking of how our climate is changing due to the effects of people and industry. So what are the facts? Do trends in Scottish weather and climate display all of the menacing signs of the effects of global warming?

Average temperature across Scotland since the start of the twentieth century shows an overall long-term rise punctuated by sudden rises and falls. The most notable change is a steep drop in temperatures centred around 1961. Thereafter, there has been a steady rise to the present, punctuated by a series of sudden falls. Invariably, western Scotland exhibits slightly higher average temperatures than the east and north of the country. To most observers, the blame for the rise in average temperatures since the early 1960s lies at the door of global warming; the average annual temperature in 2004 was higher than at any time during the twentieth century, but we also need to remember that, at present, the Sun is the coolest it has been since the scientific measurements of the Sun's temperature began in the early 1950s.

Sunspots and global warming

In the midst of media descriptions of the dire effects of global warming, astronomers and physicists around the world have started to report some astonishing observations of recent changes on the Sun's surface. For a long time, it has been known that the surface of the Sun becomes hot and cold in a cyclical manner. Periods of time when the Sun is radiating excessive amounts of heat are characterised by numerous sunspots. By contrast, periods when the Sun is relatively cold are marked by low numbers of sunspots. Such a situation existed during the seventeenth century, the lack of sunspots then being cited as a prime cause of the extreme cold of the so-called 'Little Ice Age'.

It came as a great surprise to many to learn that the Sun started to cool down dramatically during the latter half of 2008. Remarkably, no sunspots were detected on the Sun's surface between October 2008 and the summer of 2009. So many sought to explain the cold, lengthy and snowy winter of 2008–09 as being due to the occurrence of a 'cold' Sun. After all, if the Sun cools down it is entirely logical that the our planet Earth will cool down also. No one knows when this cycle in the activity of the Sun will change, with new sunspots starting to appear in greater numbers. All we know at present is that the Sun is colder now, in relative terms, than it has been since direct measurements of sunspot activity began during the 1950s. This issue is central to the global warming debate since scientists can only speculate how such a change will affect atmospheric circulation and air temperature changes across our planet.

The pattern of recent rainfall changes is equally complex. For one thing, there are strong regional differences in rainfall between east and west, with much less rain in the east. There also appears to have been a change centred around the late 1960s and early 1970s where the values seem to dip before rising

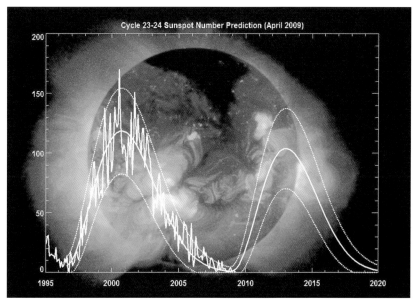

Cycle 23-24 Sunspot Number Prediction (April 2009)

Graph showing changes in sunspot activity across the surface of the Sun since 1995. The zig-zag line represents monthly changes in the absolute count of sunspots on the Sun's surface while the smoothed lines represent an 'envelope' of overall change. Note that 2009 and 2010 may be the years when the Sun is at its coldest since detailed measurements began in the 1950s. (Courtesy of NASA)

again. The rise appears to have continued throughout the 1980s before remaining fairly uniform during the 1990s and into the new millennium. Yet the trends mask important variations between individual years even for the 1990s. For example, the greatest amount of rainfall during the entire twentieth century was centred on 1990, while a period of significant drought was a characteristic of 1996. To a certain degree there are links between higher winter air temperatures and periods of heavy rainfall, since most of the rain-bearing storms are associated with relatively mild southwesterly winds.

No more snowy Goniel Blasts

As we consider recent trends in Scotland's climate, a picture starts to become clear – that of the importance of considering aspects of air-temperature change separately from other elements of the climate system that are more closely related to changes in atmospheric circulation. In terms of air temperature, we can see trends very clearly. For example, the clear trend in changing snow cover since 1961 is, much to the lament of the skiing industry, one of a progressive decrease in amounts of winter snow. The change starts with the desperately cold and snowy winter of 1962–63 and exhibits another huge peak in snowfall during the winter of 1978–79. But after that the trend has been downwards. In reality, however, it is the patterns of atmospheric circulation that determine when and where snowfall will occur during wintertime, and how long the snow will stay on the ground.

During the first weeks of 2006 it was hard to believe in global warming when blizzard conditions struck eastern and northern Scotland, and even St Andrews Old Course was blanketed in snow and passenger trains were stranded in snowdrifts between Montrose and Aberdeen.

Are winter gales really on the increase?

Were anyone to tell you that global warming had led to an increased frequency of winter gales in recent years, you could answer – not true. For many Scottish weather stations, the trend in monthly average wind speeds for each winter (when most gales take place) has been of strong variability between years and of a noticeable decline throughout the close of the twentieth century and the beginning of the twenty-first. After the tumultuous stormy winters of 1981–82 and 1982–83, gale frequency has been on the decrease. The simple explanation is that it is mostly to do with changes in atmospheric circulation and very little to do with changes in air temperature.

True, there have been some devastating storms and some great tragedies. On 13 February 1989, the strongest measured wind gust (126 knots) ever to have been measured in mainland Scotland struck Fraserburgh lighthouse. Then in 1993, the *Braer* was wrecked aground in Shetland, resulting in a damaging oilspill. Also high in the list of severe storms was the 'Great Storm' that struck the Outer Hebrides on 15 December 1996, when one of the deepest cyclones (those associated with the lowest air pressures) ever to have formed in the North Atlantic developed just south and east of Cape Farewell, Greenland. So, on the one hand the trend of winter storminess is on the decrease but the severity of individual storms may possibly be on the increase.

By the time the new millennium started, many wondered what the climate of the twenty-first century had in store. Most newspaper and TV reports discoursed endlessly about global warming and climate change. By January 2005 the worst fears of many in Scotland were realised when an enormous storm ripped through North and South Uist and Benbecula, drowning a family of five and leaving hardly a house without storm damage. By October 2006, the front page of the *Scotsman* was dominated by photos showing the effects of global warming, with two full pages of coverage inside giving warnings of future catastrophes. By 2009 we could be excused for imagining that the world's ice sheets were melting with immense speed and that we were about to be drowned by rising sea levels. But, of course, the reality is quite different and much more complex.

CHAPTER 11
WHAT CAN WE LEARN
FROM THE PAST?

INTRODUCTION

Robert Burns, like many before and after him, was profoundly influenced and inspired by Scotland's weather. But are the extremes of the seasons experienced by him now lost forever? Have the 'snawy wreeths and wild-eddying swirl' of winter blizzards disappeared from our world forever to be replaced by dour dampness and grey scudding clouds? Or does the climate have some surprises in store for us?

In today's world, powerful computers are fed weather data and predict our weather a few days in advance. But no computer exists that is sophisticated enough to predict our weather and climate months and years ahead with any degree of accuracy. Different studies have been undertaken whereby computer models are used to simulate the Earth's climate and to make predictions for the future. Most such attempts seek to replicate the interactions that take place between the Earth's ocean and atmosphere in order to learn more about the key processes that trigger significant changes in climate.

However, the data on past ocean and atmospheric conditions that the computers can use is severely limited by the length of time over which detailed observations of weather and climate have been made in the past. For most parts of the world, there is insufficient weather data for computers to use for the decades prior to the 1940s. This raises the question of how representative the weather of the last few decades has been of the last few centuries. Most would agree that it is not representative at all. So, this means that we must always be extremely cautious in accepting as gospel the results of computer models predicting future changes – the results are only as good as the data that you feed into the computer.

A constant theme throughout the preceding chapters has been how current thinking tends to link trends in air temperature to patterns of climate change. Few would argue against the view that there has been a progressive rise in air temperatures over most areas of the world during recent decades. The finger of blame is usually pointed to rising concentrations of greenhouse gases, most notably carbon dioxide, methane and water vapour. Thus we watch from our living rooms the latest pronouncements on global warming. But it is vital that we understand the scientific basis upon which this concept is based. It is simple, for example, to understand computer models simulating future climate change. Once they are fed with data about increased carbon dioxide and methane concentrations, they will always predict higher global air temperatures. And since higher air temperatures result in the accelerated melting of glaciers and ice sheets, most computer models predict rising sea levels. With this cocktail of arithmetic and computer modelling, economists are then asked to calculate what the monetary cost of the implications of the model results will be (for example the widely publicised Stern Review report of 30 October 2006).

The history of Scotland's recent weather and climate also tells this story of recent increases in air temperature – of that there can be no doubt. And with this change come other indicators of climate change across Scotland. For example, the length of the growing season appears to have increased. Similarly, the trend in the number of days each winter when there is snow points to a gloomy future for the Scottish ski industry. But we face a conundrum when we try to assess the present and future influences of the North Atlantic Ocean on our climate. On the one hand, the North Atlantic can participate in the global-warming process, leading us to expect warmer weather in future. On the other hand, we face the prospect of future cooling, due principally to a weakening in North Atlantic ocean circulation and a breakdown (or even a shutdown) of the ocean thermohaline conveyor. Some predict that such cooling would lead us quickly into a new ice age. So really, our knowledge of how global weather and climate works is quite crude.

HOW THE PAST IS LIKELY TO AFFECT THE FUTURE

As the history of Scotland's changing climate from the Ice Age to the present has unravelled, some surprising observations have come to light. It has become apparent, for example, that the timing, duration and extent of past ice ages had a great deal to do with long-term changes in the nature of the Earth's orbit around the Sun. But in disentangling the story of what happened at the close of the last ice age we run up against the enigma of the Younger Dryas cold period. This was the astonishing story of how, just as the last ice sheet across Scotland had begun to melt away, there was a sudden return to cold conditions. We learned that this change from warming to cooling was nearly instantaneous – most available evidence points to a switch to severe cooling over a matter of a few years. The lesson that the Younger Dryas cold period can teach us is a vital one. It tells us that the climate of the northern hemisphere can switch from warm to severe cold very quickly. If it happened then, it could happen again in the future.

But we also learned that the Younger Dryas cold period came to an end rather quickly and was replaced by relative warmth. All the evidence points to the fact that Scotland's first settlers took advantage of this improvement in climate as they wandered across a landscape free of ice and on which was growing luxuriant vegetation. As far as we can tell, the last 10,000 years of Scotland's history was never again associated with the growth and expansion of glaciers. In prehistory, one other time interval merits particular attention. This was around 8,200 years ago, about 3,000 years after the time when Scotland again endured, albeit briefly, a return to extreme cold conditions. It seems there was no renewed growth of glacier ice in Scotland at this time. The period of intense cold may only have been shortlived – in the order of a few hundred years – with the return to warmer conditions being as rapid as the start of the episode of cooling. For this cold 'event' there is some degree of agreement among scientists that its start was triggered by the sudden influx of large volumes of fresh water from the North American continent into the western North Atlantic Ocean. So, here is another instance of a disruption of the oceanic thermohaline conveyor plunging Scotland into a mini ice age and showing how changes in the ocean drive changes in the atmosphere.

All the indicators that have been used to gain an idea of how Scotland's climate changed after the cooling event of 8,200 years ago tell us that the magnitude of the climate changes were negligible when compared with those which occurred during the ice ages. The trend of inferred air-temperature change over time, starting with the arrival of Scotland's first settlers, points to it having been almost benign in comparison with what had gone before. Yet, when we investigate some of the climate fluctuations that took place in more detail, we learn that some of the changes were, in themselves, quite dramatic.

Our journey through Scotland's past has also told us that large volcanic eruptions, especially those from Iceland, have been important in shaping climate. Some of the eruptions we know almost nothing about – for example, those described by Hugh Miller for 1694 and 1755. For others we know a great deal. For example, the Icelandic Laki eruptions of 1783 left an unmistakable impression through their climatic impact and their association with crop failures and famine, as did later eruptions such as Krakatoa 100 years later.

We have learned also that there is a lot more to understanding climate change than simply focusing on changes in air temperature. For example, the popular impression of the Little Ice Age is of a period of severe cold. Yet we have learned that the onset of this period of cold was triggered by a remarkable reorganisation of atmospheric circulation across the northern hemisphere. Even more of a surprise is that the pattern of more vigorous circulation that coincided with the start of the Little Ice Age is still taking place today – only now with enhanced greenhouse warming of the atmosphere superimposed. We have also seen that the Little Ice Age was interrupted by brief periods of exceptional warmth (in the 1650s, for example).

All of the above leads to the observation that when trying to understand our present climate we have no period of time in the past with which to compare it. On the one hand, past periods when air temperatures were similarly warm (for example the Medieval Warm Period), were not stormy. By contrast the stormy periods of the past (for example the Little Ice Age) were for the most part colder, and definitely not warm.

How are we to understand our present climate if we are told that all changes, whether they are periods of extreme cold or intervals of exceptional warmth, are down to the effects of global warming? Consider the following – not an alternative view of climate change during recent decades but simply the facts.

First, remember that planet Earth experienced one of the strongest El Niño events of the twentieth century during 1982–83. The effects of this El Niño event extended far beyond the Pacific basin. In northern Europe, the winter of 1982–83 was one of the stormiest in recent centuries, while Greenland winter air temperatures dropped to values never experienced during the previous 500 years. The jet stream changed its direction across the northern hemisphere and brought bad weather to the Mediterranean.

By the time the 1982–83 El Niño had ended, northern Europe began to experience quite different weather and climate. Several of the warmest summers occurred during the mid and late 1980s. The headlines and front-page pictures in the Scottish papers showed photos of deck chairs out in their thousands along the Clyde coast beaches and soaring temperatures matched only by the sales of ice cream. But the 1980s was a time when the temperature across the surface of the Sun was much higher than normal – a time of exceptional solar flaring. The effects were widespread, the circulation of the stratosphere changed dramatically, the position and size of the ozone layer also changed, satellites were displaced out of their normal orbits, the Northern Lights (the Aurora Borealis) were seen in the night sky over Scotland on a regular basis and even military communications systems were disrupted by the effects of the Sun's radiation on the atmosphere

By the start of the 1990s, as the episode of solar flaring came to an end, our climate was hit by another environmental catastrophe. During 1991 a huge volcanic eruption took place in Indonesia. The eruption of Mt Pinatubo in the Phillipines was so violently explosive that it sent huge volumes of ash nearly 50km high into the stratosphere. It was the biggest volcanic eruption of recent centuries and the erupted material passed through the troposphere and into the overlying stratosphere, with profound effects on the Earth's climate. Scientists measuring air temperatures at different levels in the atmosphere showed quite clearly that, for at least five years after the eruption, a distinct cooling took place. Many observed at the time that this cooling was sufficiently strong to offset and even reverse the trend of global warming that had become such a big talking point after the warm years at the end of the 1980s. Some even said that Pinatubo had 'bought the world some time' in its attempt to offset global warming. Another strong El Niño followed during 1997 and again disrupted the world's weather.

The point of the above observations is a simple one. If we are to model global climate change with any accuracy, scientists need to develop computer models that are sufficiently powerful to incorporate *all* of the major effects on climate described above. Yes, there are climate models that attempt to simulate El Niño conditions. Yes, there are others that can simulate the effect of large volcanic eruptions on the Earth's climate. There are even computer models that can simulate changes in the Earth's climate caused by variations in the amount of heat received from the Sun. There are plenty of models, of course, that simulate changes to our climate based on changes over time in the concentration of greenhouse gases linked to emissions dictated by a variety of geopolitical scenarios. Other models have been relatively successful in simulating how changes in the complex interactions between the world's oceans and atmosphere can influence our climate. But there is no model in existence that can do all of these things simultaneously – simply because present technology is unable to accomplish such an enormous task. If this is the case, how much reliability can we place in any computer model to predict future changes in the Earth's climate?

We end with this challenging question. Is our society blinkered in respect of understanding climate change? Is this because of the widely publicised view that changes taking place to our weather and climate can only be explained as a result of the concept of global warming to the exclusion of all other explanations? Perhaps we would be well advised to shake off the simple explanations of climate change and recognise that the science of climate change is, in fact, very complex. This is abundantly clear when trying to unravel the history of Scotland's weather and climate. Perhaps this book also teaches us how important a part past changes in weather and climate may have played in Scotland's turbulent history.

The story of Scotland's weather and climate leaves one with an impression of all the amazing twists and turns of water, wind, fire and ice that have conspired to shape a remarkable story. We might close the book and reflect on how much we know about the remarkable changes in weather and climate that have taken place in Scotland's past. In fact we know very little indeed. And for the sake of our children and their future we need to be able to explain what the words 'climate change' really mean.

FURTHER READING

Much of the literature that has been written on Scotland's weather and climate history can be found on the shelves of libraries and local archives. It is a great irony that the classic textbooks on Scottish history contain only very limited information on past weather and climate extremes, so one has to do a great deal of digging around to unearth relevant material. There are jewels of information in many of the texts, however, with a number of these focused on episodes of famine and dearth. Some of the most important books are listed below and these will allow the reader to become acquainted with this fascinating subject – one that is inextricably entwined with the history of the Scottish people.

THE SCIENCE OF WEATHER AND CLIMATE

Extreme Weather: a Guide and Record Book. C.C. Burt. 2004. W. W. Norton and Co. (A well-written account of how weather works and focusing on weather and climate extremes.)

Frozen Earth, The Once and Future Story of Ice Ages. D Macdougall. 2004. University of California Press. (An easy to read account of the causes and effects of ice ages and some of the scientists involved in the climate change debate.)

Ice Ages: Solving the Mystery. J. Imbrie and K.P. Imbrie. 1979. Macmillan. (A classic text on how our understanding of ice ages changed from Victorian times to the present.)

Ocean Circulation. 1989. Open University Course Team. Pergamon Press. (An excellent book that explains the most important links between ocean circulation and climate.)

An Online Handbook of Climate Trends Across Scotland. 2006. Scotland and Northern Ireland Forum for Environmental Research (SNIFFER). (A handbook of climate data for Scotland showing patterns of changes in temperature, snow cover, growing season, rainfall etc. – can also be viewed online at www.sniffer.org.uk.)

Palaeoclimatology: Reconstructing Climates of the Quaternary. 1999. R.S. Bradley. Harcourt. (A detailed account both of the methods used to reconstruct Quaternary climate changes and also of the main findings of Quaternary research.)

The Quaternary Ice Age. W.B. Wright. 1914. Macmillan and Co., Ltd. (One of the all-time greats – providing an elegant description of the last ice age with a very valuable historical perspective.)

The Two-Mile Time Machine. R.B. Alley. 2000. Princeton University Press. (A classic and one of the first books to give an account of what the study of ice cores has taught in respect of global climate change.)

Weather, Climate and Climate Change. G. O'Hare, J. Sweeney and R. Wilby. 2005. Pearson. (A comprehensive and up-to-date account of weather, how it works and its relations to climate and climate change.)

The Weather Makers. T. Flannery. 2005. Allen Lane (Penguin). (Plenty of information on weather processes written in an easy-to-read style.)

ICE AGES AND GEOLOGY

The Evolution of Scotland's Scenery. J.B. Sissons. 1967. Oliver and Boyd. (An all-time classic that includes descriptions and explanations of Scotland's changing landscape during and after the last ice age.)

The Great Ice Age – Climate Change and Life. R.C.L. Wilson, S.A. Drury and J.L. Chapman. 2000. Routledge Press. (A heavyweight and authoritative account of the environmental changes that took place on Earth during the last Ice Age.)

Ice Age Earth. A.G. Dawson. 1992. Routledge Publishers. (A detailed description of fluctuations in the Earth's climate since the last ice age together with accounts of the accompanying geomorphological changes.)

Land of Mountain and Flood: the Geology and Landforms of Scotland. A. McKirdy, J. Gordon and R. Crofts. 2007. Birlinn. (A beautifully-produced account of the evolution of Scotland's landscape.)

Little Ice Ages. J.M. Grove. 2005. Routledge, London. (A classic text describing the climate change processes associated with the Little Ice

Age as well as the human impacts of climate changes over this intriguing period of the Earth's history. An earlier book *The Little Ice Age* was published in 1988 by the same author.)

The Little Ice Age: How Climate Made History 1300-1850. B Fagan. 2000. Basic Books. (A fascinating account of the interactions between weather, climate and history and considered from a global perspective.)

Reflections on the Ice Age in Scotland. J.E. Gordon (ed.). 1997. Scottish Association of Geography Teachers and Scottish Natural Heritage. (A collection of papers addressing various aspects of the last ice age in Scotland.)

Scotland After the Ice Age: Environment, Archaeology and History 8000 BC–AD 1000. K.J. Edwards and I.B.M. Ralston. 2003. Edinburgh University Press. (A highly regarded collection of papers that describe the environmental and cultural changes that took place in Scotland since the end of the last Ice Age.)

HISTORICAL WEATHER

The Buik of the Croniclis of Scotland: Or, A Metrical Version of the History of Hector Boece. William Stewart. 1858. 3 vols, Rolls Series. (One of the earliest accounts for Scotland of historical weather events.)

Climate, History and the Modern World. H.H.Lamb. 1982. Methuen. (A classic text by one of the most highly regarded scholars of his generation. Hubert Lamb's text should be pored over time and time again.)

Climate since AD 1500. R.S. Bradley and P.D. Jones (eds). 1992. Routledge. (A collection of papers by international experts on climate change that seek to explain patterns of climate change that have taken place around the world since AD 1500.)

Earth's Climate: Past and Future. W.F. Ruddiman. 2000. W.H. Freeman and Co. (A comprehensive explanation of what we can learn from the pattern of past climate changes on Earth.)

Historic Scotland Book of Scotland's First Settlers. C. Wickham-Jones. 1994. B.T. Batsford Ltd., London. (an exceptionally vivid account of the archaeology of Scotland's first settlers – where they lived and how they lived their lives.)

Historic Storms of the North Sea, British Isles and Northwest Europe. H.H. Lamb. 1991. Cambridge University Press. (A highly detailed account of many of the greatest storms of recent centuries.)

Medieval Scotland: Kingship and Nation. A. Macquarrie. 2004. Sutton
Publishing. (A fine account of Medieval Scotland that sets in context the
social and cultural changes associated with a period of time in Scotland's
history when the climate was significantly different from present.)

A Meteorological Chronology to AD 1450. C.E. Britton. 1937. Meteorological
Office Geophysical Memoir No. 70. His Majesty's Stationery Office. (A
truly remarkable compilation of all extraordinary weather and climate
phenomena that took place in the UK up to AD 1450)

Scotland's Weather: An Anthology. A. Martin. 1995. National Museums of
Scotland. (A fascinating compilation of extreme weather events for
Scotland, several of which are referred to in the 'catalogue of disasters'.)

The Stone Age in Scotland. A.D. Lacaille. 1954. Oxford University Press. (A
classic archaeological text on Scotland's ancient settlers, partly out-of-date
but essential reading nonetheless.)

Wild Harvesters: the First People in Scotland. B. Finlayson. 1998.
Canongate/Historic Scotland. (A fascinating account of the lives of the
first people to live in Scotland covering the period from about 8000 to
4000 BC.)

SCOTTISH HISTORY

Cargoes of Despair and Hope: Scottish Emigration to North America 1603–1800. I.
Adams and M. Somerville. 1993. John Donald. (Detailed accounts of the
emigrant ships and their passengers.)

Eskimos in Scotland c. 1682–1924. D. Idiens. In C. Feest (ed.) *Indians in Europe,*
University of Nebraska Press. 1999. pp. 161–74. (A wonderful account of
the various reports of Eskinos having reached Scotland.)

Feast and Famine, Food and Nutrition in Ireland 1500-1920. L Clarkson and M.
Crawford. 2001. Oxford University Press (A comprehensive account of
famines in Ireland together with information on weather and climate
extremes.)

A Gathering of Eagles: Scenes from Roman Scotland. G. Maxwell. 1998. Birlinn
with Historic Scotland. (A description of the period in Scotland's history
when Caledonia was at the northern frontier of the mighty Roman
Empire.)

The Isles: a History. N Davies. 1999. Macmillan. (A wonderful account that
integrates the separate histories of Scotland, England, Wales and Ireland

and one that does not forget to mention the most important times of dearth and famine.)

Last of the Free: a Millennial History of the Highlands and Islands of Scotland. J Hunter. 1999. Mainstream Publishing. (An inspired and authoritative account of the history of the Highlands and Islands – a classic account that enables one to set in context the importance of weather and climate on the precarious existence faced by Highlanders and Islanders through the centuries.)

The Lighthouse Stevensons. B. Bathurst. 1999. HarperCollins. (A wonderfully evocative account of the lives of the Stevenson lighthouse builders containing numerous vivid descriptions of some of the worst storms experienced during the construction phases of several of Scotland's lighthouses.)

The Lords of the Isles. R.C. Paterson. 2001. Birlinn. (A detailed history of Clan Donald and the Lordship. The book begins with Somerled and ends with the deposing of the Lordship during the 1490s. The historical accounts span the period during the early 1400s when Scotland's climate changed dramatically.)

The Orkneyinga Saga. J. Anderson (ed.). 1999. Mercat Press. (A fascinating account that begins with the conquest of the Isles and the later history of the Earldom.)

The Prophecies of the Brahman Seer. A. Mackenzie. 1935. Eneas Mackay. (The well-known account in which can be found numerous instances foretelling extreme weather events.)

Scenes and Legends of the North of Scotland. H. Miller. 1834. Nimmo, Hay and Mitchell. (A classic text with numerous accounts of extreme weather events, including reports of volcanic eruptions in Iceland during historical times.)

Scotland: A History, 8000 BC–AD 2000. F. Watson. 2002. Tempus. (A contemporary account of Scotland's history – accessible, scholarly, lively and concise.)

The Scottish Nation: 1700–2000. T.M. Devine. 1999. Penguin. (One of the most highly acclaimed accounts of Scotland's history over the last three centuries.)

Shipwrecks of North-East Scotland 1444–1990. D.M. Ferguson. 1991. The Mercat Press. (A comprehensive and exhaustive discussion by one of Scotland's foremost shipwreck experts. This book is one of a series that describe wrecks around Scotland's waters.)

The Sutherland Book. D. Omand (ed.). 1982. Northern Times Limited. (A graphical account of the history of Sutherland containing vivid descriptions of the changing social conditions.)

Times of Feast, Times of Famine: a History of Climate since the Year 1000. E. Le Roy Ladurie. 1971. Doubleday and Co. Inc. (A wide-ranging and global account of times of feast and famine since medieval times.)

A tour in Scotland and voyage to the Hebrides. 1776. Thomas Pennant privately printed, London.

Walter Bower's Scotichronicon. D.E.R. Watt (ed.) 1991. Aberdeen University Press. (A lengthy treatise on Scotland's history including numerous descriptions of past weather.)

LOCAL SCOTTISH HISTORIES

The Beautiful Railway Bridge of the Silvery Tay. P. Lewis. 2004. NPI Media Group. (One of several books written about the Tay Bridge disaster, this one by a professor of engineering explains how and why the bride collapsed in such a dramatic manner.)

Boswell's Journal of A Tour to the Hebrides with Samuel Johnson. F.A. Pottle and C.H. Bennett (eds). 1936. William Heinemann. (A transcript of the original text that includes fascinating descriptions of the 'sand drift' that overwhelmed many coastal areas during the late eighteenth century.)

Chronicles of the Frasers: The Wardlaw Manuscript, entitled 'Polichronicon Seu Policratica Temporum, or, the true genealogy of the Frasers', 906–1674. James Fraser. W. Mackay (ed.). 1905. Scottish History Society, First Series, Edinburgh.

A Description of the Islands of Orkney. Rev. J. Wallace. 1700. London. (One of the earliest detailed written accounts of the natural history of Orkney.)

Description of ye Country of Zetland. Printed for private circulation 1908, copied from original in the Advocates' Library, Edinburgh, by the late Mr Bruce of Sumburgh. Bruce, S. 1908. Shetland Archives, Lerwick. Additional material is provided by Bruce (1925) in a letter dated 19 January 1925 to the *Shetland Times.* Newspaper Cuttings, Shetland Archives, pp. 93–5.

Disaster at Dundee. J. Prebble. 1957. Harcourt Brace Publishers. (One of John Prebble's most famous early books with graphic accounts of the disaster. A similar book was also published as *The High Girders* by the same author, published in 1956 by Secker and Warburg, London.)

The Discovery of the Hebrides. Elizabeth Bray. 1996. Birlinn. (The story of the exploration and exploitation of the Hebrides containing numerous evocative descriptions of seafaring and winter storms and covering the period 1745–1883.)

Easdale, Belnahua, Luing and Seil: The Islands that Roofed the World. M Withall. 2001. Luath Press. (An account of the famous slate quarries and their abandonment following the great storm of 1881.)

The Great Highland Famine. T.M. Devine. 1988. John Donald. (Provides an account of the potato famine that affected the Highlands and Islands during the middle decades of the nineteenth century. The effects of the potato blight are inextricably linked with weather and climate extremes that, together, caused so much suffering at this time.)

Guide to Ben Nevis: with an Account of the Foundation and Work of the Meteorological Observatory. 1893. John Menzies and Co. (An authoritative account of the story of the Ben Nevis Observatory.)

'The Haff Deckers'. T Henderson. In J.J. Graham and J. Tait (eds.), *Shetland Folk Book*, vol.7. 1980. Shetland Times, Lerwick.

The History of Islay from Earliest Times to 1848. C.N. Jupp. 1994. Museum of Islay Life, Port Charlotte. (A detailed account of the history of Islay that includes descriptions of the most important famine episodes.)

History of Orkney. W.P.L. Thomson. 1987. Mercat Press. (One of the most authoritative and best researched books on Orkney's turbulent history. The book describes some of the horrible famines that caused so much suffering.)

The History of the Orkney Isles. G. Barry. 1805. Constable and Co. (A remarkable account of Orkney during historical times that includes descriptions of volcanic ashfalls.)

The Hjaltland Miscellany. E.S. Reid Tait (ed.). 1947. Shetland Archive, Lerwick. (Contains an account by Rev. James Kay of sand drift at Quendale.)

Instructions from the heritors of the cuntrey of Zetland to Allexander Brand, stewart and justiciar of Orkney and Zetland for representing ther conditione to the Lords of His Majesties Councill and Thesaurie. P. Umphray et al. 1696. Scottish Records Office, Edinburgh. (An account that describes the petition of James Oliphant of Ure.)

Jura : Island of Deer. P Youngson. 2001. Birlinn. (A voluminous tome providing a highly detailed account of social change. This case study of a

Hebridean island, through the detailed descriptions that are provided, helps us to visualise the links between weather, climate and making a living from the land.)

Lewis: a History of the Island. D. Macdonald. 1978. Gordon Wright Publishing. (A detailed history of the island with numerous accounts showing the precarious links between livelihood and changes in weather and climate.)

Lindores Abbey and its Burgh of Newburgh: Their History and Annals. Alexander Laing. 1876. Edmonston and Douglas Publishers. (A fascinating historical account of a once-famous abbey. The accounts for the late 1690s describe extreme poverty and conditions of severe cold.)

The Meteorology of Edinburgh. R.W. Mossman. 1895–1903. Transactions of the Royal Society of Edinburgh, Part 1, pp. 38, 681–756; Part 2, pp. 29, 63–175 and 39, 476–83; Part 3, 40, 469–510. (A classic treatise summarising the history of Edinburgh weather.)

An Old-Time Fishing Town: Eyemouth: Its History, Romance, and Tragedy with an Account of the East Coast Disaster, 14th October 1881. D. McIver. 1906. John Menzies and Co. Ltd. (A classic description of Eyemouth history and culture including graphic descriptions of the tragedy at sea.)

The Orcadian Book of the Twentieth Century. H. Hazell. 2000. The Orcadian Limited, Kirkwall Press. (A wonderful compilation of newspaper cuttings from the *Orcadian* covering the twentieth century.)

Orkney and the Sea: an Oral History. K. Towsey. 2002. Orkney Heritage. (A wonderful compilation of the oral history of Orkney with numerous references to climate and weather.)

The Outer Hebrides: the Shaping of the Islands. S. Angus. 1997. White Horse Press. (A highly detailed and informative account of the history of the Outer Hebrides that includes sections on the islands' weather and climate history.)

Reliquiae Divi Andreae or the State of the Venerable and Primitial See of St Andrews. George Martine. 1797. James Morrison printers for St Andrews University. (A well-known document summarising earlier writings on St Andrews and surrounding areas.)

The Reverend Dr John Walker's Report on the Hebrides of 1764 and 1771. M.M. McKay. 1980. John Donald. (An illuminating transcription of the Rev. Walker's observations that includes descriptions of weather and climate for the latter part of the eighteenth century.)

The Road to Apocalypse. R. Black. 9 May. 1997. West Highland Free Press.

Scenes and legends of the North of Scotland or The traditional history of Cromarty.

Hugh Miller. 1851. Nimmo, Hay and Mitchell. (Centenary edition of the writings of one of Scotland's foremost natural scientists containing hundreds of accounts pertaining to the natural history of Cromarty.)

'Snowstorms in Scotland – 1729–1861'. M.G. Pearson, in *Weather* 33. 1978. pp. 392–99. (A rare paper that describes remarkable patterns of snowstorm occurrences across Scotland between 1729 and 1861.)

The Weather in North Skye. D. A. Maclean. 1977. Highland Herald Limited. (A rare compilation of past weather in Skye.)

Whalehunters: Dundee and the Arctic Whalers. M. Archibald. 2004. Mercat Press. (An expansive description of Scotland's whaling industry that highlights the climatic severity of the eighteenth and nineteenth centuries and the changing sea ice conditions in northern waters.)

Wick of the North. F. Foden. 1996. North of Scotland Newspapers. (A very detailed account that traces the history of Wick from earliest times to present. The book contains numerous contemporary descriptions of weather and climate, including many destructive winter storms.)

Wrecks and Reminiscences of St Andrews Bay. G. Bruce. 1884. John Leng and Co. (Another classic text with descriptions of all of the major shipwrecks in Fife during historical times as well as numerous additional accounts of extreme weather including blizzards and frosts.)

DIARIES

The diary of Alexander Brodie of Brodie, MDCLII-MDCLXXX, and of his son, James Brodie of Brodie, MDCLXXX-MDCLXXXV. David Laing (ed.) 1863. Spalding Club (Scottish History Society). (Another of the famous diarists of the seventeenth century – the diary contains very detailed accounts of past weather.)

The Diary of Patrick Fea of Stove, Orkney, 1766–1796. W.S. Hewison (ed.). 1997. Tuckwell Press. (Patrick Fea's diary provides a day-to-day record of farming and weather conditions on the Isle of Sanday in Orkney – an incredibly detailed account.)

The diary of Andrew Hay of Craignethan, 1659–1660. Alexander G. Reid (ed.). 1901. Scottish History Society, First Series. (The last of the famous diarists of the seventeenth century – this diary contains detailed records for a short period only.)

The diary of Mr John Lamont of Newton, 1649–1671. George R. Kinloch (ed.).

1830. Maitland Club (Scottish History Society). (A famous diary containing fascinating weather records set alongside notes of the tumultuous social and political changes taking place at this time.)

A diary of public transactions and other occurrences, chiefly in Scotland, from January 1650 to June 1667. J. Nicoll, edited by David Laing. 1836. Bannatyne Club (Scottish History Society). (One of Scotland's most famous diarists of the seventeenth century, his writings contain remarkably detailed accounts of the weather.)

The diary of the Rev. George Turnbull, Minister of Alloa and Tyninghame, 1657–1704. Robert Paul (ed.), in *Miscellany of the Scottish History Society,* 295–445. 1893. Scottish History Society, First Series. (Another well-known diary that although mostly consisting of ecclesiastical records also contains gems of information on the weather the author experienced.)

The Masterton Papers, 1660–1719. Victor A. N. Paton (ed.), in *Miscellany of the Scottish History Society.* 1893. Scottish History Society, First Series, (A rare account of political and social changes in Scotland for the 17th century – including weather descriptions.)

More Frost and Snow: the Diary of Janet Burnett 1758–1795. M. Pearson (ed.). 1994. Canongate. (The diary of a remarkable lady who lived in Kenmay, Aberdeenshire, and at Disblair House in the parish of Fintray and who kept a daily account of weather and farming conditions.)

GLOBAL WARMING AND CLIMATE CHANGE

Climate Change: a Multidisciplinary Approach. W. Burroughs. 2001. Cambridge University Press. (A very informative description of the most important climate and weather processes supplemented by up-to-date discussion of the key topics in the climate change debate.)

Climate Change 1995: The Science of Climate Change. J. Houghton et al. (eds.). 2001. Cambridge University Press. (The 'holy grail' of climate change research – used by policymakers and planners worldwide in all deliberations regarding global climate change. The latest (2007) report is in the process of being published. At present an 18-page 'Summary for Policymakers' is available for download at the IPCC website.)

Climate Change: The Challenge to All of Us. S. McDonagh. 2007. Columba Press. (A popular account of the climate change debate followed by a discussion of what the individual can do to help combat climate change.)

Climate Variability, Climate Change and Fisheries. M.H. Glantz (ed.). 1992. Cambridge University Press. (One of the few books that considers the issues of climate change in respect of fisheries and the response of the world's oceans to changes in the atmosphere.)

Earth in the Balance. A. Gore. 1992. Plume/Penguin. (A graphical and contemporaray account of global climate change issues.)

Forecasting the Weather. Alan Rodgers. 2007. Heinemann. (A lucid explanation of how professionals use weather data to predict future weather and climate.)

Global Warming: Causes, Effects and the Future. Mark Maslin. 2002. Voyageur Press. (A valuable text for the lay reader where the complex science of climate change is synthesised down to a pacy narrative.)

Global Warming: The Hard Science. D. Harvey. 2000. Prentice Hall Inc. (A concise text that breaks through the hype about global warming and focuses on the key scientific issues.)

The Greenhouse Delusion : a Critique of 'Climate Change 2001'. V. Gray. 2004. Multi-Science Publishing Company Ltd. (A controversial account of climate change science in which a number of misconceptions are challenged. The criticism is principally directed at the IPCC.)

The Ice Chronicles: The Quest to Understand Global Climate Change. P.A. Mayewski and F. White. 2002. University Press of New England. (One of the best books around that describes and explains the historical context of the present global climate-change debate. The book focuses on the amazing results of recent climate-change research based on ice cores.)

The Last Generation – How Nature Will Take Her Revenge for Climate Change. F. Pearce. 2007. Eden Books, Transworld. (A wide-ranging and articulate account covering some of the key issues in the climate-change debate.)

Revenge of Gaia: Earth's Climate Crisis and the Fate of Humanity. J. Lovelock. 2006. HarperCollins. (In this book, the author explain his theory of Gaia and its importance to the concept of global climate change.)

Stormy Weather: a Forecast of Increased Storms, Worsening Weather and Detailed Explanations of the Causes. M. Maslin. 2002. Apple Press. (An illustrated description of various forms of extreme weather focusing on the issue of climate change. Well-known examples of extreme events form the core of the narrative.)

Thin Ice. M. Bowen. 2006. Henry Holt and Company Inc. (Tells the story of

Lonnie Thompson, who has devoted his life to the study of ice cores in remote areas such as China and South America.)

With Speed and Violence: Why Scientists Fear Tipping Points in Climate Change. F. Pearce. 2007. Beacon Press. (A wide-ranging discussion on the many issues concerning climate change. The author pays particular attention to thresholds in the system and ways in which climate change may take place rapidly.)

INDEX